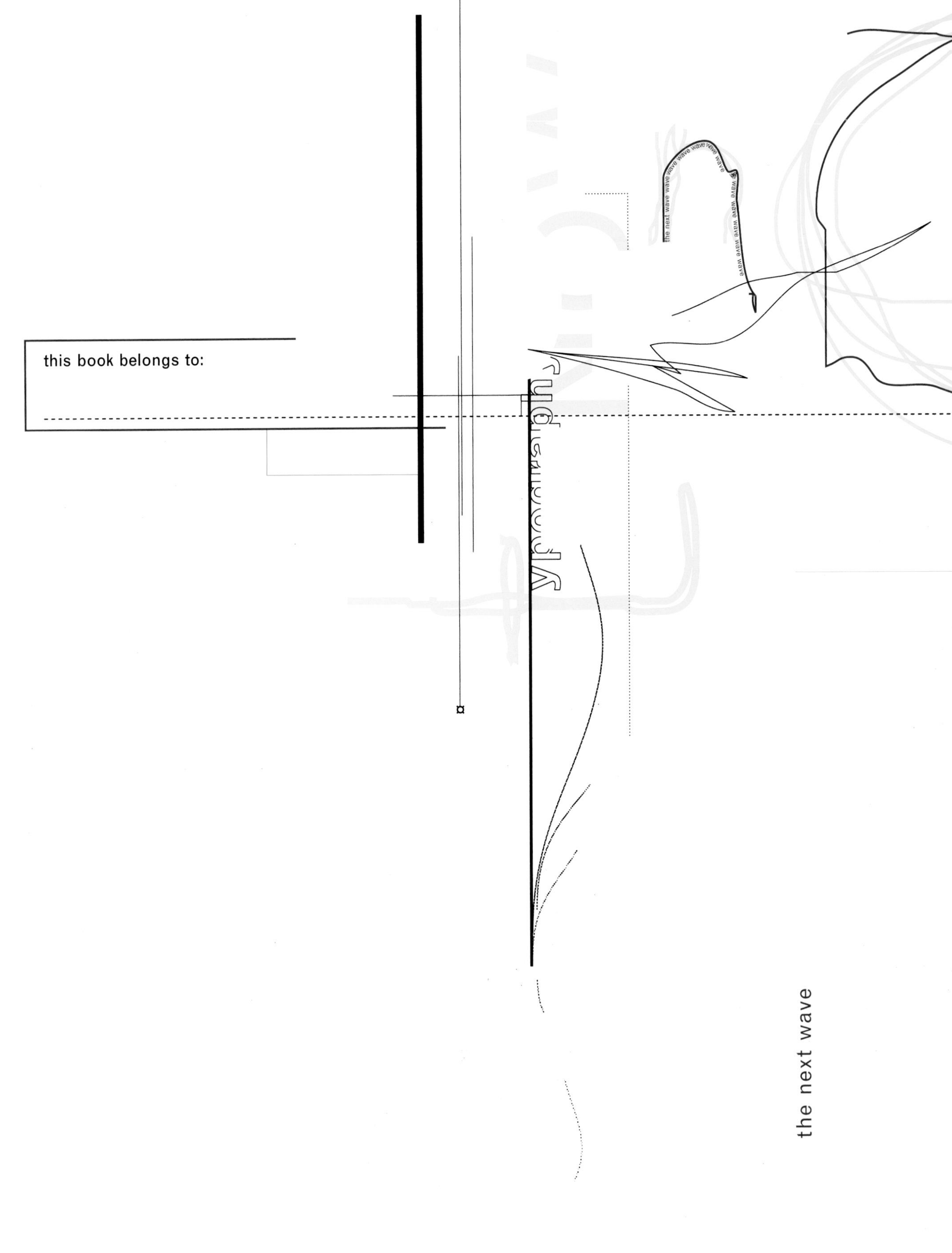
this book belongs to:
the next wave

typography
NOW
the next wave

editors

rick poynor
edward booth-clibborn

book design

why not associates

cover photograph by why not and rocco redondo.
end paper photography by pirco wolfframm & alistair lever.
computer-generated wave on cover by simon scott.
set in monotype grotesque by alphabet set.
printed and bound in japan by dai nippon printing

captions and artwork in this book have been supplied by the entrants. while every effort has been made to ensure accuracy, booth-clibborn editions do not under any circumstances accept any responsibility for errors or omissions.

first distributed in the united states of america in 1992 by north light books,
an imprint of f&w publications, inc., 1507 dana avenue, cincinnati, ohio, 45207. world direct rights: internos books. isbn no. 0 904 866 904

rest of the world distribution:
hearst books international
1350 avenue of the americas, new york ny 10016 usa.

the typefaces beowolf, brokenscript, lunatix, oakland, matrix, modular, scratch, totally gothic, triplex and vortex were kindly supplied by fontworks, a division of fontshop international.

1st reprint 1992.
2nd reprint 1992.
3rd reprint 1992.

introduction

contents

"Type is going to be as abstract as sand on a beach. In that sense type doesn't exist anymore."

MAX KISMAN

type and deconstruction in the digital era

by rick poynor

In the age of the desktop computer, font design software and page make-up programs, type has acquired a fluidity of physical outline, an ease of manipulation and, potentially, a lack of conceptual boundaries unimaginable only a few years ago. Everyone agrees that the new **digital tools** remove typography from the exclusive domain of the specialist – whether type designer, typefoundry or typesetting company – and place it (not always firmly) in the hands of the ordinary graphic designer. The results of this freedom, however, are the subject of intense and continuing debate. Traditionalists argue that the accessibility of the technology will accelerate the decline in typographic standards that started when the first clumsy photocomposition systems began to replace lead type. Evangelists enthuse about a soon to be realised **digital paradise** in which everyone will compose letters in personally configured typefaces as idiosyncratic as their own handwriting.

¶*Typography now: the next wave* is an interim report on these changes, filed while they are still under way. It collects new work – from America, Britain, Germany, France and The Netherlands – which is redefining our approach to typography. Some of these designs are entirely dependent on the new technology; in production terms it would be simply too time-consuming, costly or awkward to generate them in any other way. Some of them anticipate the aesthetic concerns of the new **digital typography,** or reflect the freedoms that the technology makes possible, while still being produced at the drawing board, or by letterpress. Some will stand the test of time; others will prove to have been representative of their period, but of no greater significance. All of them demonstrate their designers' reluctance to accept that the conventions of typography are inscribed inviolably on tablets of stone.

¶Among these articles of faith, legibility is perhaps the first and most emotive. If there is one characteristic that links the many visual strategies of the new typographers, it is their combined assault on this most sacred of cows. Swiss-school modernism composed orderly, linear, well-tempered messages using supposedly objective, and certainly inexpressive, sanserif letterforms. The new typographers, reacting against this bloodless neutrality, justify their experiments by arguing that

no typeface is inherently legible;

rather, in the words of type designer **ZUZANA LICKO** of Emigre Graphics,

"it is the reader's familiarity with faces that accounts for their legibility".[1]

We might find it impossible to read black letter with ease today, but in pre-war Germany it was the dominant letterform. Baskerville, rejected in 1757 as ugly and unreadable, is now regarded as one of the most serviceable typefaces for long text setting.

¶Type design in the **digital era** is quirky, personal and unreservedly subjective. The **authoritarian voices of modernist typography,** which seem to permit only a single authorised reading, are rejected as too corporate, inflexible and limiting, as though typographic diversity itself might somehow re-enfranchise its readers.

"I think there are a lot of voices that have not been heard typographically,"

says Californian type designer **JEFFERY KEEDY**

"Whenever I start a new job and try to pick a typeface, none of the typefaces give me the voice that I need. They just don't relate to my experiences in my life. They're about somebody else's experiences, which don't belong to me."[2]

¶Another American type designer, **BARRY DECK**, speaks of trading in the

"myth of the transparency of typographical form for a more realistic attitude toward form, acknowledging that form carries meaning".[3] -

1. "Do you read me?", *Emigre*, No.15, 1990, p.12.
2. *Emigre*, No.15, pp.16-17.
3. Designer's statement, August 1991.
4. *Emigre*, No.15, p.17.

The aim is to promote multiple rather than fixed readings, to provoke the reader into becoming an active participant in the construction of the message.

Later modernist typography sought to reduce complexity and to clarify content, but the new typographers relish **ambiguity,** preferring the provisional utterance, alternative take and delayed punchline to the finely honed phrase.

"If someone interprets my work in a way that is totally new to me, I say fine," says Keedy. "That way your work has a life of its own. You create a situation for people to do with it what they will, and you don't create an enclosed or encapsulated moment."[4]

Citizen Light
Citizen Bold

Zuzana Licko. Citizen typeface. 1990

as a designer i realized there is no escaping being post-modern, since the typefaces available are very old or are based on very old models. Even when you try to do something contemporary, you rely on these old typefaces and conventions.

Jeffery Keedy
Application of Keedy typeface
Emigre magazine, 1990

¶For Keedy, Deck, Emigre Graphics and colleagues such as NEVILLE BRODY and JONATHAN BARNBROOK in Britain, and MAX KISMAN in The Netherlands, designing typefaces for personal use is a way of ensuring that graphic design projects carry their own specific

identity

and tone of voice. The pre-digital typefaces that Brody drew for *The Face* emphasised the new perspectives on contemporary culture embodied in the magazine's editorial. They also functioned as a medium through which Brody could develop a socio-cultural

commentary

of his own. Typeface Two, designed in 1984, was deliberately authoritarian in mood, in order, Brody said, to draw a parallel between the social climate of the 1930s and 1980s. The typeface's geometric rigidity was persistently undermined by the light-hearted manner in which it was applied. Other designers take an even more idiosyncratic approach. For Barry Deck, the starting point for a type design is not traditional notions of legibility or elegance, but a highly subjective and seemingly arbitrary

narrative

founded on the supposed correlation between sexuality and letterforms.

Neville Brody
12" single cover
1984

Neville Brody
Typeface Two
1984

Neville Brody
Application of Typeface Two
The Face magazine, 1984

5. Designer's statement.

"With this in mind, I began imposing narratives of sexual angst, deviation and perversion on the design of my type. Because the F is a particularly important letter in the language of sexuality, it came to be a major point of activation in all of the alphabets."[5]

¶In this polymorphous **digital realm,** typefaces can cross-fertilise each other or merge to form strange new **hybrids.** Kisman's Fudoni Bold Remix mixes Futura and Bodini; Barnbrook's Prototype is collaged together from the parts of ten other typefaces, among them Bembo, Perpetua and Gill; and Deck's Canicopulus Script is Gill Sans Serif with the satirical addition of puppy-dog tails. Other typeface designs are more polemical than practical in their acknowledgement of the contingency, impermanence and potential for chaos which is a basic condition of the **digital medium.** ERIK VAN BLOKLAND and JUST VAN ROSSUM's Beowolf is a family of unpredictable **random fonts** programmed for three levels of randomness whose broken, antique outlines shift and reform every time a letter is produced so that no character is ever the same twice. Van Blokland and van Rossum, mavericks with a semi-serious message about the shortcomings of computerised perfection, speculate on the possibility of developing fonts that will cause characters to drop out at random, or to print upside down, and typefaces that will slowly decay until they eventually become illegible in a **digital parody** of hot-metal type. Jonathan Barnbrook goes a step further by extending this nihilistic randomising principle to the text itself. His typeface Burroughs (named after the novelist with a penchant for textual "cut-ups") replaces whatever is typeset with a **stream of gibberish** generated at random by the software.

¶Hand in hand with this investigation of the new aesthetic possibilities of the computer comes **a revaluation of the**

the hand-made and the ready-made.

For designers who are dissatisfied with the glib solutions and formulaic perfection of professional graphics, naive **vernacular** approaches to type (and imagery) appear to offer a rich seam of authenticity, allusion, expression and meaning. HARD WERKEN, THE THUNDER JOCKEYS, JOHN WEBER and BARRY DECK value letterforms – hand-drawn and mechanical – for their impurities and flaws.

"I am really interested in type that isn't perfect," says Deck. "Type that reflects more truly the imperfect language of an imperfect world inhabited by imperfect beings."[6]

Deck's typeface Template Gothic, based on an old sign he found in a laundromat, is an attempt to capture the spirit of crude lettering templates by using truncated strokes, erratic, tapered letterforms, and letters that look like they are the degraded product of photomechanical reproduction.

EDWARD FELLA, a former commercial artist, creates posters that break every known rule of typographic decorum and designer good taste. In Fella's agitated hands, type is spun, tilted, stretched, sliced, fractured, drawn as if with a broken nib, and set loose among fields of ink-blotter doodles and networks of rules. He is perhaps the most extreme example in these pages of the typographer as artist – an innovator who assumes and achieves the same level of creative freedom as the painters and sculptors whose exhibitions he promotes in catalogues and posters.

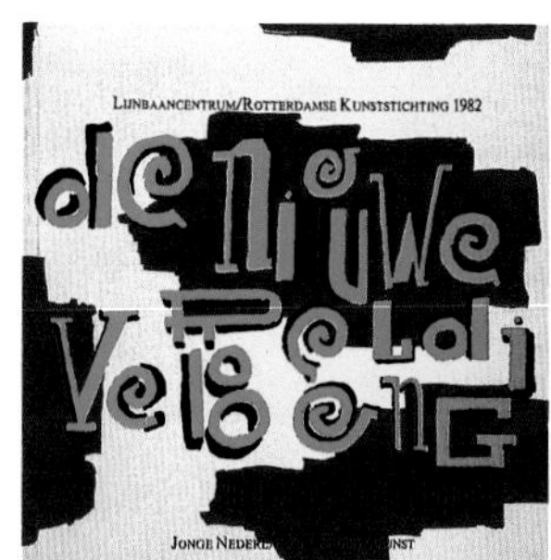

Hard Werken
Hand-drawn type
1982

¶Fella, significantly, is a graduate of the Cranbrook Academy of Art, the source of many of the most interesting developments in new typography. Few Cranbrook exercises, however, are entirely typographic; the most typical concentrate on the relationship of **image and text.** Cranbrook has been at the forefront in exploring the dense, complex **layering of elements** that is one of the most salient (and frequently criticised) characteristics of the new typographic design. Unlike the earlier work of the New Wave designers, this is not simply a formal exercise in collage-making; the method arises directly from **an engagement with content.** The Cranbrook theorists' aim, derived from French philosophy and literary theory, is to **deconstruct,** or break apart and expose, the **manipulative visual language** and different levels of meaning embodied in a design, in the same way that a literary critic might deconstruct and decode the verbal language of a novel.

6. *Emigre*, No.15, p.21.

7. "A brave new world: understanding deconstruction", *Print*, XLIV:VI, November/ December 1990, p.83. See also: Katherine McCoy and David Frej, "Typography as discourse", *ID*, Vol. 35 No. 2, 1988, p.34-37.

"When the deconstructionist approach is applied to design,"

write the American critics Chuck Byrne and Martha Witte,

"each layer, through the use of language and image, is an intentional performer in a deliberately playful game wherein the viewer can discover and experience the hidden complexities of language."[7]

The work that results (seen in this book in examples by KATHERINE McCOY, ALLEN HORI and P. SCOTT MAKELA) is a direct challenge to its audience, which must learn to "read" these layered, allusive, open-ended image/type constructions with the same close attention that it would bring to a difficult piece of text.

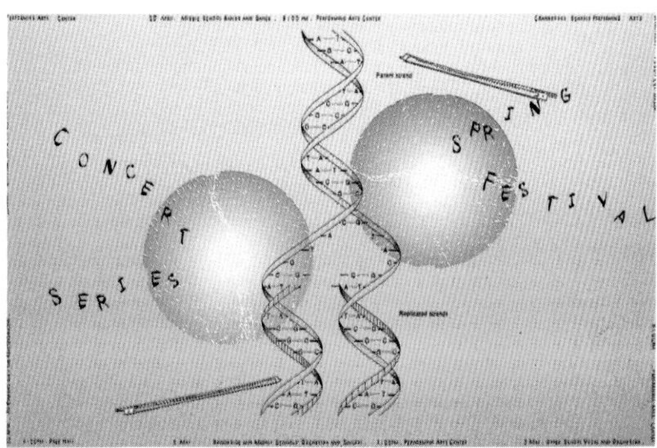

Lisa Langhoff Vorhees,
Cranbrook Academy of Art
Concert poster
1990

¶Although the idea of deconstruction is gaining ground among designers in the US, and enjoys some currency in Europe where it originated, few typographers, at this point, would feel sufficiently confident of the theoretical basis of the term to describe themselves as deconstructionists. Yet the visual strategies of deconstruction, driven by the

two faces for the 90's— john wesley harding (singer-songwriter) , beach culture magazine.

Santa Monica pier

mary;'s danish on bottled w
plus the u s u a l mix of art, places st Yle

on the Road in jamaica, ZANZIBAR, Hawaii and kentucky

the ULTIMATE: A sport

rd st

TIMATE: A sport that lives up to its name.

the j e s u s and mary chain on the S
anta Monica pier

b o o k stores

RFSHOPS and the beach

David Carson
Beach Culture magazine
1990

layering capabilities of the computer, are already widely dispersed. The Californian surfing magazine *Beach Culture* rapidly became both *cause célèbre* and designer's *bête noire* for the deconstructive

frenzy

with which its art director, DAVID CARSON dismantled the typography of contents pages, headlines and text. In London, WHY NOT ASSOCIATES bring a similar typographic abandon to their catalogue dividers and covers for the clothing company Next. In each case the visual

delirium

is formally stunning, but its relevance to the content is not always clear. Both in their different ways are examples of what Andy Altmann of Why Not Associates calls

type as entertainment.

The designs function decoratively as a means of engaging, amusing, persuading and no doubt sometimes infuriating the reader, rather than as vehicles for extending meaning or exploring the text.

¶Such issues are unavoidable when it comes to the design of long pieces of prose. The questions of legibility and personal expression that preoccupy the new typographers become far more acute when the aim is to hold the reader's attention over the course of many pages. Are the new fonts suitable for any purpose other than exotic display? Or is it time, perhaps, to re-examine the rigidly drawn distinction between typefaces for text and titles? Emigre Graphics, which is able to road-test its typefaces in its own magazine, has demonstrated the surprising readability of even the most bizarre and apparently

unpromising fonts,

given a little familiarity with their quirks. *Emigre*'s designer RUDY VANDERLANS mixes seemingly

incompatible faces,

varies point size and line depth, centres text over extra-wide measures, changes column width within articles, and runs two or more text-strands in parallel – most of the time

without

undue

loss of legibility.

Phil Baines
Postcard
1986

PHIL : J THING NG TO EARS C
anuary 1986. LO s happening and w lift a seven foot H ompletion. 5: (At
OKING ONE ork being done, a AIRY CIRCLE last). A red, moun
WAY, pounds st good spirit. 3: An made of Silver Bir tain BIKE, lost fo
erling; design as h dy Goldsworthy on ch. 25th January.' r a moment, IN S
igh street fashion Hampstead Heath 4: A Map of THE NOW at 1100 fe
as design. LOO , 'Very cold. Helpi CITY of London n et, and rememberi
KING ANOT o develop my idea(ng the running I c
HER, 1: Re the a an no longer do: 'I
bove, remembered I)s. . . . DESIGNERS PLAYI
card from May 19
84, (EXTRAC POSITIVE ROLE IN SOCI
T RIGHT) at od
ds but still an aspi . . I LIKE that; it's a t is the caged taki
ration. 2: Another ng wing but it is n
term. Feels like an good stART. ot space encompas
other college with sed'. (K. Gibran).

¶But *Emigre* remains the exception. Most designers experimenting with radical approaches to page structure and typographic hierarchy work with a far more restricted and conventional selection of typefaces. The British typographer and letterpress exponent PHIL BAINES has turned to

medieval manuscripts,

Marshall McLuhan's *The Gutenberg galaxy,* concrete poetry and artists' books for

alternative models of textual organisation.

Baines's autobiographical postcards and his undergraduate thesis, "The Bauhaus mistook legibility for communication", combine editorial rigour and sensitivity to language with a playful sense of typographic possibility.

"Legibility, presents information as facts rather than as experience,"[8] says Baines. There is nothing wrong with logic and linearity, he argues, but these qualities satisfy only the rational side of the brain. For Baines and his colleagues, it is equally important that

typography should address our capacity for intuitive insight and simultaneous perception, and stimulate our senses as well as engaging our intellect.

¶Baines's most experimental work is still to be found in his personal projects, but in the last two years there have been a number of striking attempts to redefine the syntax of the conventional book. TIBOR KALMAN's catalogue for an exhibition about chaos theory and the arts subjects the essays to extremes of typographic distortion in an attempt to embody the exhibition's theme. In one essay, the word-spacing increases progressively until the

text disintegrates into particles;

in another, bold and under-sized characters are sprinkled randomly throughout the text. Avital Ronell's *The telephone book*, a discourse on the history, philosophy and psychoanalytical implications of the telephone, subverts the traditional elegance of a university press publication with a catalogue of

typographic mishaps

and metaphorical wrong numbers. Lines of type ripple with size changes, sections of text are crossed out or tilted at angles, whole pages are obscured by over-setting or

photographic erosion,

fragments of setting float free of the grid, and arguments break off and are never resumed. It is as though the entire book – a collaboration between "switchboard operator" Ronell, designer RICHARD ECKERSLEY and compositor Michael Jensen – is in the grip of some fiendish gremlin playing havoc with the telephone system.

8.
"The first consideration of typography is to be clearly read", debate, Chartered Society of Designers, London, 11 March 1991.

Wolfgang Weingart
Poster. 1977

¶Ambitious publishing projects such as *Emigre* and *The telephone book* suggest that the tradition of experimental typography initiated by Futurism, Dada and the Bauhaus, and sustained by the work of

ROBERT MASSIN
WOLFGANG WEINGART
WARREN LEHRER

and others, is still being refreshed. None of these projects is part of the typographic mainstream, or reaches a particularly wide readership, yet they are exerting an influence well beyond their milieu. The textual designs and many of the posters featured in *Typography now: the next wave* make large demands on their readers, but they make equally large demands on their designers. If this kind of typography is not to become simply an exercise in style, or fashionable deconstruction, then **designers must** be able to **function as visual editors** who can bring acute perception to their readings of the text. In some cases (*Emigre* and 8vo's magazine, *Octavo*, are examples) the designer might combine the role of editor and typographer. If this is not possible, then author and typographer must work together much more closely than is usually the case **to establish and amplify textual meaning.** Only then will there be a satisfying relationship between typographic expression and text.

Robert Massin
Page from Ionesco's play,
The bald prima donna

type
and andandand
image
K TMY 5053

Van dag tot dag (From day to day). Festival magazine cover
Holland Festival, the Netherlands, 1987
Design Robert Nakata Studio Dumbar
Photography: Lex van Pieterson

Concertos for Orchestra. CD cover
Decca, UK, 1989
Design **Nick Bell**
Art director: Ann Bradbeer
Photography: Jim Friedman

Newsprint. Magazine cover. VRG
The Netherlands, 1990
Design **Will de l'Ecluse**
Ingeborg Bloem, UNA

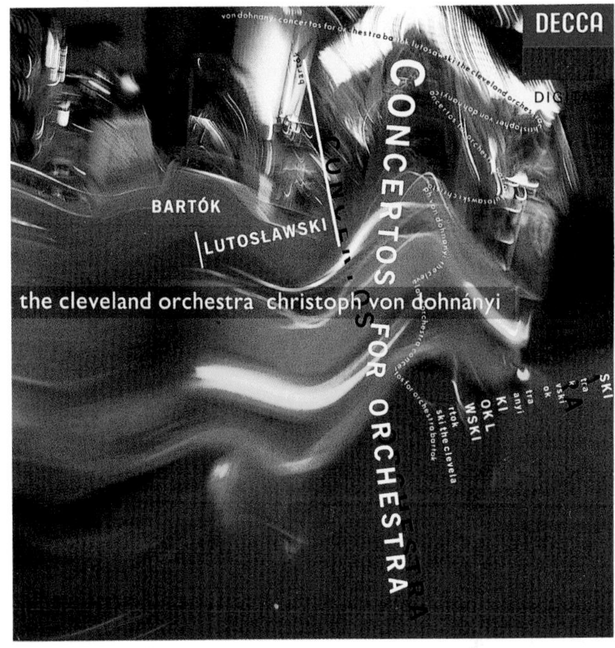

left: *De voor-verkoop is al begonnen!*
(The pre-sale has begun!)
Poster. Holland Festival, The Netherlands, 1988
Design Vincent van Baar, Hans Meijboom
Studio Dumbar
Photography: Lex van Pieterson

below: Farewell party invitation. Rijksmuseum, The Netherlands, 1989
Design Eric Nuyten
Studio Dumbar

opposite: *Programme 1987*. Cover
Holland Festival, The Netherlands, 1987
Design Robert Nakata
Studio Dumbar
Photography: Lex van Pieterson

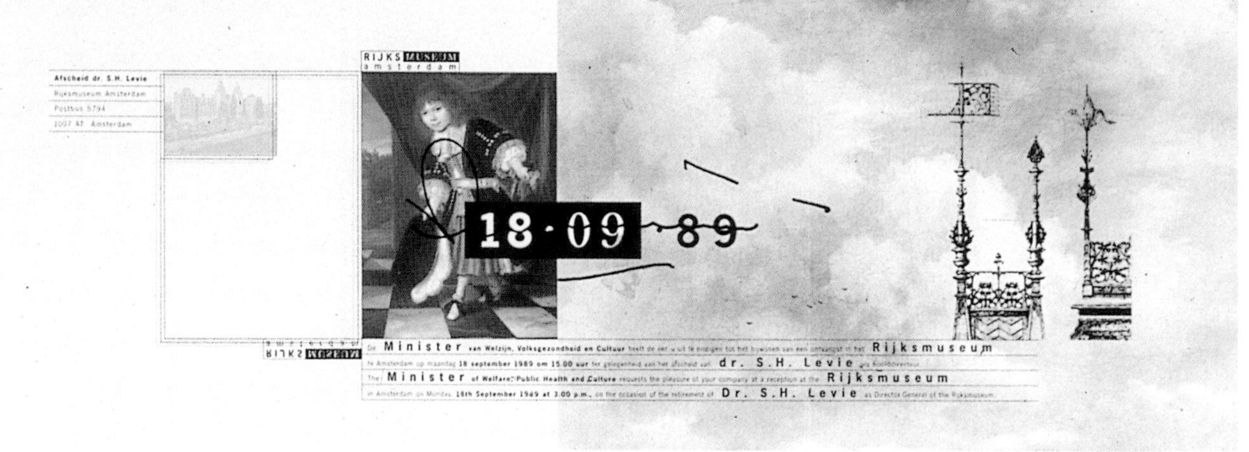

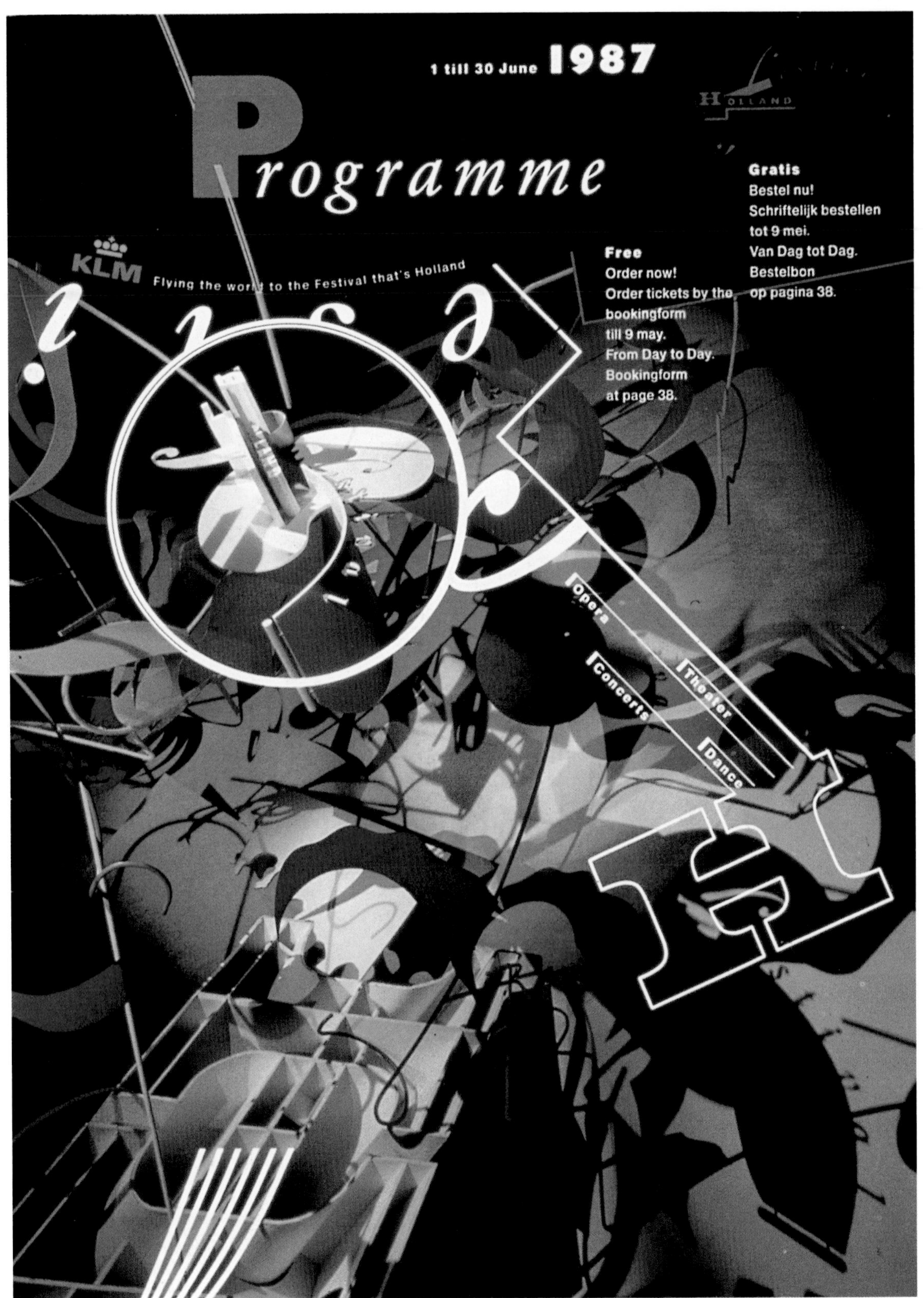
1 till 30 June 1987
Holland
Programme
Gratis
Bestel nu!
Schriftelijk bestellen
tot 9 mei.
Van Dag tot Dag.
Bestelbon
op pagina 38.
KLM
Flying the world to the Festival that's Holland
Free
Order now!
Order tickets by the
bookingform
till 9 may.
From Day to Day.
Bookingform
at page 38.
Opera
Theater
Concerts
Dance

Paper stories. Promotional poster
Zanders, Germany, 1990
Design Helene Bergmans
Ton van Bragt
Alan Chandler
Studio Dumbar
Illustration: Henk Bank
Photography: Lex van Pieterson

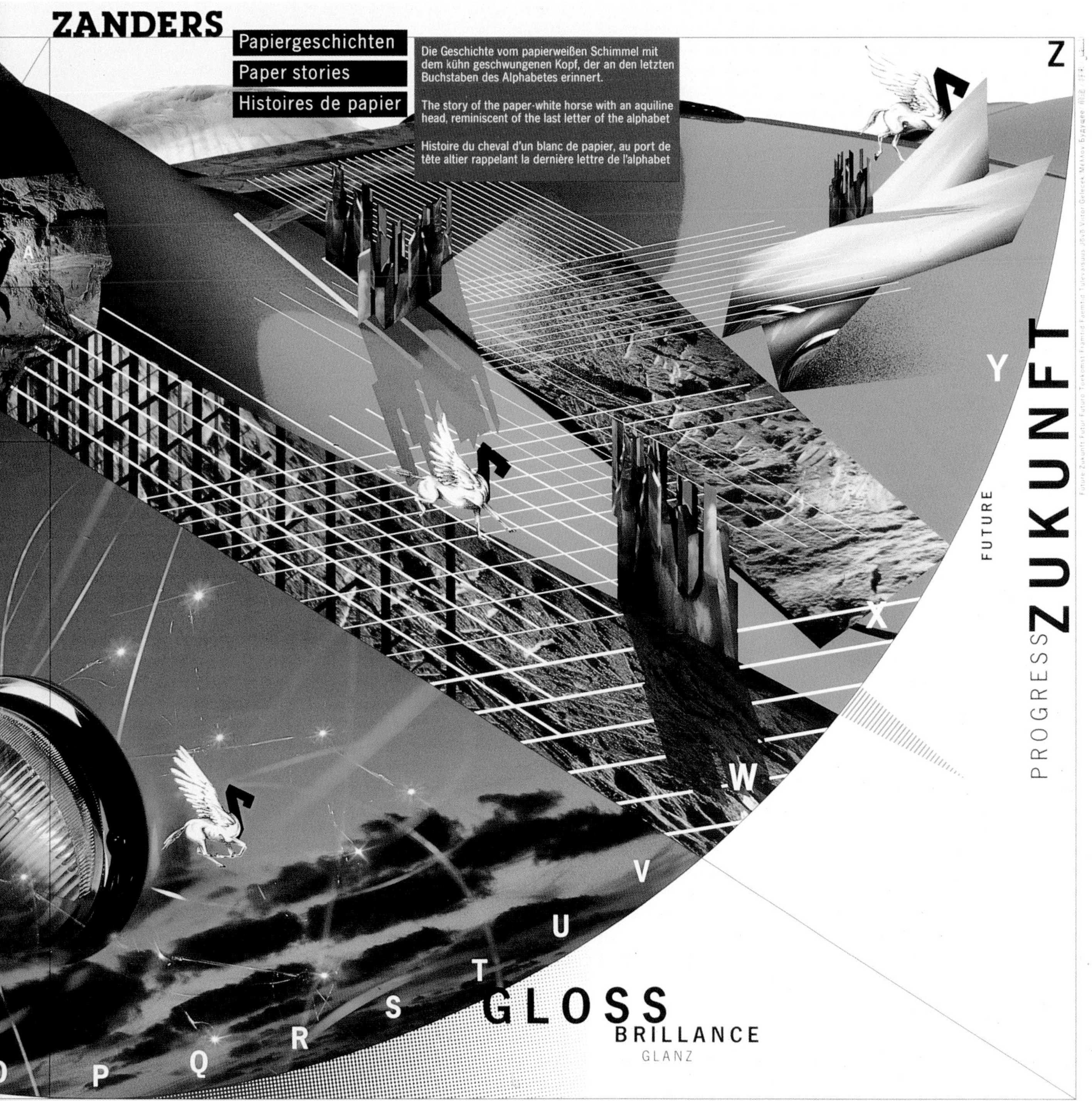
ZANDERS
Papiergeschichten
Paper stories
Histoires de papier
Die Geschichte vom papierweißen Schimmel mit dem kühn geschwungenen Kopf, der an den letzten Buchstaben des Alphabetes erinnert.
The story of the paper-white horse with an aquiline head, reminiscent of the last letter of the alphabet
Histoire du cheval d'un blanc de papier, au port de tête altier rappelant la dernière lettre de l'alphabet
Z
Y
X
W
V
U
T
S
R
Q
P
FUTURE
PROGRESS ZUKUNFT
GLOSS
BRILLANCE
GLANZ
Gloss/Glanz/Brillance/Brillantezza/Brillo/Brilho/Glans/Loisto/Fény/Strălucire/Parlak
ikonofix 170 g/m² ZANDERS Feinpapiere AG
Impression: Sechsfarben Offsetdruck/Six colour offset printing/Offset 6 couleurs

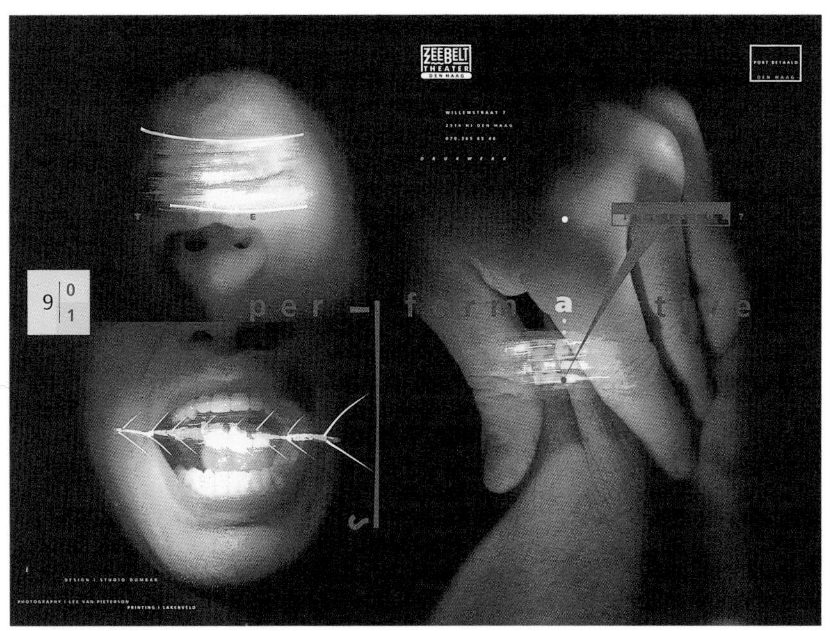

above: *Performative - Incision?*
Monthly mailer. Zeebelt Theatre,
The Netherlands, 1990
Design **Allen Hori**
Studio Dumbar
Photography: Lex van Pieterson

opposite: *Largo Desolato.* Poster
Bristol Old Vic, UK, 1986
Design **Hans Bockting**
Photography: Reinier Gerritsen

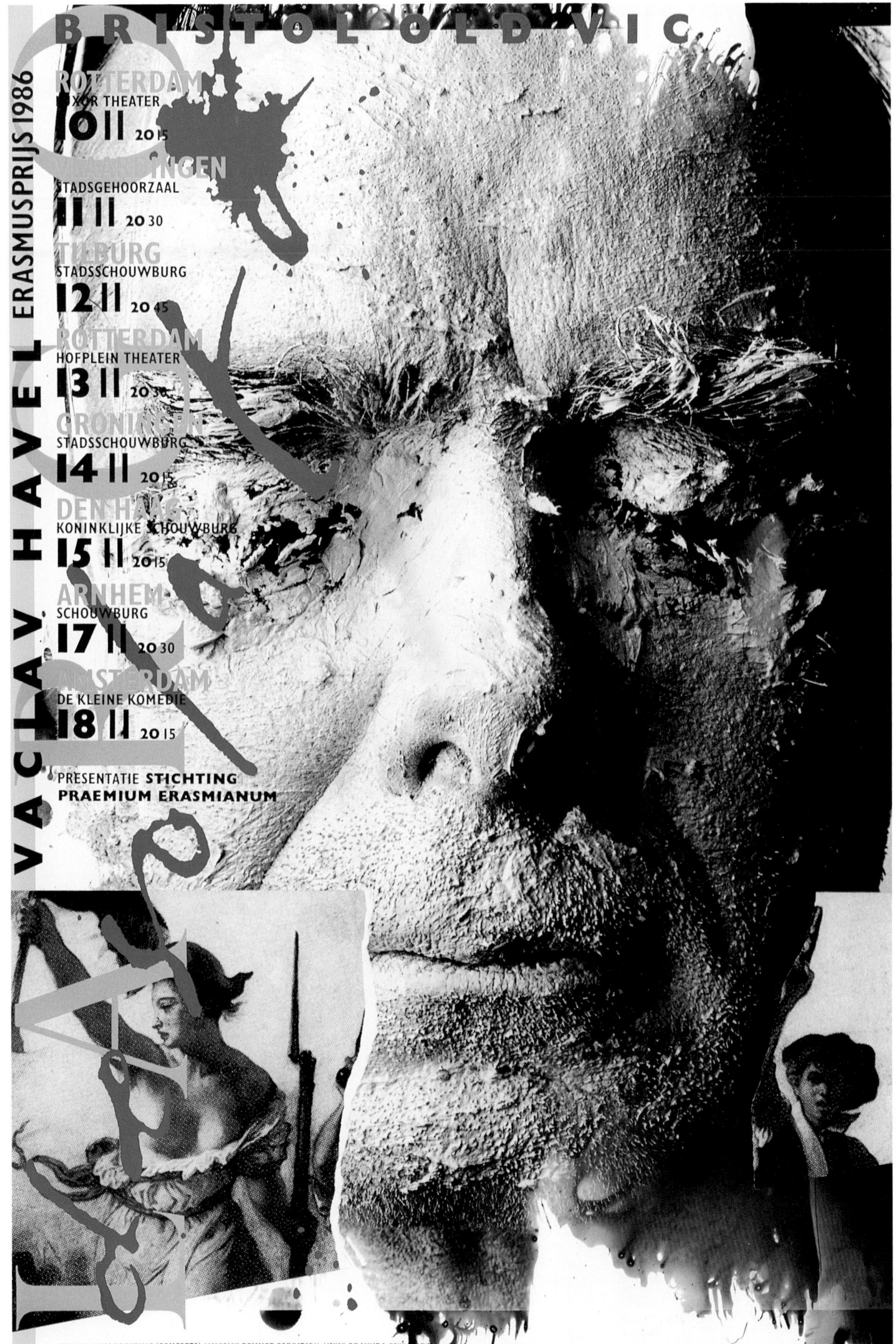
BRISTOL OLD VIC
VACLAV HAVEL ERASMUSPRIJS 1986
ROTTERDAM
XOR THEATER
10 11 20 15
INGEN
STADSGEHOORZAAL
11 11 20 30
TILBURG
STADSSCHOUWBURG
12 11 20 45
ROTTERDAM
HOFPLEIN THEATER
13 11 20 30
GRONINGEN
STADSSCHOUWBURG
14 11 20 15
DEN HAAG
KONINKLIJKE SCHOUWBURG
15 11 20 15
ARNHEM
SCHOUWBURG
17 11 20 30
AMSTERDAM
DE KLEINE KOMEDIE
18 11 20 15
PRESENTATIE STICHTING
PRAEMIUM ERASMIANUM
ONTWERP HANS BOCKTING (CONCEPTS) FOTOGRAFIE REINIER GERRITSEN LITHO'S GRAVURA

Componist
david dramm
Toneelbeeld
edwin kolpa
Licht
marc van gelder
Kostuums
bianca van dillen
Choreografie
1 phil griffin
2 dries van der post en
3 guido severien
dansproduktie

above: *Het Arsenaal/Dolf Stekhoven.* Posters
Icograda, The Netherlands, 1987
Design **Armand Mevis, Linda van Deursen**

opposite: *Tiga.* Poster. The Netherlands, 1990. Design **Koweiden Postma**
Photography: Hans Verschuuren

American piano sonatas. CD cover. Virgin Classics, UK, 1990 Design Nick Bell
Photography: Andy Rumball

Letterhead (back). UK, 1991
Design Nick Bell

Architects' brochure/poster
Daryl Jackson International, UK, 1990
Design Siobhan Keaney
Photography: Robert Shackleton

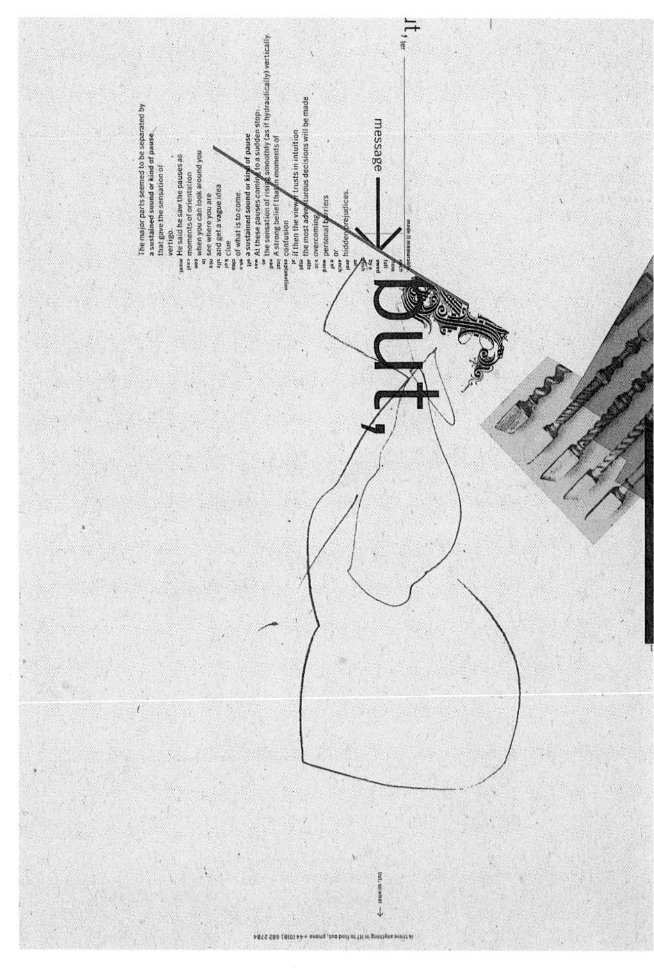

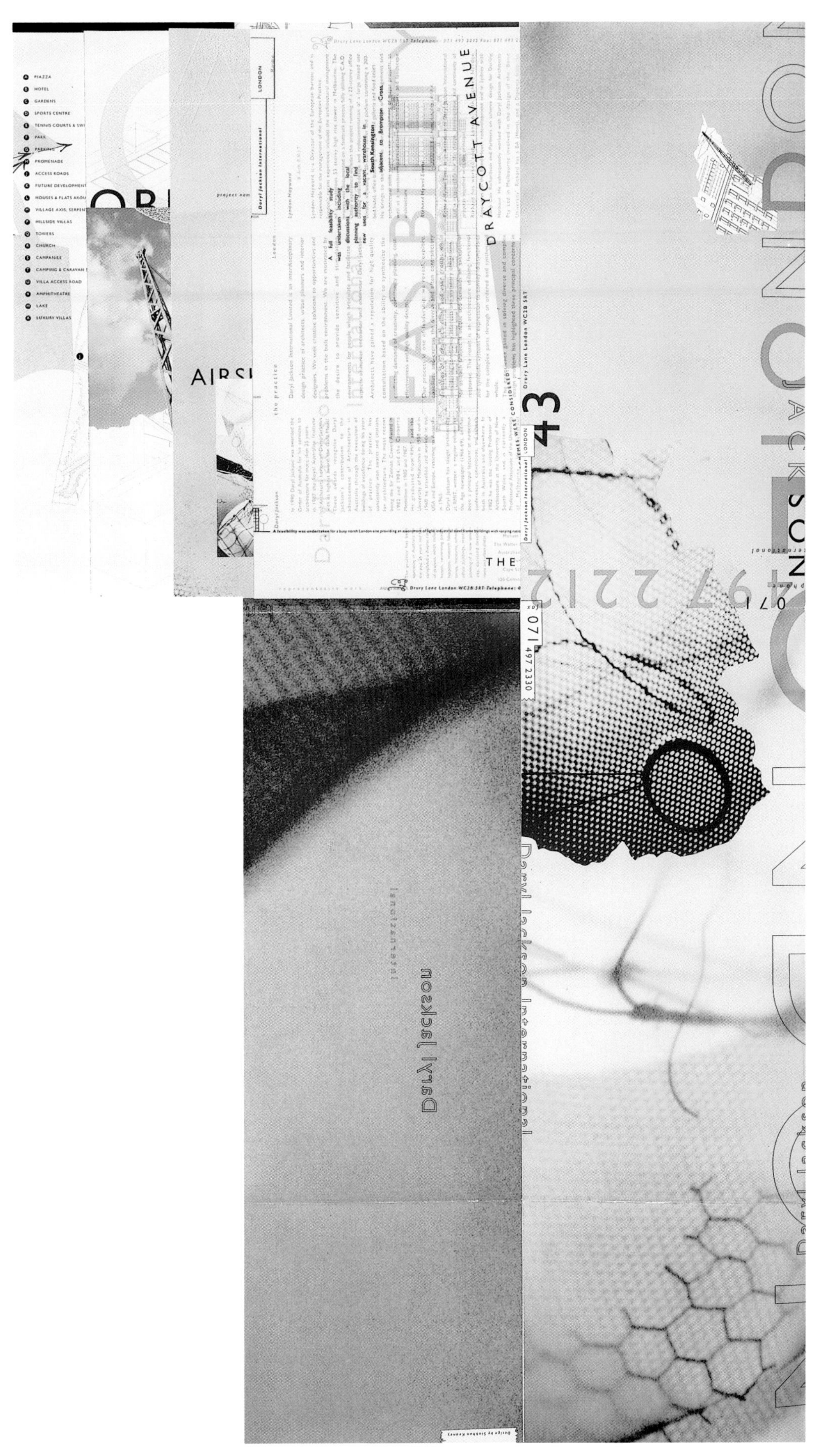

PIAZZA
HOTEL
GARDENS
SPORTS CENTRE
PARK
PROMENADE
ACCESS ROADS
HILLSIDE VILLAS
TOWERS
CHURCH
CAMPANILE
VILLA ACCESS ROAD
AMPHITHEATRE
LAKE
LUXURY VILLAS
AIRS
THE
DRAYCOTT AVENUE
43
071 497 2330

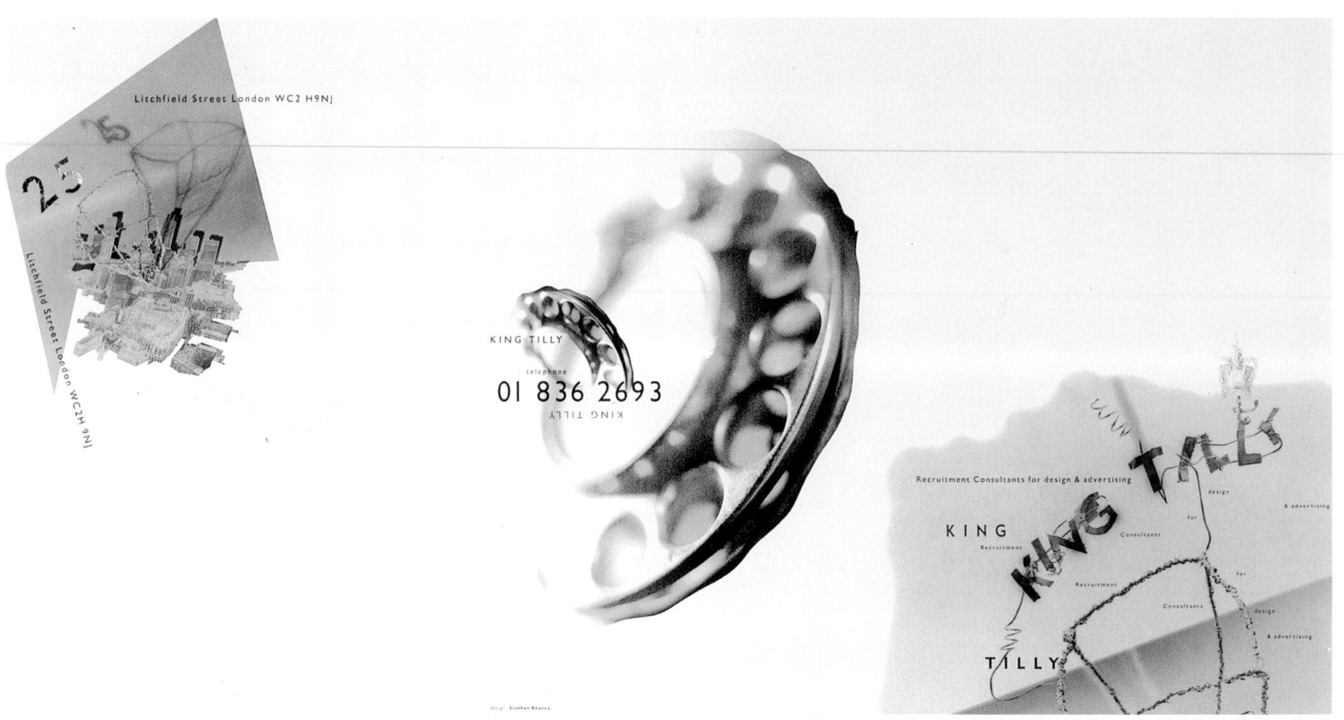

Brochure/mailer. King Tilly, UK, 1990
Design **Siobhan Keaney**
Photography: Robert Shackleton

Annual report. Cover. Apicorp, UK, 1988
Design **Siobhan Keaney**
Photography: Robert Shackleton

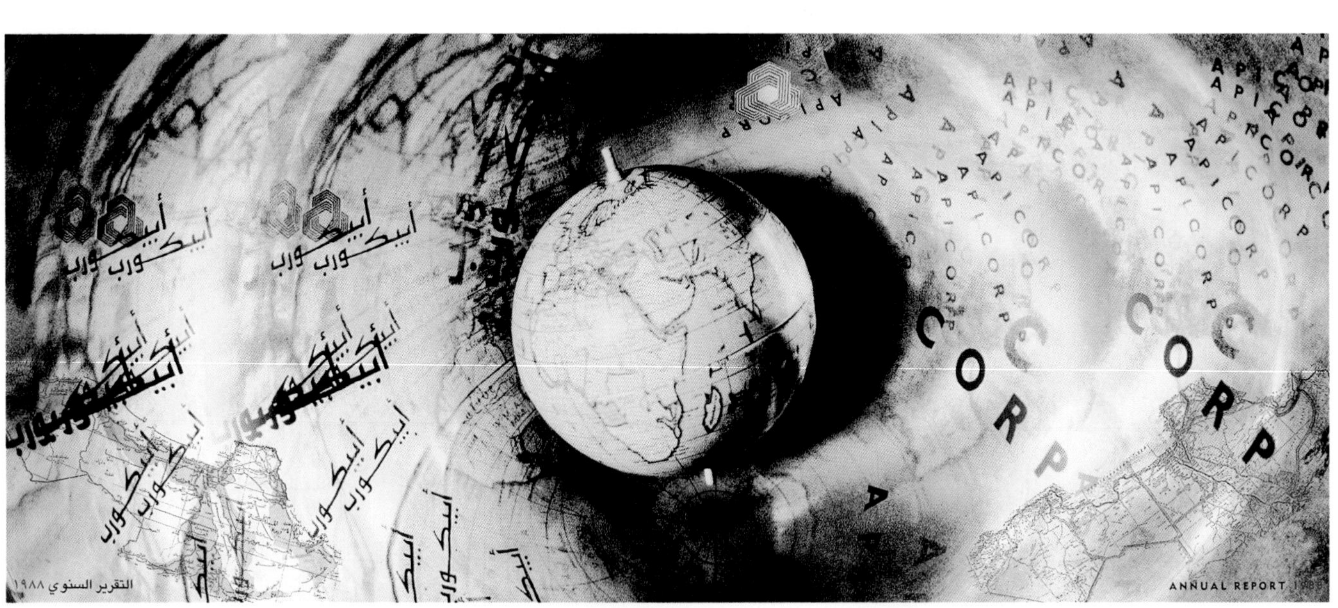

Annual review. Illustration. IBM, UK, 1991
Design **Nick Bell**
Photography: Andy Rumball, Nick Bell

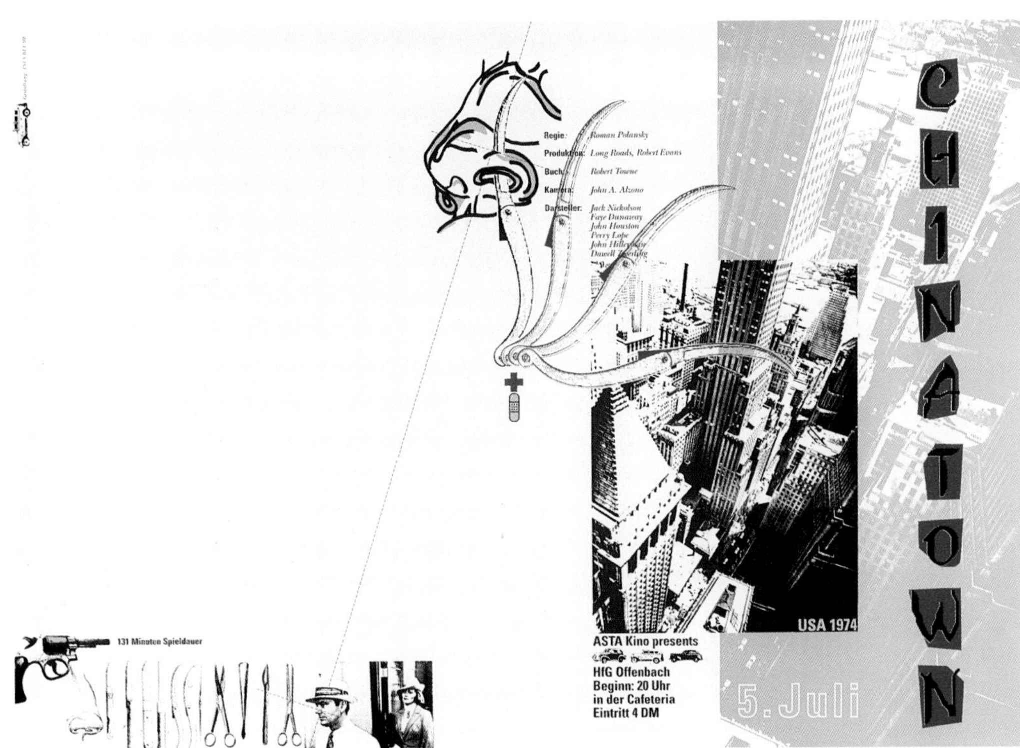

Chinatown. Film poster. Germany, 1989
Hochschule für Gestaltung
Offenbach
Design **Ines Blume**

opposite: 1990 calendar. PTT, The Netherlands, 1989
Design **Vorm Vijf**

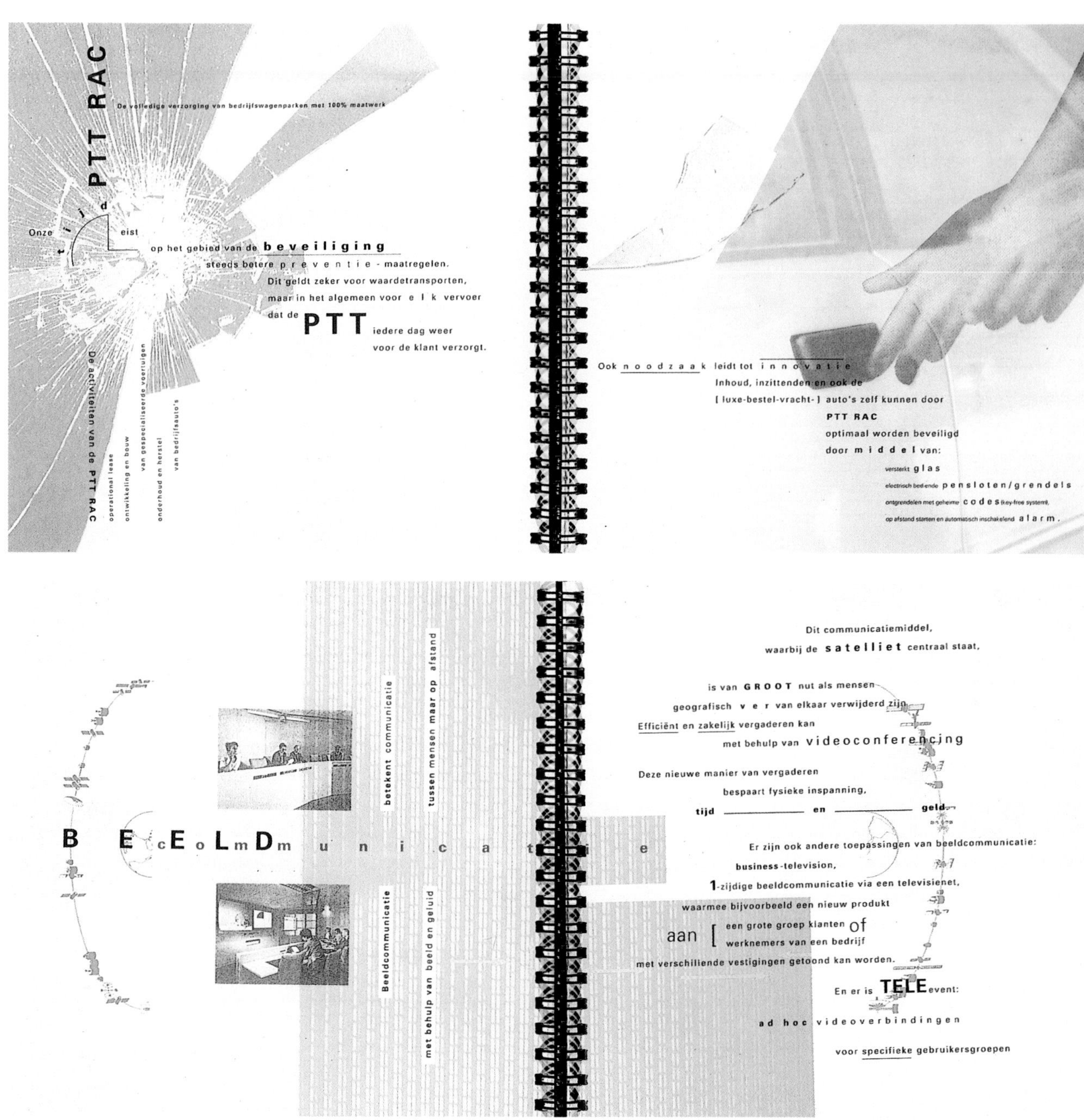
PTT RAC
De volledige verzorging van bedrijfswagenparken met 100% maatwerk
Onze tijd eist
op het gebied van de beveiliging
steeds betere preventie - maatregelen.
Dit geldt zeker voor waardetransporten,
maar in het algemeen voor elk vervoer
dat de PTT iedere dag weer
voor de klant verzorgt.
De activiteiten van de PTT RAC
operational lease
ontwikkeling en bouw
van gespecialiseerde voertuigen
onderhoud en herstel
van bedrijfsauto's
Ook noodzaak leidt tot innovatie
Inhoud, inzittenden en ook de
[luxe-bestel-vracht-] auto's zelf kunnen door
PTT RAC
optimaal worden beveiligd
door middel van:
versterkt glas
electrisch bediende pensloten/grendels
ontgrendelen met geheime codes (key-free system),
op afstand starten en automatisch inschakelend alarm.
BEELDcommunicatie
betekent communicatie
tussen mensen maar op afstand
Beeldcommunicatie
met behulp van beeld en geluid
Dit communicatiemiddel,
waarbij de satelliet centraal staat,
is van GROOT nut als mensen
geografisch ver van elkaar verwijderd zijn.
Efficiënt en zakelijk vergaderen kan
met behulp van videoconferencing
Deze nieuwe manier van vergaderen
bespaart fysieke inspanning,
tijd en geld
Er zijn ook andere toepassingen van beeldcommunicatie:
business-television,
1-zijdige beeldcommunicatie via een televisienet,
waarmee bijvoorbeeld een nieuw produkt
aan [een grote groep klanten of werknemers van een bedrijf
met verschillende vestigingen getoond kan worden.
En er is TELEevent:
ad hoc videoverbindingen
voor specifieke gebruikersgroepen

jaarkalender 1990
ptt: goede zaak!
post
ptt nederland
ptt|post

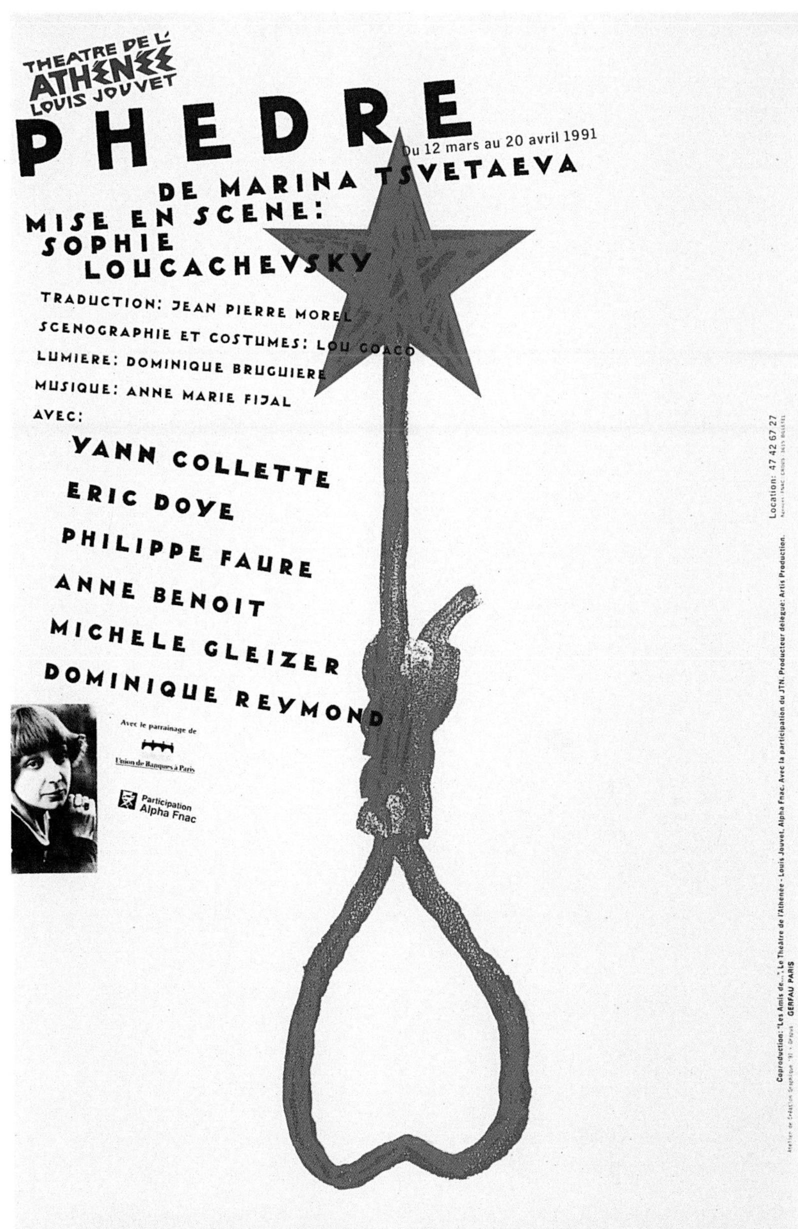

Phedre. Poster. Theatre de l'Athénée Louis Jouvet, France, 1991

Design Dirk Behage
Pierre Bernard
Fokke Draaijer
Atelier de Création Graphique-Grapus

opposite: 1990 calendar. Poster. PTT, The Netherlands, 1990

Design Vorm Vijf

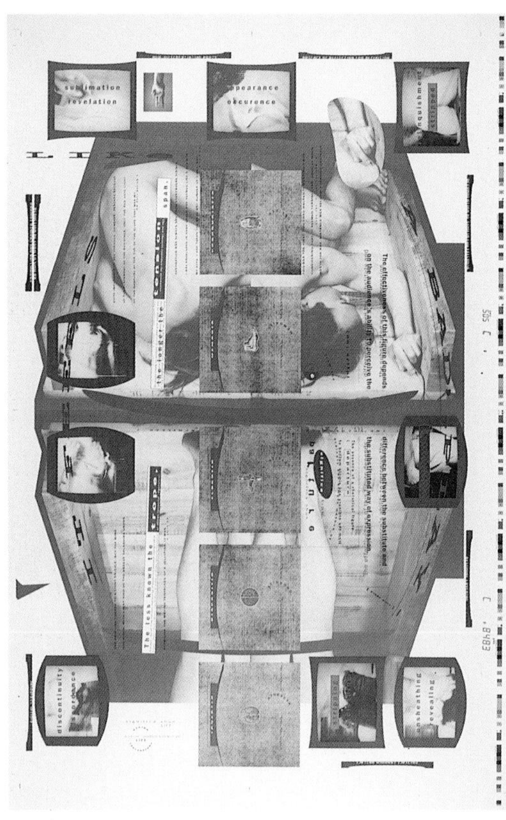

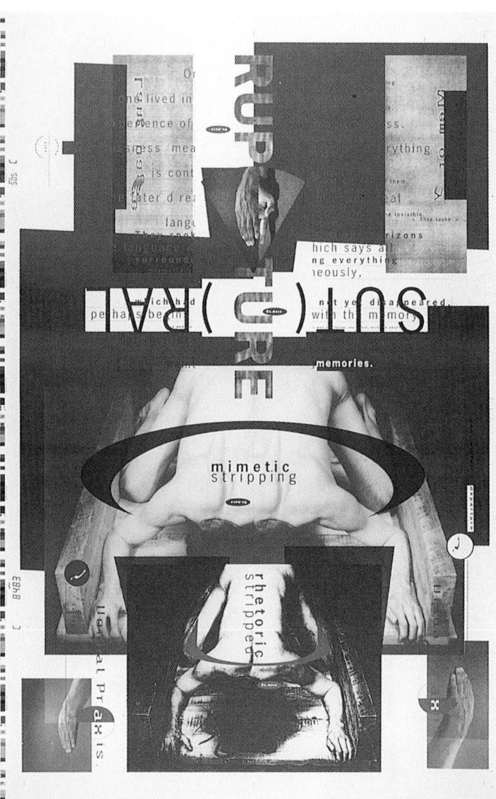

It feels like a bad play. Two-sided poster
Emigre Graphics, USA, 1989
Design/photography Allen Hori

opposite: *Cranbrook design: the new discourse*
Poster. USA, 1990
Design P. Scott Makela
Cranbrook Academy of Art

Art science

Nothing pulls you into the territory between art and science quite so quickly as design.

Mathematics

Mythology

Technology

Poetry

Dangerous

Rigorous

Desire necessity

Watching the process of students

Mythology technology

the new

Systematic

discourse

Desire

necessity

reading

finding

the new
CRANBROOK DESIGN
discourse

Computer related design. Poster

Royal College of Art, UK, 1991

Design 

Photography: Nick Harrington

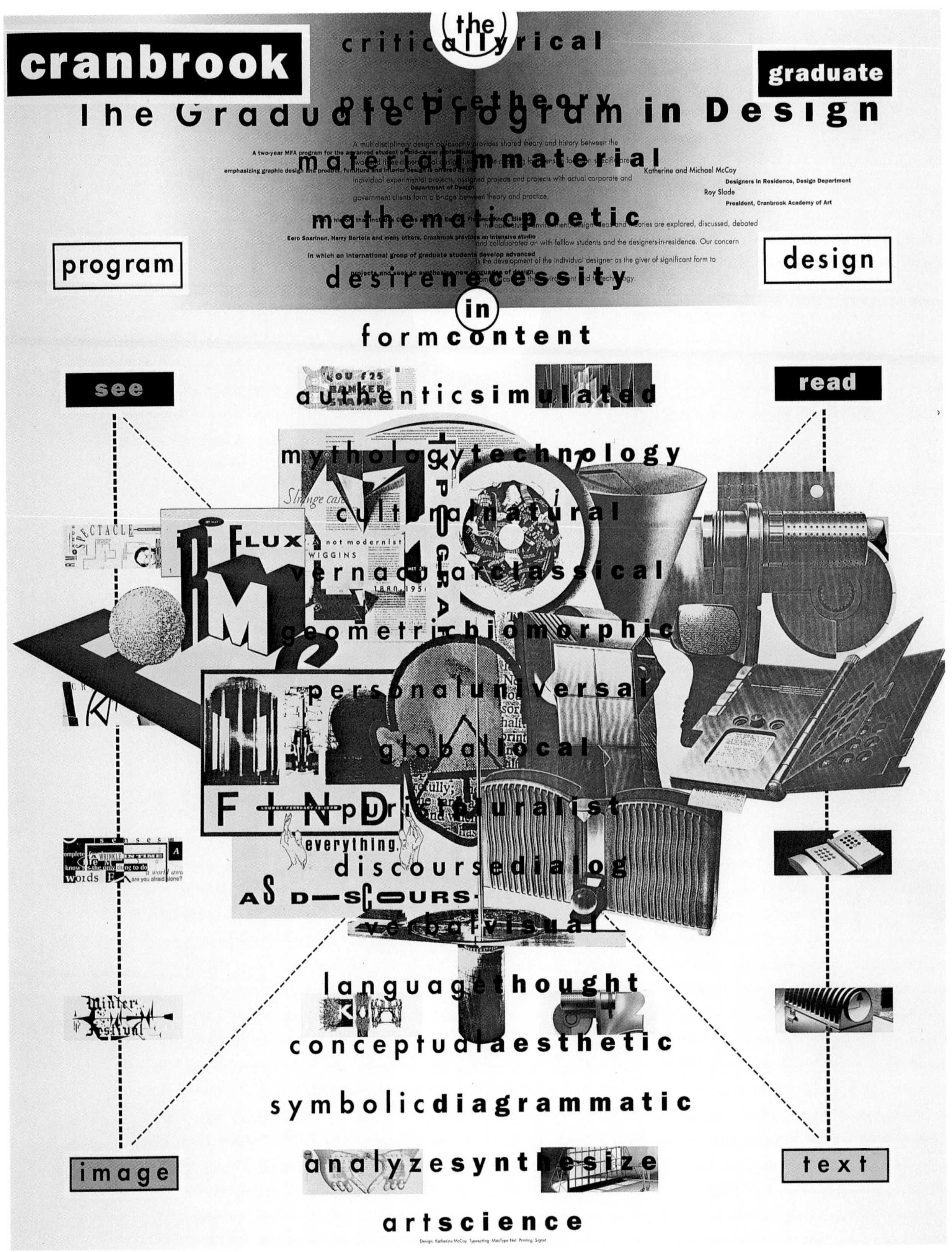

The Cranbrook graduate program in design. Poster
Cranbrook Academy of Art, USA, 1989
Design **Katherine McCoy**

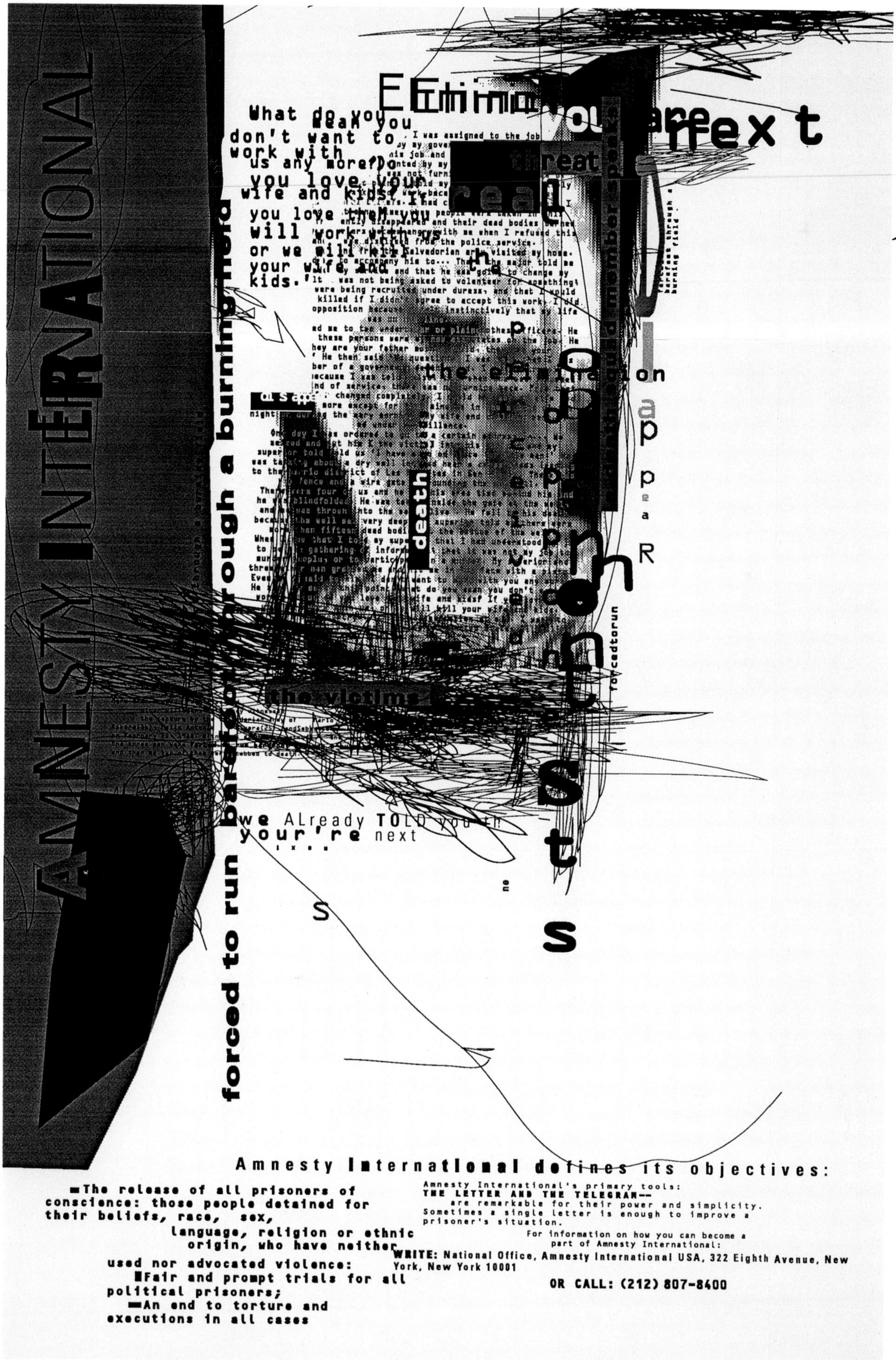

AMNESTY INTERNATIONAL

What do you mean you don't want to work with us any more? Do you love your wife and kids? If you love them you will work with us or we will kill your wife and kids.'

forced to run barefoot through a burning field

the elimination

death

the victims

we ALready TOLD you, your're next

Amnesty International defines its objectives:

■The release of all prisoners of conscience: those people detained for their beliefs, race, sex, language, religion or ethnic origin, who have neither used nor advocated violence:

■Fair and prompt trials for all political prisoners;

■An end to torture and executions in all cases

Amnesty International's primary tools:
THE LETTER AND THE TELEGRAM-- are remarkable for their power and simplicity. Sometimes a single letter is enough to improve a prisoner's situation.

For information on how you can become a part of Amnesty International:

WRITE: National Office, Amnesty International USA, 322 Eighth Avenue, New York, New York 10001

OR CALL: (212) 807-8400

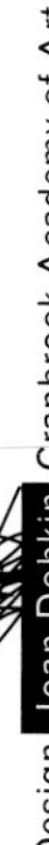

Amnesty International. Poster. USA, 1991. Design Joan Dobkin Cranbrook Academy of Art

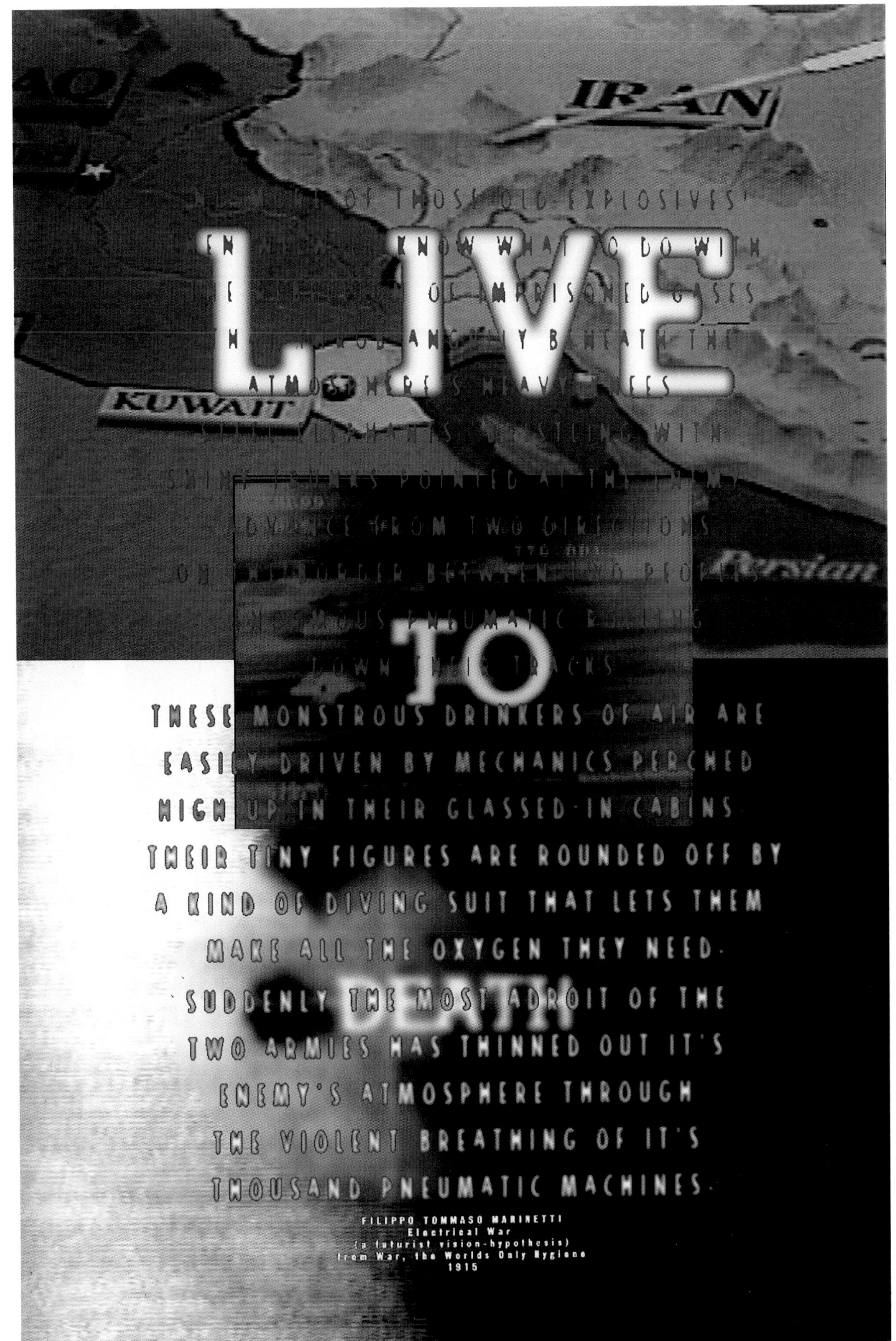

Live to Death. Poster. USA, 1991. Design P. Scott Makela Cranbrook Academy of Art

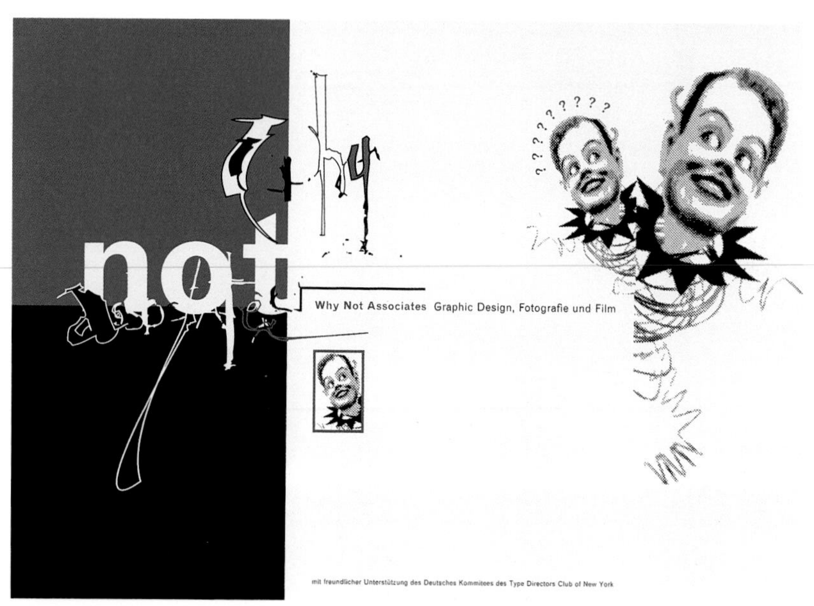

above: Exhibition invitation. UK, 1991
right: *Next Directory Preview*. Catalogue cover. Next, UK, 1991
Design Why Not Associates
Photography: Why Not Associates, Rocco Redondo

Lamp/Feel. Poster. USA, 1991
Design Mark D. Sylvester
Cranbrook Academy of Art

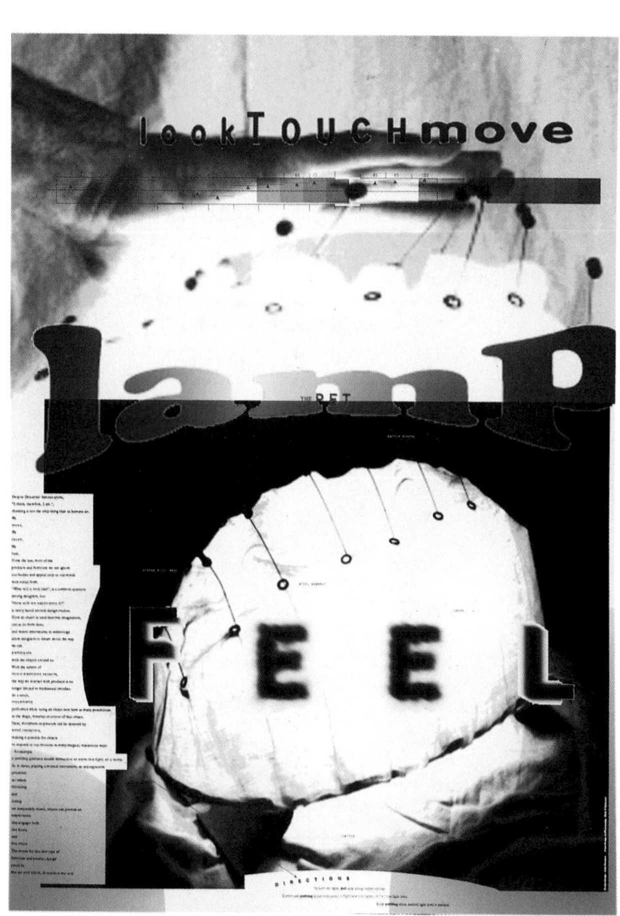

NEXT
VII
1991
EDITION
S P RING
SUMMER
DIR ECT ORY
preview
1991
S E V E N
VII
NEXT DIRECTORY
SPRING SUMMER

Next Directory 5. Section divider. Next, UK, 1990
Design Why Not Associates
Photography: Why Not Associates,
Rocco Redondo

opposite: *Morris Brose: a sustained vision*
Poster/mailer (front)
Detroit Focus Gallery, USA, 1987
Design Edward Fella

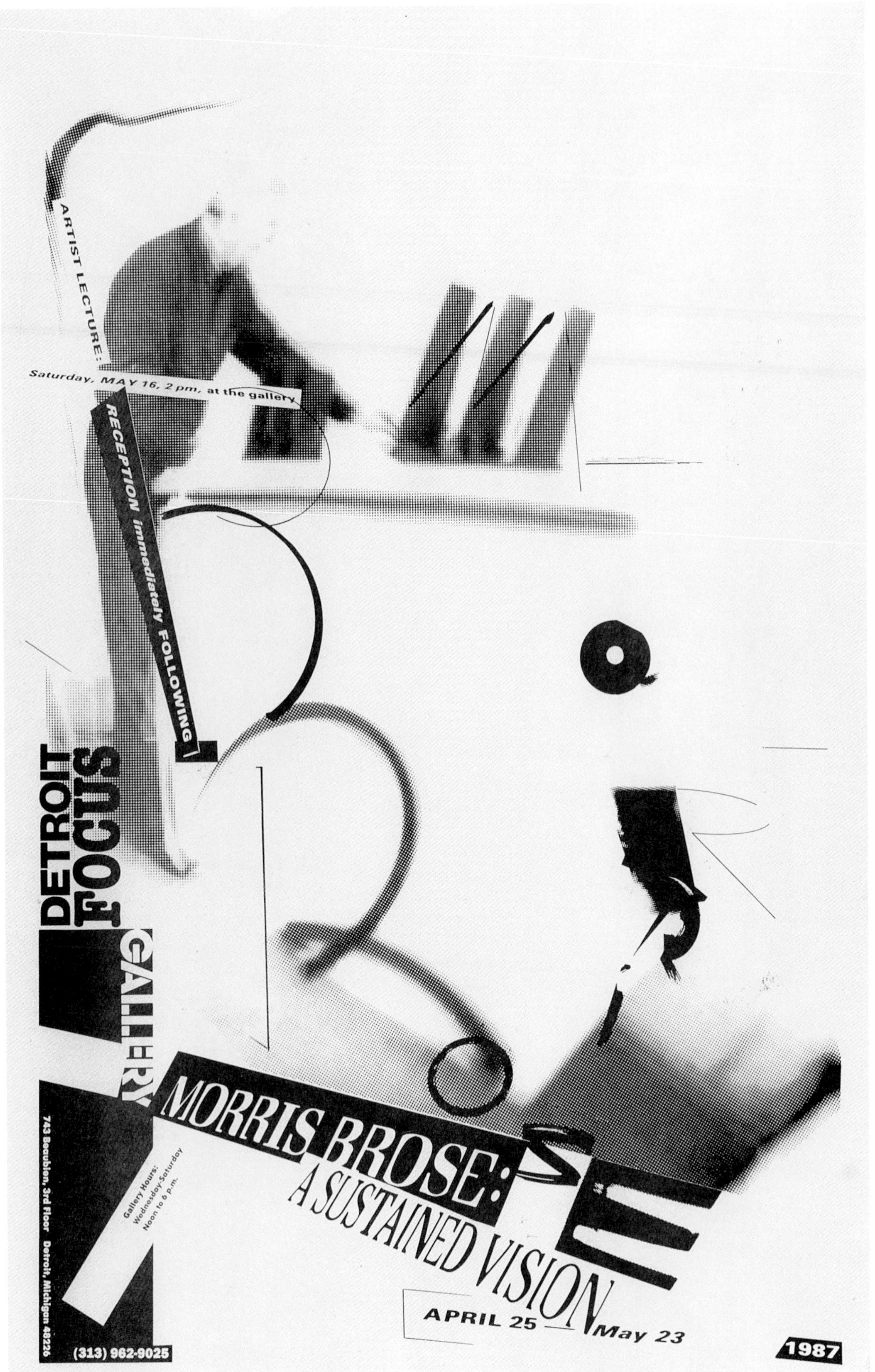
ARTIST LECTURE:
Saturday, MAY 16, 2 pm, at the gallery
RECEPTION immediately FOLLOWING
DETROIT FOCUS GALLERY
MORRIS BROSE:
A SUSTAINED VISION
APRIL 25 — May 23
1987
Gallery Hours: Wednesday-Saturday Noon to 6 p.m.
743 Beaubien, 3rd Floor Detroit, Michigan 48226
(313) 962-9025

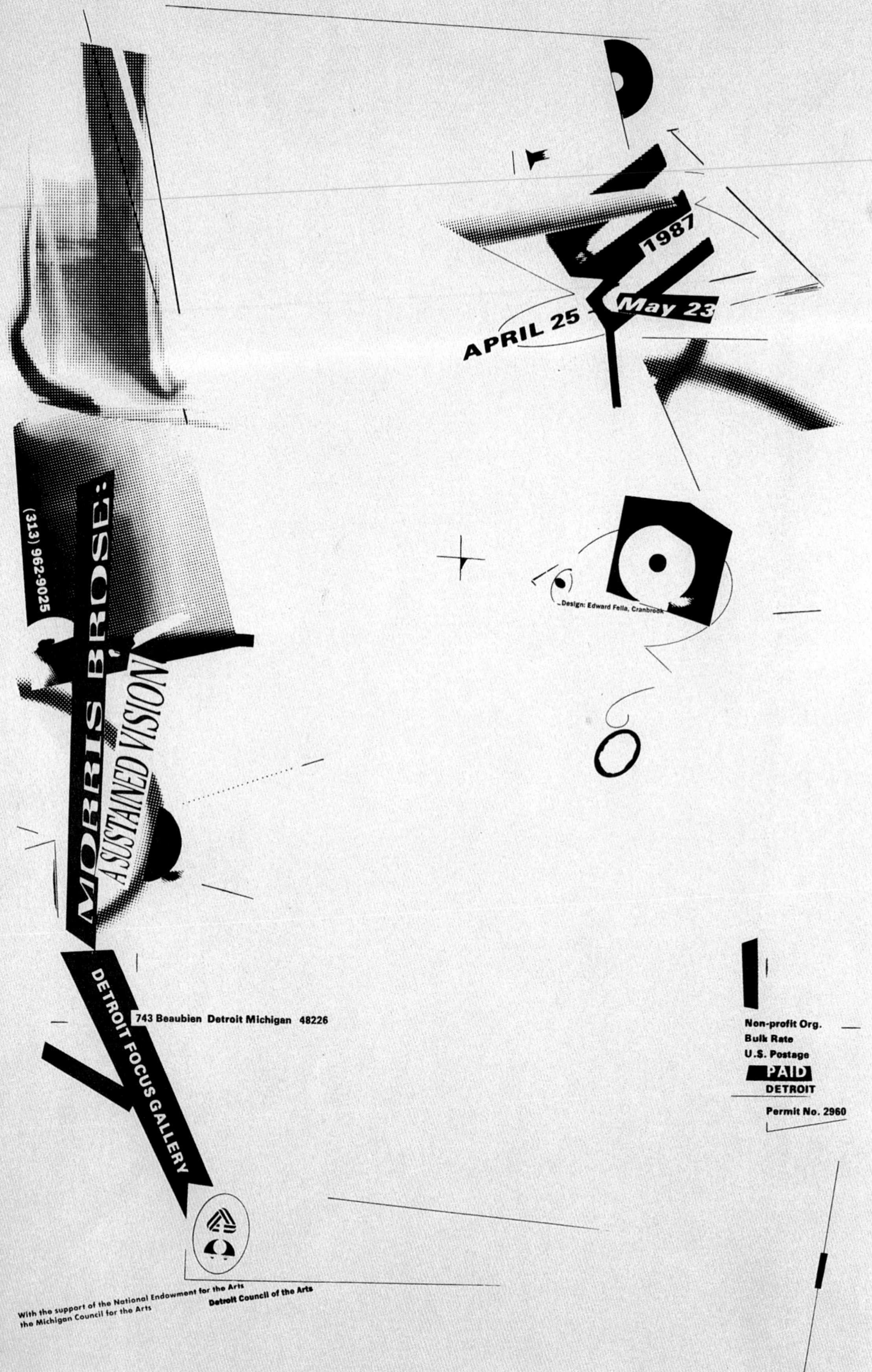

1987
APRIL 25
May 23
Design: Edward Fella, Cranbrook
(313) 962-9025
MORRIS BROSE:
A SUSTAINED VISION
DETROIT FOCUS GALLERY
743 Beaubien Detroit Michigan 48226
Non-profit Org.
Bulk Rate
U.S. Postage
PAID
DETROIT
Permit No. 2960
With the support of the National Endowment for the Arts
the Michigan Council for the Arts
Detroit Council of the Arts

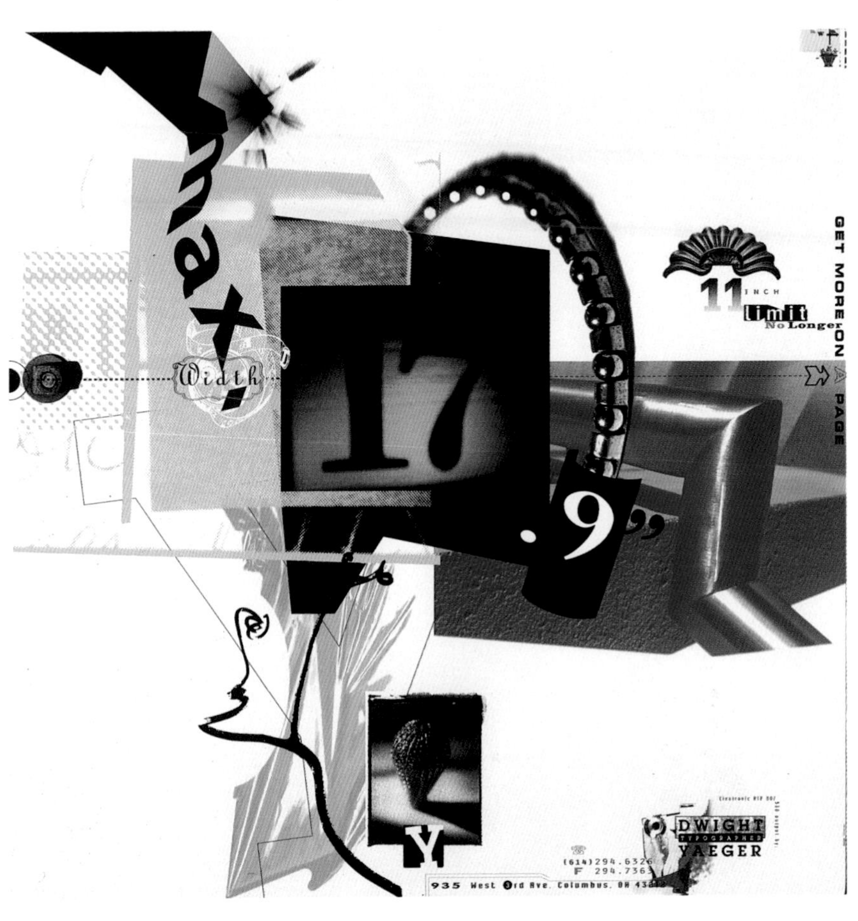

Promotional poster. Dwight Yaeger Typographer, USA, 1991
Design John Weber

opposite: *Morris Brose: a sustained vision*
Poster/mailer (back)
Detroit Focus Gallery, USA, 1987
Design Edward Fella

International call for proposals. Poster. San Francisco Artspace, USA, 1990. Design **John Weber**

Poster/flyer. Columbus Society of Communicating Arts, USA, 1990. Design **John Weber, Rudy VanderLans**

Creator/ designer/ editor/ keeper of the flame?

Non-Stop

design circus

(non-stop design)

CSCA Guest Speaker

RUDY

VANDERLANS

(em'ə grā')

m a g
azin
e

April 19
THURSDAY

6:30 Social hour
7:30 ANNOUNCEMENTS
7:45 *presentation*

AT
THE PHOTOGRAPHIC ILLUSTRATORS
GREEN MEADOWS CORPORATE PARK
404 ENTERPRISE DRIVE
WESTERVILLE

oh

NS REGARDING AT&T
DETAIL OF LONG
TIME PLACE AREA-NUMBER CODE AMOUNT
1022AM TO TORONTO ON 416 362-1913 D
151PM TO BERKELEY CA 415 845-9021 D
446PM TO NEW YORK CA 415 807-4000 D
158PM TO BERKELEY NY 212 845-9021 N
231PM TO BERKELEY CA 415 845-9021 N
238PM TO BERKELEY CA 415 845-9021 N
246PM TO NEW YORK CA 415 845-9021 N
1034AM TO LOSANGELES CA 415 279-2000 D
NEWHALL NY 212 932-0400 D

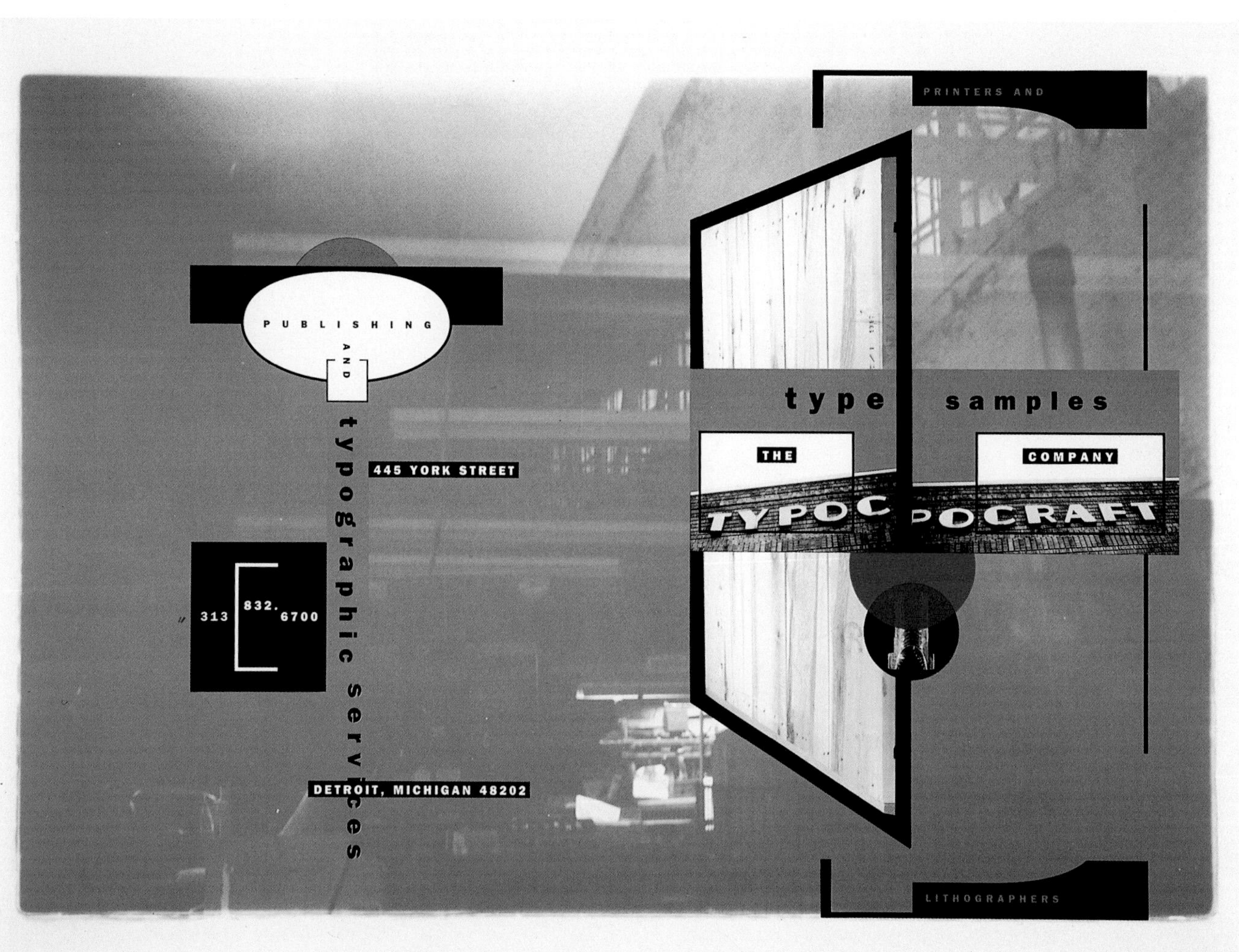
PRINTERS AND
PUBLISHING
AND
typographic services
445 YORK STREET
313 832. 6700
DETROIT, MICHIGAN 48202
type samples
THE
COMPANY
TYPOCRAFT
LITHOGRAPHERS

left: Type samples poster
The Typocraft Company, USA, 1990
Design Allen Hori

right: Advertisement
Gonzgraphics, USA, 1990
Design Barry Deck
Photography: Charles Field

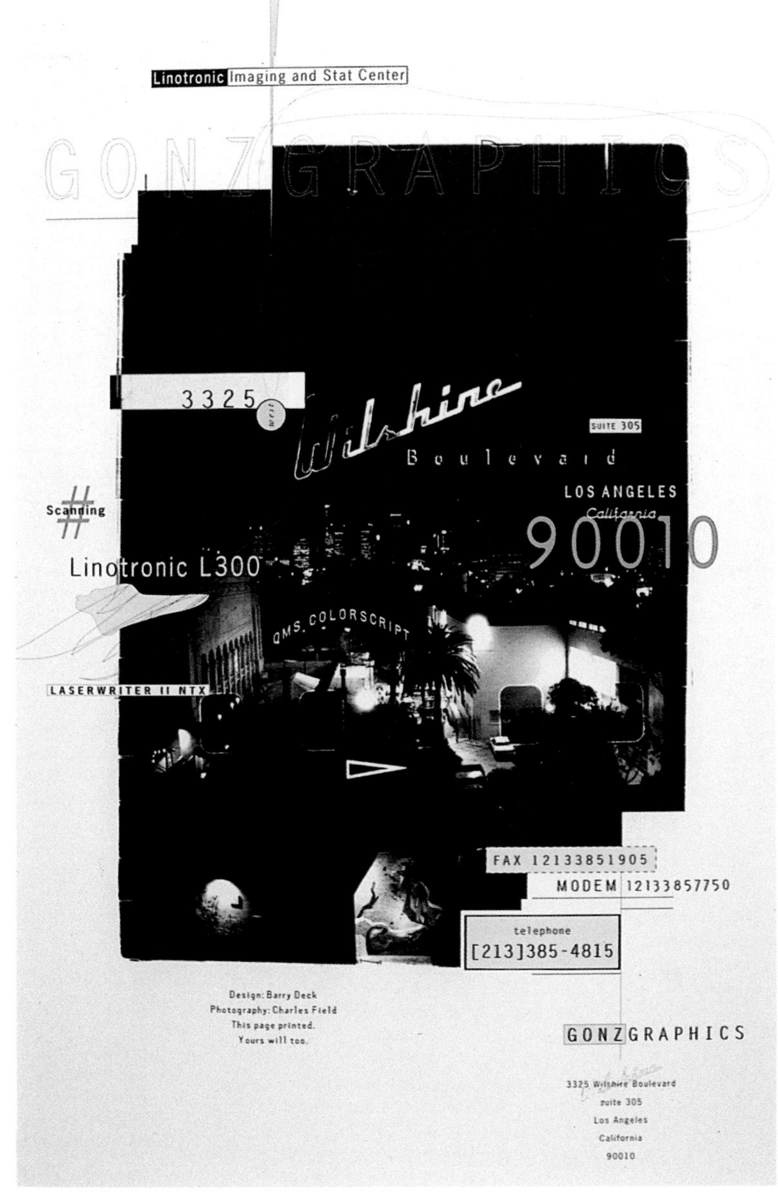

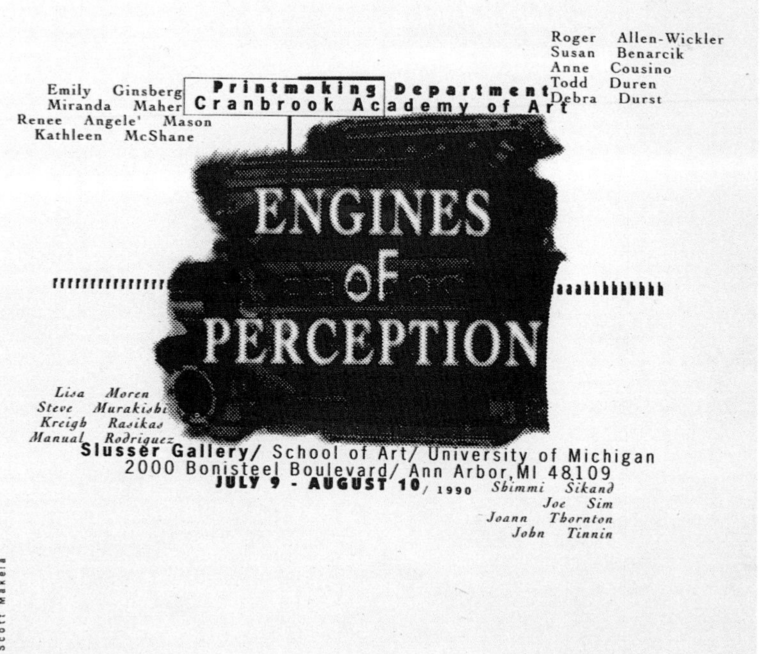

Engines of perception. Exhibition invitation
Cranbrook Academy of Art, USA, 1990
Design P. Scott Makela

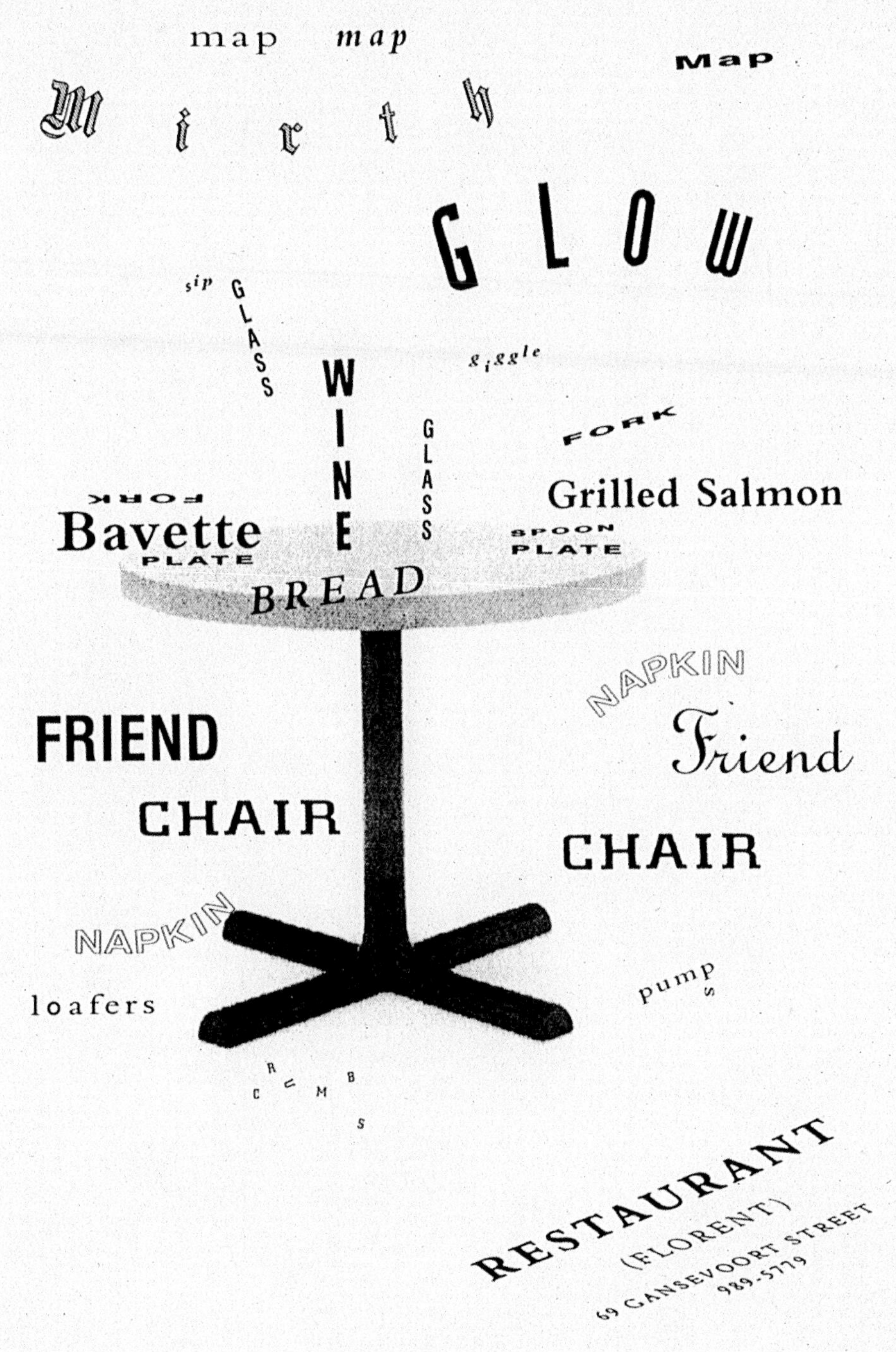

Mirth. Postcard
Restaurant Florent, USA, 1989
Design Marlene McCarty, Tibor Kalman M&Co

above: *Vout:oroonie*

Club poster/flyer. UK, 1990

Design Designers Republic

opposite: *Fact Twenty Two*. Poster. USA, 1990. Design Rudy VanderLans, James Towning

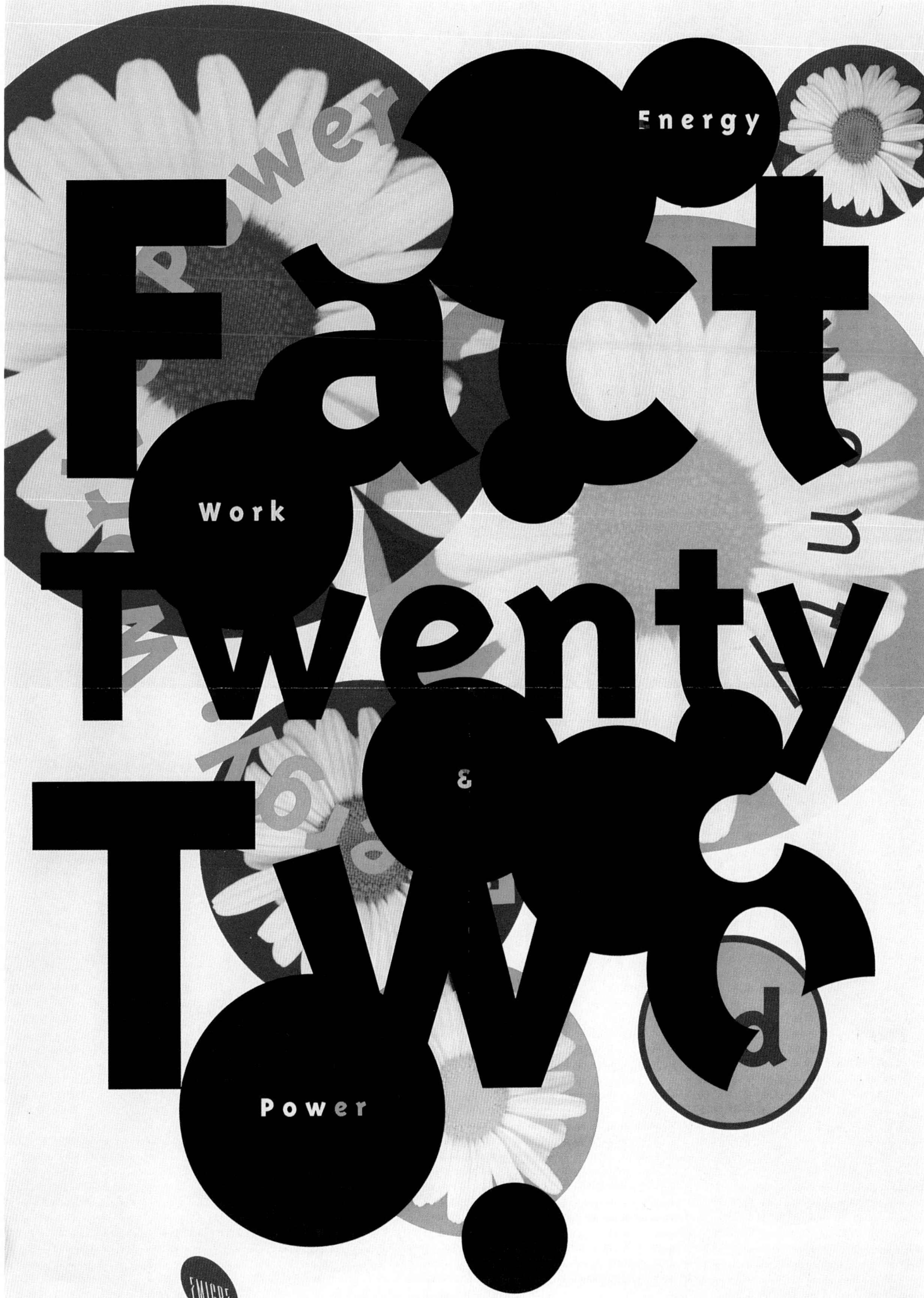
Energy
Fact
Work
Twenty
&
Two
Power
EMIGRE

Public Enemy's first record, *Yo! Bumrush the Show*, went gold. Their second record, *It Takes a Nation of Millions to Hold Us Back*, went platinum. The single "Fight the Power" (from their third and most recent album, *Fear of a Black Planet*) was the musical theme of Spike Lee's *Do the Right Thing*. *Fear of a Black Planet* went platinum in one week. These figures might not be so impressive if the act were a middle-of-the-road act, but Public Enemy pulls no punches, and there is no shortage of controversy over their lyrics. They have become cultural heroes, representing the truth of urban youth in no uncertain terms: "Elvis was a hero to most/but he never meant shit to me you see/Straight up racist that sucker was/Simple and plain/Motherfuck him and John Wayne"—from the single "Fight the Power."

In early 1983 a mobile D.J. collective known as Spectrum City was roaming around Roosevelt, Long Island, playing hip-hop in the parks and broadcasting their highly influential Super Spectrum Mixx Show on the Long Island radio station WBAU every Saturday night. At the forefront of all the action was a powerhouse jester/M.C. named Flavor Flav, whose antics and energy brought him into local prominence. It was also in Spectrum City that **Flavor Flav** began his collaboration with producer Hank Shocklee and another resident of the 'Velt, named Chuck D. Chuck had studied the speech patterns of minister Louis Farrakhan, and by blending this dynamic oratory with a keen political consciousness and a Madison Avenue knack for phrase-mongering, Chuck established himself as one of the most powerful voices in rap. In 1986 Flavor Flav, Chuck D. and a D.J. named Terminator X formed Public Enemy. As his name suggests, Flavor Flav was the perfect counterpart to Chuck D's heavily militant, hard-core approach to rap. Sometimes Flavor Flav adds spice, accent, or salt, but most often his voice is inserted as a kind of hydraulic adrenaline boost, loopy and cartoonlike against Chuck's straight-ahead drilling. A master at playing "the dozens" (a ritual requiring speedy wit to out-insult your opponent), Flavor Flav can be as biting as he is hilarious. But as he proves on the recent hit single "911 Is a Joke," when Flavor Flav takes over the role of lead rapper, he commands serious respect.

i'm black
and i'm
proud
i'm ready
and hyped plus I'm
amped
most of my
heroes don't appear
on no stamps
sample
a look back
you look
and find
nothing but rednecks
for 400 years
if you check
don't worry
be happy
was a
number
one jam...

above: *Interview*. Magazine pages
Brant Publications, USA, 1990

Creative director **Tibor Kalman**
Design **Kristin Johnson**
Photography: Josef Astor

athol fugard gives the impression that doing the right thing is easy, that doing the right thing makes you feel alive, that it is as easy as breathing to know the right way from the wrong way.

Interview. Magazine pages
Brant Publications, USA, 1990
Creative director Tibor Kalman
Design Kristin Johnson
Photography: David Lee

above: *Just slam it*

Advertising campaign. Nike, USA, 1989

Design **Neville Brody**

Agency: Wieden and Kennedy

Interview. Magazine pages
Brant Publications, USA, 1990
Creative director **Fabien Baron**

Photography:
Wayne Maser

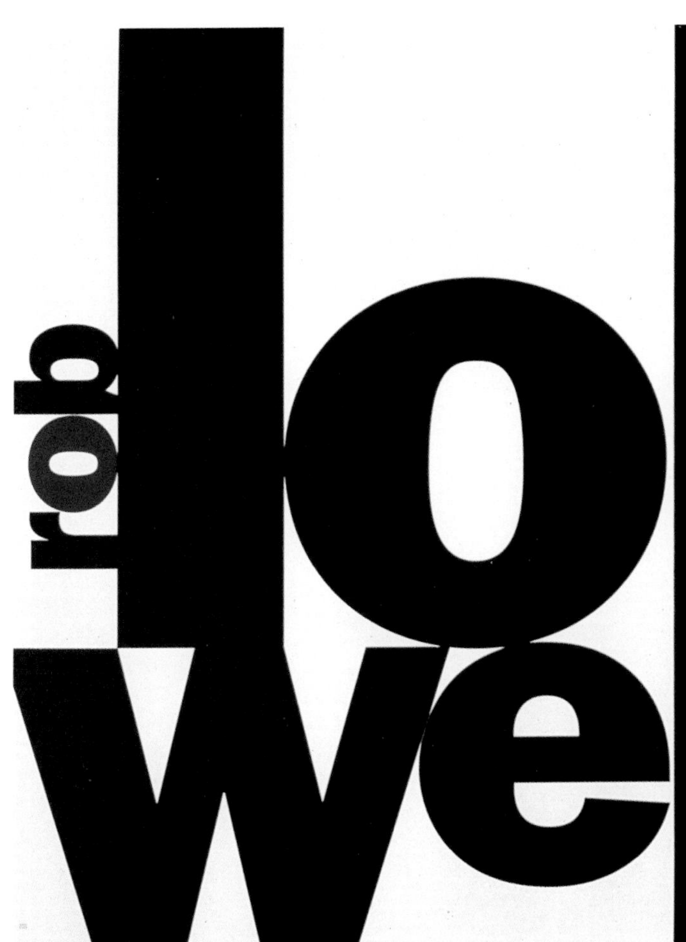

left: *Interview*. Magazine pages
Brant Publications, USA, 1990
Creative director **Fabien Baron**
Photography: Albert Watson
below: *Per Lui*. Magazine pages
Condé Nast, Italy, 1990
Art director **Neville Brody**

neighborhood
di
dilemma
l
e
m
m
a
dilemma

opposite: *Howl* by Allen Ginsberg (German translation)
Book pages. Germany, 1991
Design **Lars Ohlerich**
Hochschule für Gestaltung
Offenbach

below: *Howl* by Allen Ginsberg
Book pages. Germany, 1991
Design **Peter Biler**
Hochschule für Gestaltung,
Offenbach

Moloch,
Moloch,
In dem ich mir Engel erträume!
Verrückt in Moloch
Schwanzlutscher in Moloch!
M o l o c h !
Ohne Liebe und Männerfreundschaft in
Moloch, der mir früh in die Seele drang!
Moloch, in dem ich ein Bewußtsein ohne Körper bin!
Moloch, der mich aus meiner natürlichen Extase schreckte!
Moloch, von dem ich mich lossage!
In dem ich wieder aufwache! Im Licht, das aus dem Himmel strömt!
Moloch!
M o l o c h !
Roboter-Apartments!
unsichtbare Vorstädte!
Skelette in den Tresoren!
blinde Hauptstädte!
dämonische Industrien!
gespenstische Nationen!
unbesiegbare Irrenhäuser!
Schwänze aus Granit!
monströse Bomben!
Sie brachen sich das Kreuz, als sie Moloch zum Himmel hoben!
Straßenpflaster, Bäume, Radios, tonnenschwer!
Die ganze Stadt hoben sie in den Himmel, der existiert und uns überall umgibt!
Visionen!
Vorahnungen!
Halluzinationen!
Wunder!
Extasen!
Anbetungen!
Illuminationen!
Religionen!
Scheiße!
Durchbrüche!
über den Fluß!
ausgeflippt und gekreuzigt!
fortgespült mit der Flut!
Rausch!
Epiphanien!
Verzweiflung!
Animalische Schreie und Selbstmorde von zehn Jahren!
Genies!
Neue Liebschaften!
Verrückte Generation! gestrandet auf den Felsen der Zeit!
Echtes heiliges Gelächter im Fluß!
Sie sahen es alle!
die wilden Augen!
die heiligen Schreie!
Sie verabschiedeten sich!
Sie sprangen vom Dach!
in die Einsamkeit!
winkend!
mit Blumen in den Händen!
Hinunter zum Fluß!
Hinaus auf die Straße!

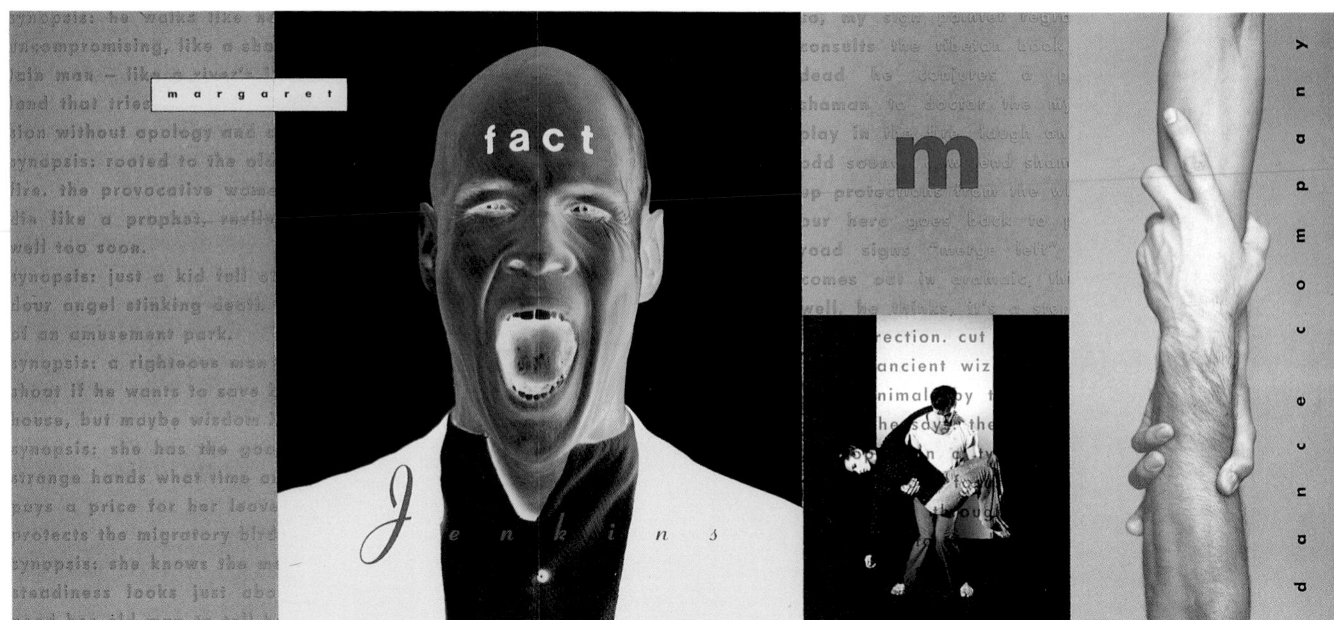

above: *Dance for the new decade*
Margaret Jenkins Dance Company, USA, 1988
Design Tom Bonauro
Photography: Ken Probst

right: *Rearrange.* Greetings card
Pillow Talk Cards, USA, 1991
Design Tom Bonauro

Tocsin. Album cover. 4AD, UK, 1984. Design Vaughan Oliver
Photography: Nigel Grierson

Fetisch. Album cover (back)
4AD, UK, 1983
Design Vaughan Oliver

above: *L'Esclave endormi.* 12" single (front and back). 4AD, UK, 1986
Design Vaughan Oliver
Photography: Nigel Grierson

left: *Le mystère des voix Bulgares*
Album cover. 4AD, UK, 1988
Design Vaughan Oliver
Photography: Simon Larbalestier

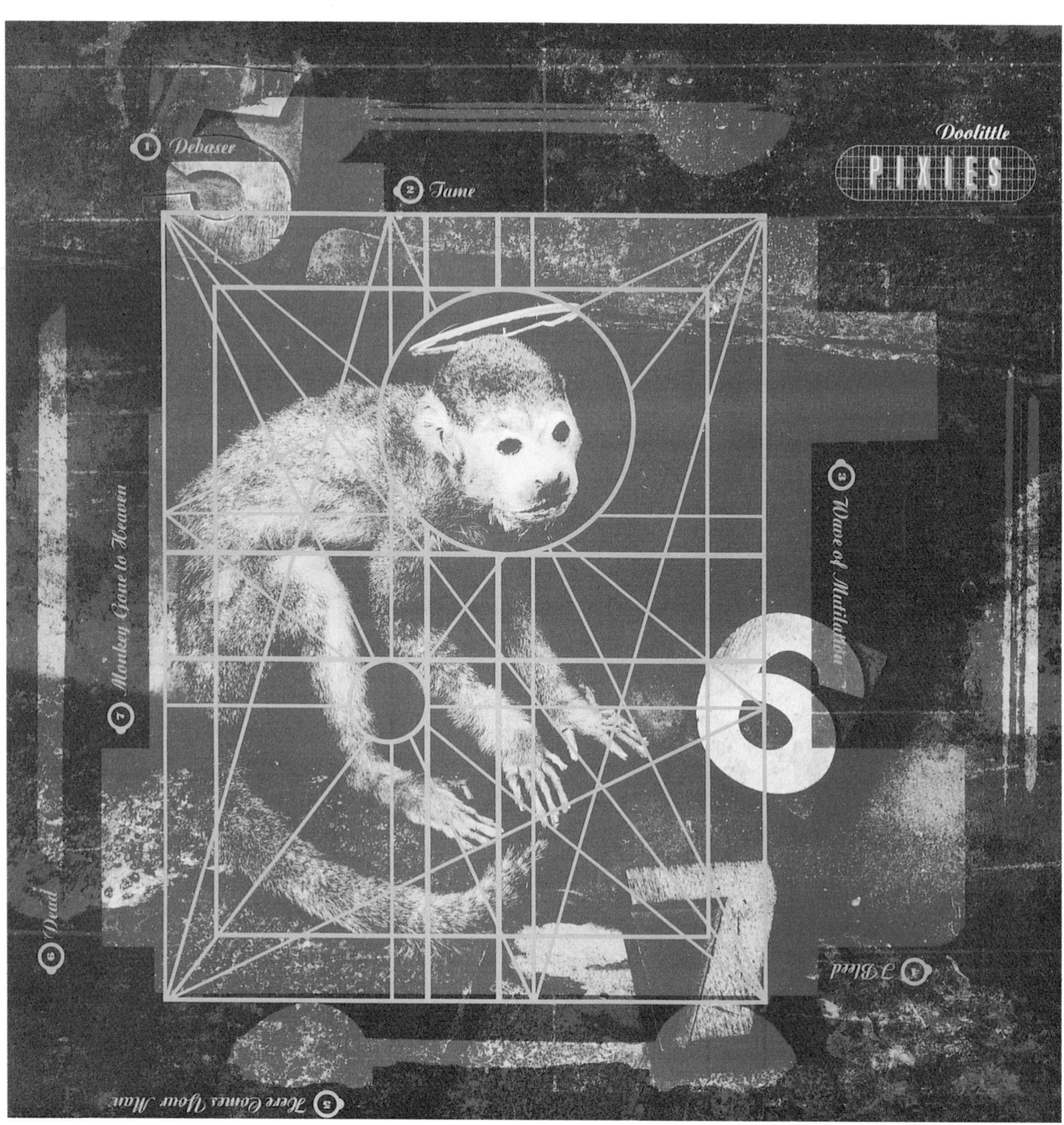

Doolittle. Album cover. 4AD, UK, 1989
Design Vaughan Oliver
Photography: Simon Larbalestier

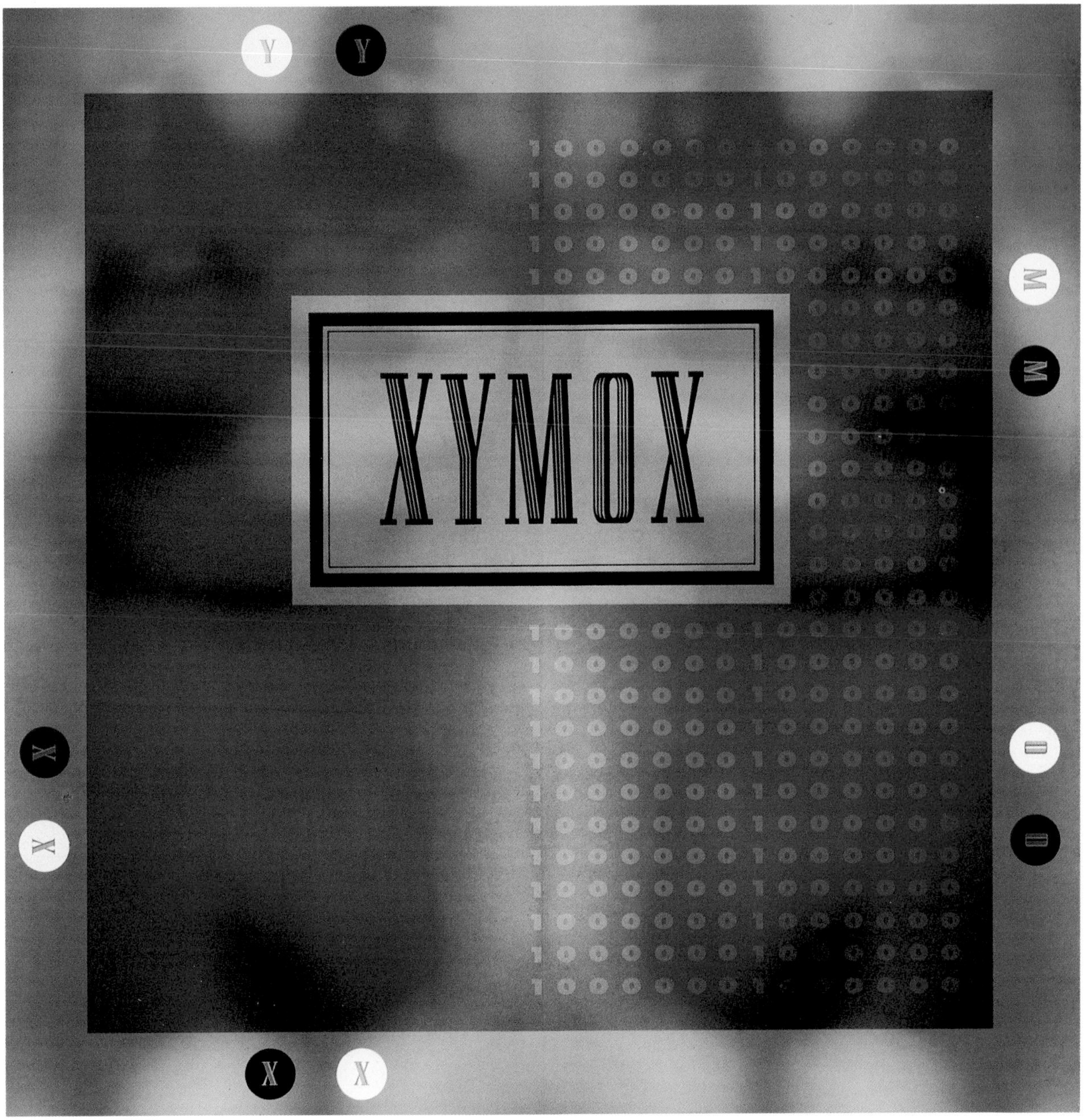

Xymox. 12" single cover. 4AD, UK, 1987
Design Vaughan Oliver
Photography: Jim Friedman

Velouria. 12" single cover (back). 4AD, UK, 1990. Design **Vaughan Oliver** Photography: Simon Larbalestier

right: Brochure. Seymour Powell. UK, 1989
Design Siobhan Keaney
Photography: Robert Shackleton

below: Price card. P.Inks LA. USA, 1989
Design Tom Bonauro

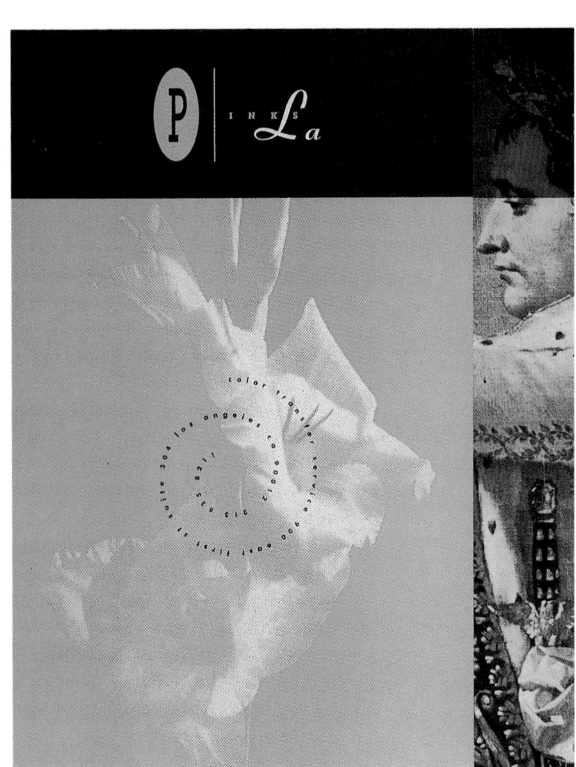

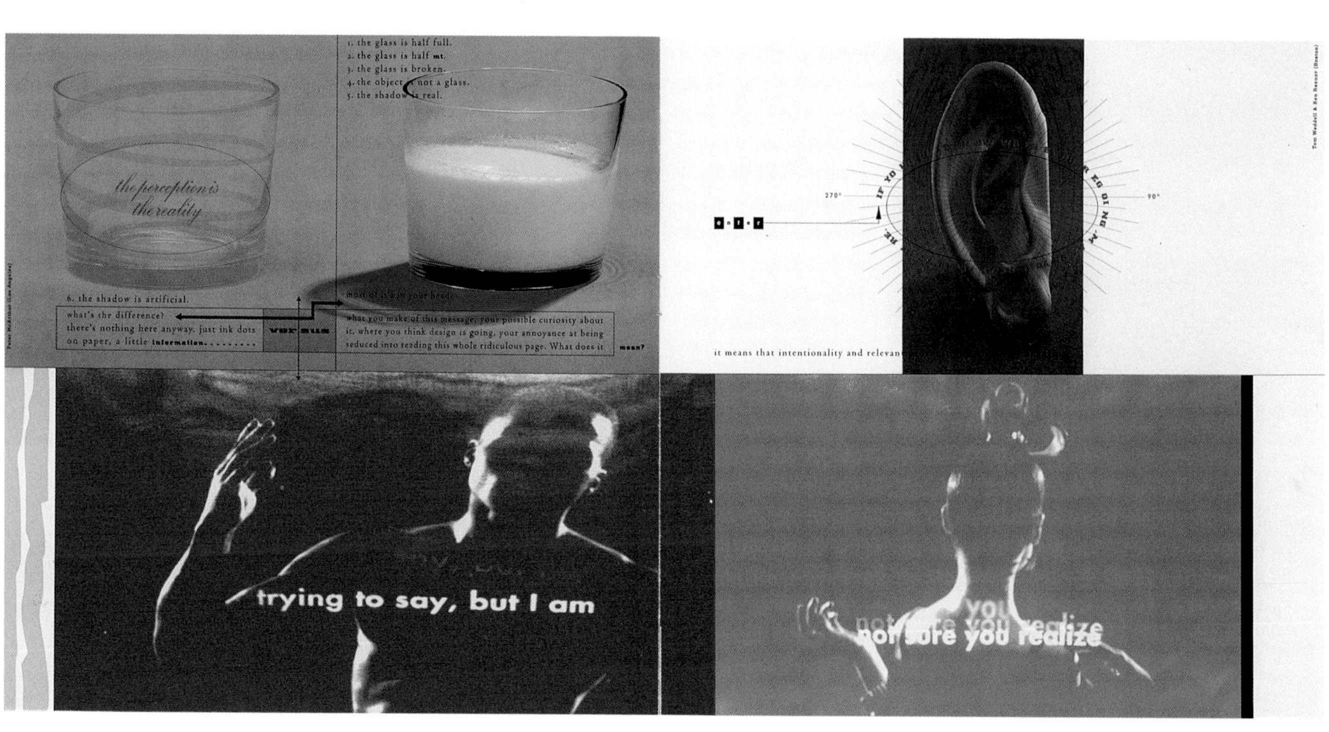

Enter. Call for entries
American Center for Design, USA, 1989
Design Rick Valicenti Thirst

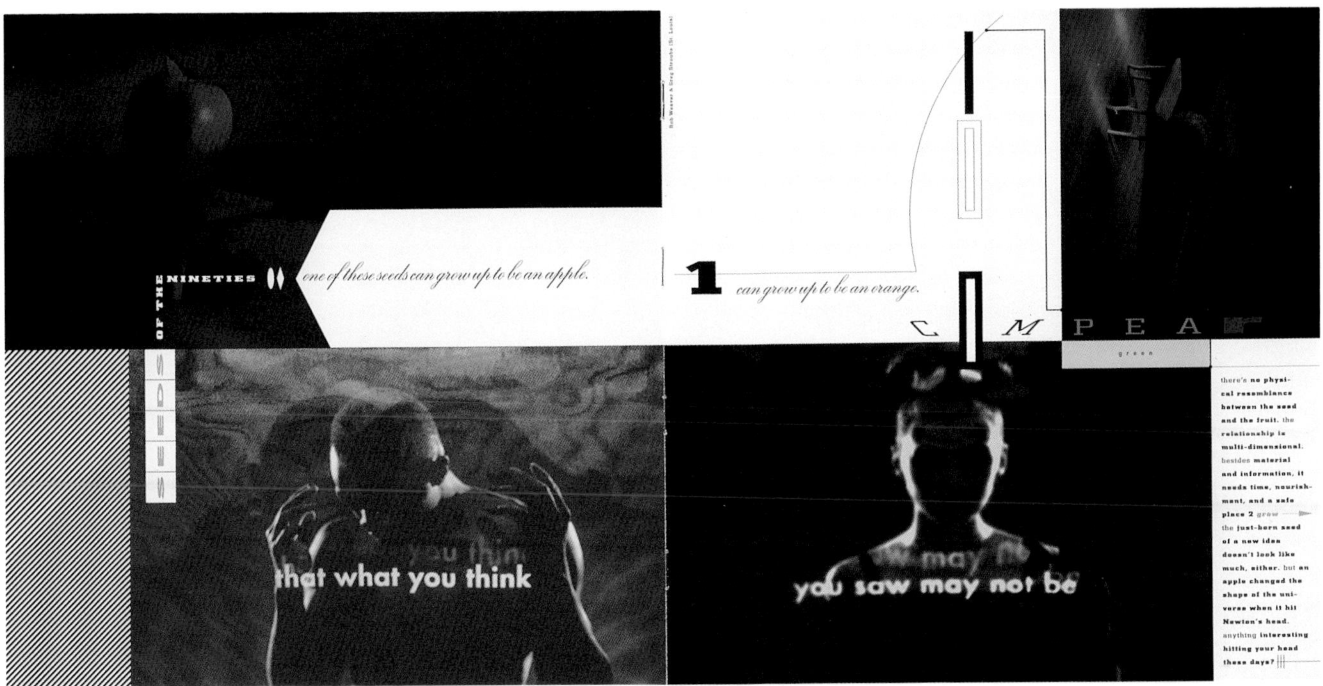
SEEDS OF THE NINETIES
one of these seeds can grow up to be an apple.
1 can grow up to be an orange.
that what you think
you saw may not be
green
there's no physical resemblance between the seed and the fruit. the relationship is multi-dimensional. besides material and information, it needs time, nourishment, and a safe place 2 grow
the just-born seed of a new idea doesn't look like much, either. but an apple changed the shape of the universe when it hit Newton's head.
anything interesting hitting your head these days?

thread
spontaneity
solitude
gradual
impurity
discipline
connection
intimacy
responsibility freedom
crystal smoke
risk fascinating
global local
TIME
WILL.
TELL
5
Mildred Friedman
design curator walker art center minneapolis
Tibor Kalman
m & co. new york
Gert Dumbar
studio dumbar holland
Michael Mabry
michael mabry design san francisco
Eric Martin
consultant in information theatre los angeles
Rick Valicenti
1989 STA 100 SHOW chairperson
what I meant unless
2
you believe that I
so does resistance which leads to friction which leads to fire which leads to transformation
friction makes a light bulb shine.

In each case, in order to achieve this distinctive aesthetic quality we worked at the limits of the technology of the day. In some instances the frontiers were extended by some innovations. I have already mentioned the use of epoxy glued joints and pre-stressing on the Opera House, the essential role of computers, and developments in glass technology. There was also the development of non-ferrous metals for certain fixings (we even used titanium), as well as in the surveying techniques which were complex as a consequence of the geometry of the building. But above all, while the basic sculptural composition was an architectural or artistic concept, the subsequent geometric discipline to which we subjected the building resulted in a clear expression of the underlying engineering forms.
What I have spoken about is engineering in the service of architecture. It is an activity that can of course have its frustrations — I suppose all human endeavour has its trials as well as its tribulations. And in these days of specializations, it is more important than ever to concentrate on human qualities as much as on technical ones. However brilliant the engineer and architect, if they cannot or will not communicate or work together effectively, the building will suffer. We must learn to understand the problems of our collaborators and when we do and they understand ours, engineering is or should be a creative and challenging activity. And when it is associated with interesting, or even better, great architecture, it can be exciting and very rewarding."
Excerpt from a lecture given by Jack Zunz at the Royal College of Art, London, on December 17, 1987 in association with the College's 150th Anniversary "Great Engineers" Exhibition
Ove Arup & Partners California
invites you to a reception in honor of Sir Jack Zunz
Sir Jack Zunz
246 FT RADIUS
Monday, October 29, 1990
5:30 pm to 8:00 pm
The Atrium
901 Market Street
San Francisco
RSVP by October 26
415 957 9445
An exhibit featuring the work of Ove Arup & Partners California will be on display in The Atrium Gallery, October 29 through December 7, courtesy of The Luria Company.
On Tuesday, October 30, Sir Jack Zunz will speak on the Aesthetics of Technology at the twelfth annual lecture series on contemporary architecture sponsored by the San Francisco Museum of Modern Art and the San Francisco American Institute of Architects.
Michael Lewis, Ove Arup, and Jack Zunz at the Sydney Opera House site, 1966
architecture
integration
technology
engineering

opposite:
Sir Jack Zunz. Invitation
Ove Arup & Partners, USA, 1990

Workspirit. Magazine cover. Vitra, Switzerland, 1988
Design **April Greiman**

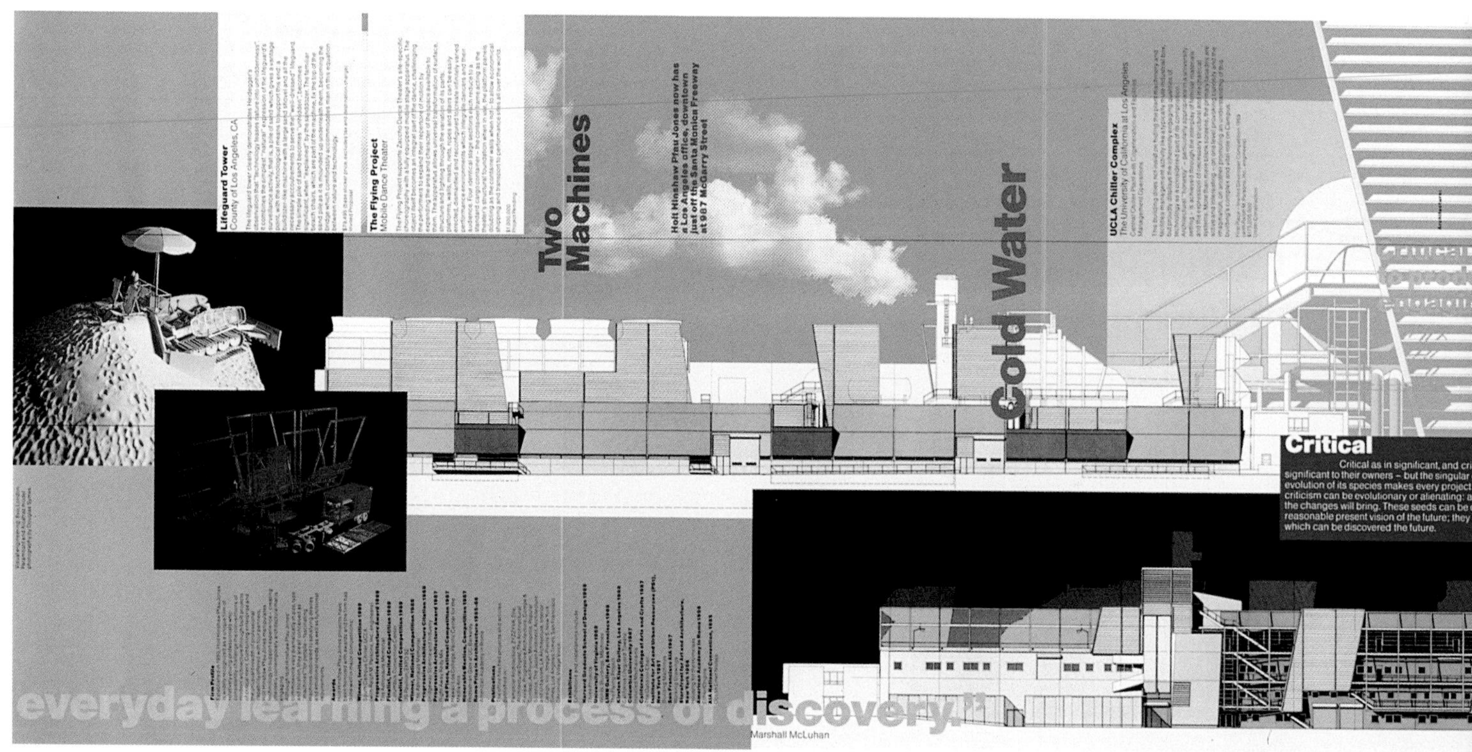

Holt Hinshaw Pfau Jones

Architecture

Two Working Buildings

Paramount Pictures
Hollywood, CA

Right Away Redy Mix
Oakland, CA

Contemporary

The cultural omnipresence of technology defines the horizon along contemporary buildings must stand. As public statements living within the world circumscribed by this horizon, all buildings should find the source of their highe expression there. Those which inhabit this world enthusiastically, embracing tod reality with energetic awareness, will be more technically sophisticated, express therefore inherently engaging.

the possibility of arranging the entire human environment as a work of art, as a teaching machine

Architects' brochure/poster (front and back). Holt Hinshaw Pfau Jones, USA, 1989
Design 8vo

m a k i n g

Ched Reeder
Electronic Empowerment

Joseph Fenzl
Tricking the Eye: The Art of Faux Painting

The Joyful Play of Forms in Light
Judith Crook

Tom Farrage
Bob Cunningham
David Hertz

1990

Professional Development

S C I ARC

Southern California Institute of Architecture

Summer

at SCI ARC offers an opportunity for working directly with the most actively creative people in the discipline.

SCI ARC courses combine the activities of making and thinking in an open experimental interchange.

Coy Howard
Psst, Psst - The Four Best Kept Secrets of the Creative Life

Louis Naidorf
Major Highrise Office Building Workshop

George Sumner
Putting it All Together

Michael Andrews
Fundamentals of Architectural Model Making

In the Spirit of Wood: A Day with a Master Craftsman
Sam Maloof

Graham Powell
User Friendly Tools

Charles Calvo

Sam Hall Kaplan

The Path of Light - Designing
Steven D. Ehrlich

Peter Shire
Art Furniture Design

Designing Lighting Systems
Ron Mendleski

Nader Khalili

Kenneth Breisch
American Cities: The Chicago School

Peter Shapiro
The Finely Crafted Drawer
Wood Finishing

t h i n k i n g

Sci Arc: summer programs. Poster
Southern California Institute of Architecture,
USA, 1991

opposite:

Sci Arc: making/thinking. Poster
Southern California Institute of Architecture,
USA, 1990

Design **April Greiman**

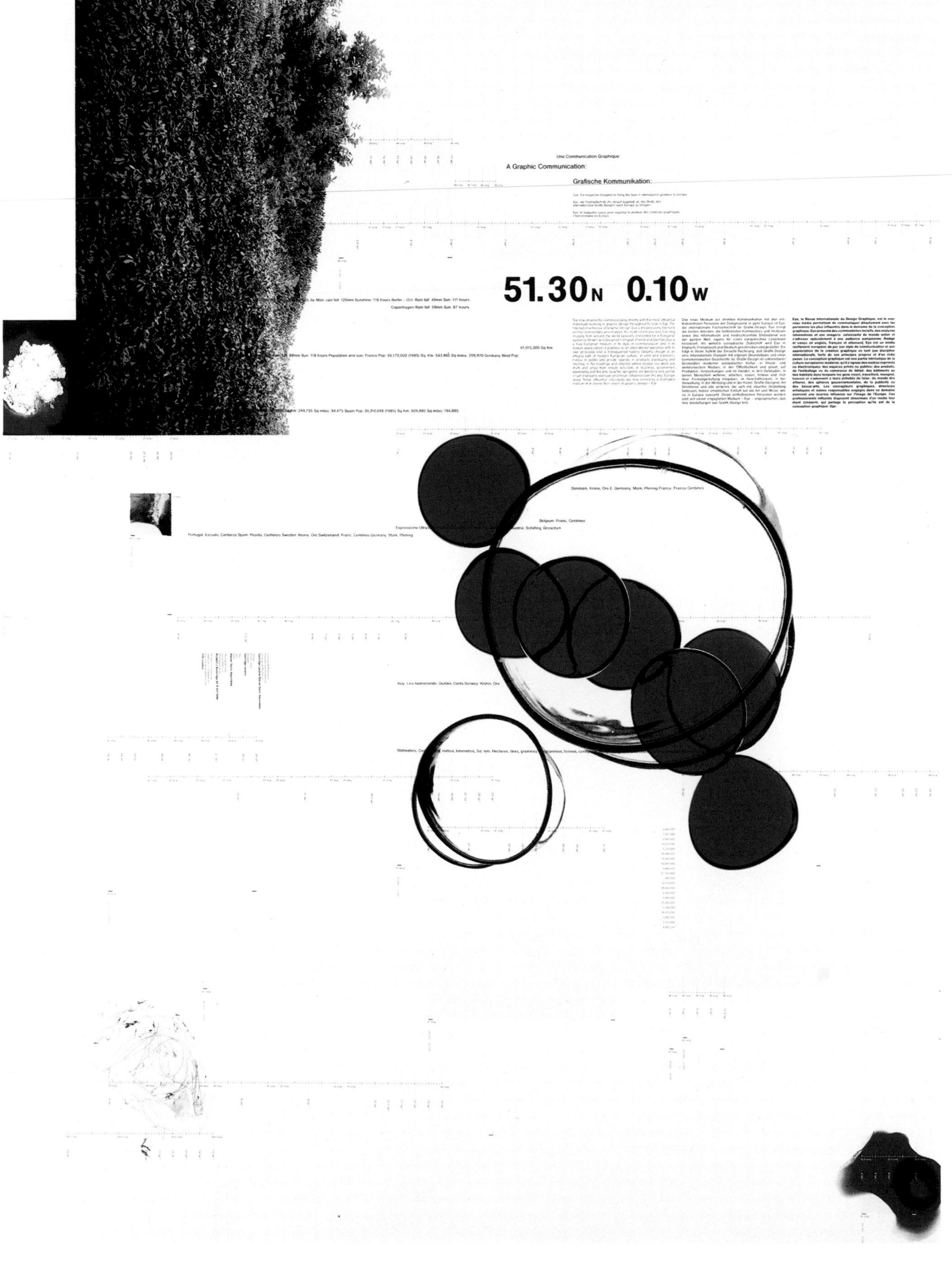
Une Communication Graphique
A Graphic Communication:
Grafische Kommunikation:
51.30N 0.10W

opposite: *Eye magazine: a graphic communication*
Promotional poster. Wordsearch, UK, 1990
Design Cartlidge Levene
Photography: Richard J. Burbridge

Issue. Magazine pages
Design Museum, UK, 1991
Design Cartlidge Levene
Photography: Richard J. Burbridge

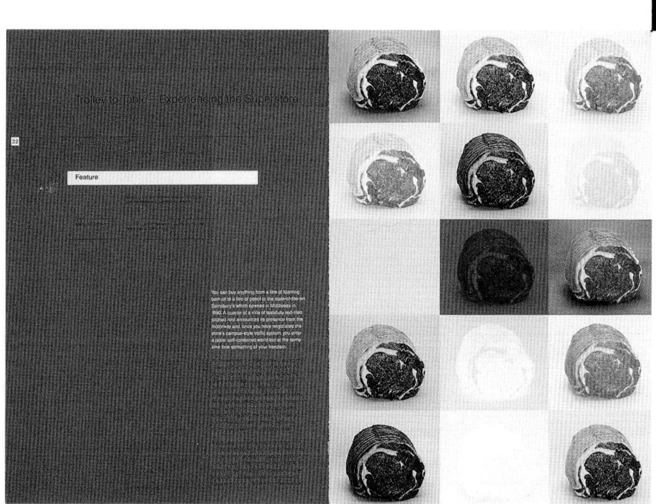

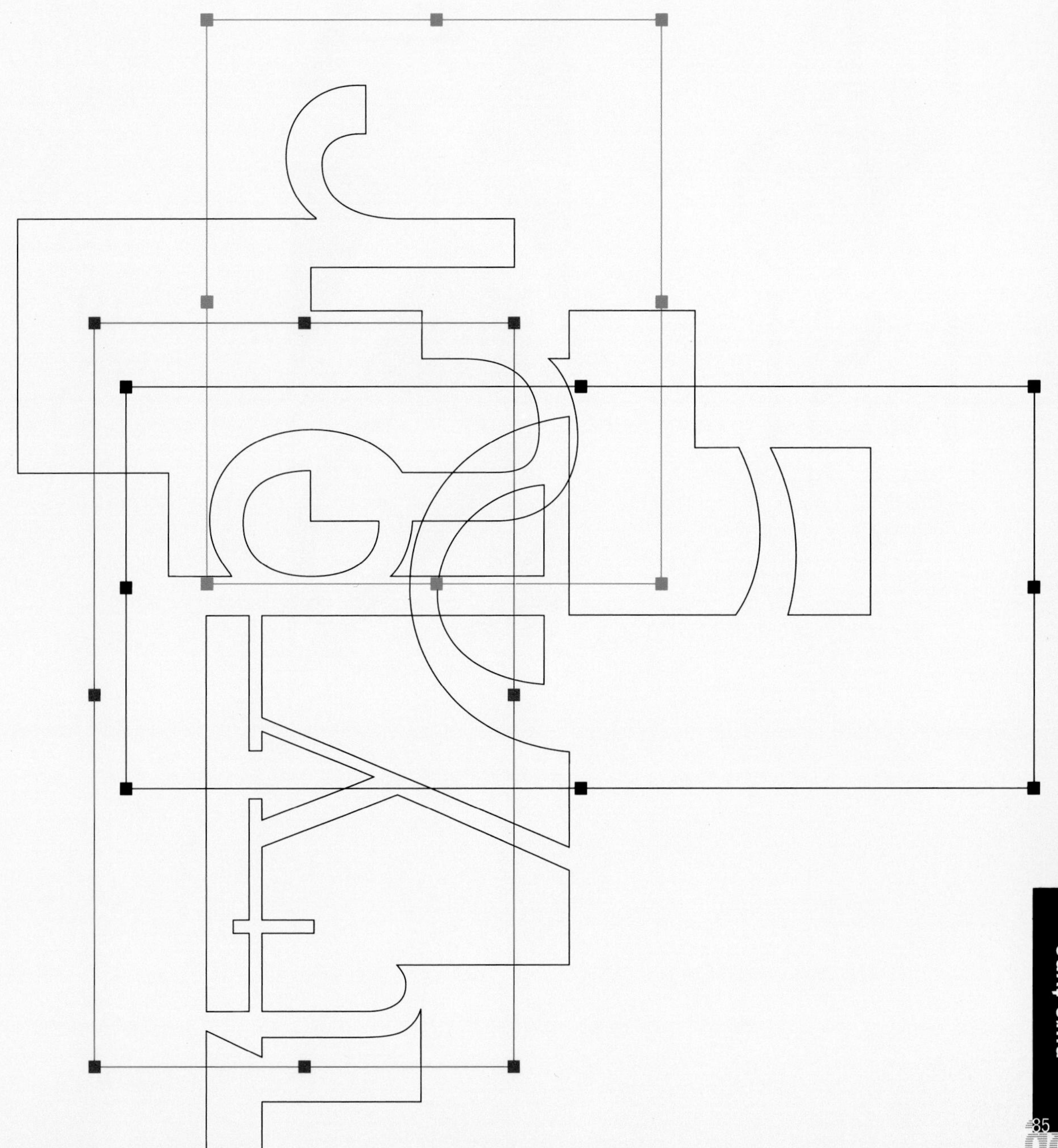

Copyright Phil Baines, 1988. Published by Northern Heights.

Paschal candles
Letterpress and silk screen
to fit 3' x 3" candle. UK, 1987-91
Design Phil Baines

This is the night… This is the night… This is the night…

HÆC NOX EST

1 9 9 1

…when Jesus Christ broke the chains of death & rose triumphant from the grave.

…when Christians everywhere, washed clean of sin & freed from all defilement, are restored to peace & grow together in holiness.

…when first you saved our fathers: you freed the people of Israel from their slavery & led them dry-shod through the sea. *Exsultet*

Designed & printed by Phil Baines, iii 1991.

a l l e l u i a

EX
SUL
TET
iam A
ngelic
a Jesu
s CHR
IST tu
rba
is RIS
EN.
caelo
rum.

REJ
OICE heav
nly po
wers. S
ING, c
hoirs of
angels
.EXU
LT, al
l creat
i
o
n
a
ro
u
n
d
God
's th
rone

O
happy
fault
,O necessary
sin of Adam,
which gained
for us so great
a redeemer. Mos
t blessed of all nig
hts, chosen by Go
d to see CHRIST
ris
ing fro
m the
dead.

CHR
IST yesterday and today, t
he beginning and the end,
Alpha
and O
mega,
al
l t
i
m
e belongs to him
, and all the age
s, TO HI
M BE GL
ORY and power thro
ugh every age f
or ever, AMEN.

OUR
KiNG

Sound th
e trum
pet of salv
ation....

Acc
ep
t this
EAsT
eR can
dle, a fl
ame di
vided,
but undimmed, A PILLAR
OF FIRE that gro
ws to the glory of G
od. Let it mingle w
ith the lights of hea
ven and c
ontinue b
ravely bu
rning TO
DIS
PEl
tHe
Dar
KNESS
of this ni
ght. May
the morn
ing star which never sets fin
d this flame still burning: C
HRIST that morning star,
WHO CAME BACK FRO
M THe
DEAD.

O
vere
beata
nox.

1986

PhilBaine
s: March,

opposite: *F Can You . . . ?*

Poster for typographic magazine. *Fuse* issue 1, UK, 1991

Paschal candle

Letterpress to fit 3' x 3" candle. UK, 1986

Design Phil Baines

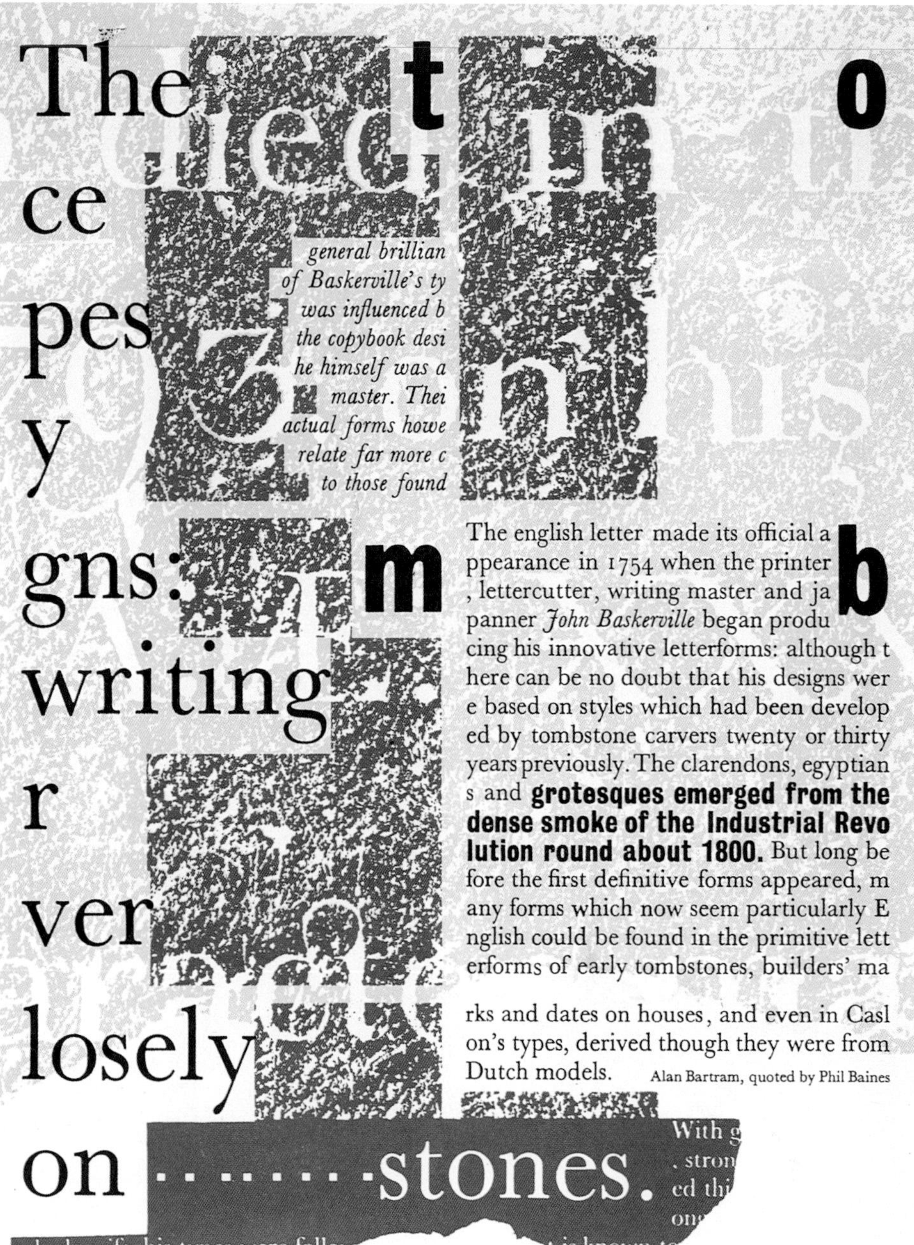

Bound image. Page from an artists' book. Spacex Gallery, UK, 1988

Design Phil Ba
ines

opposite:

Machine-generated stone-carving. UK, 1990

Design Jonathan Barnbrook

ONLY WHEN THE
TECHNOLOGY
IS INVISIBLE IS
IT OF ANY USE

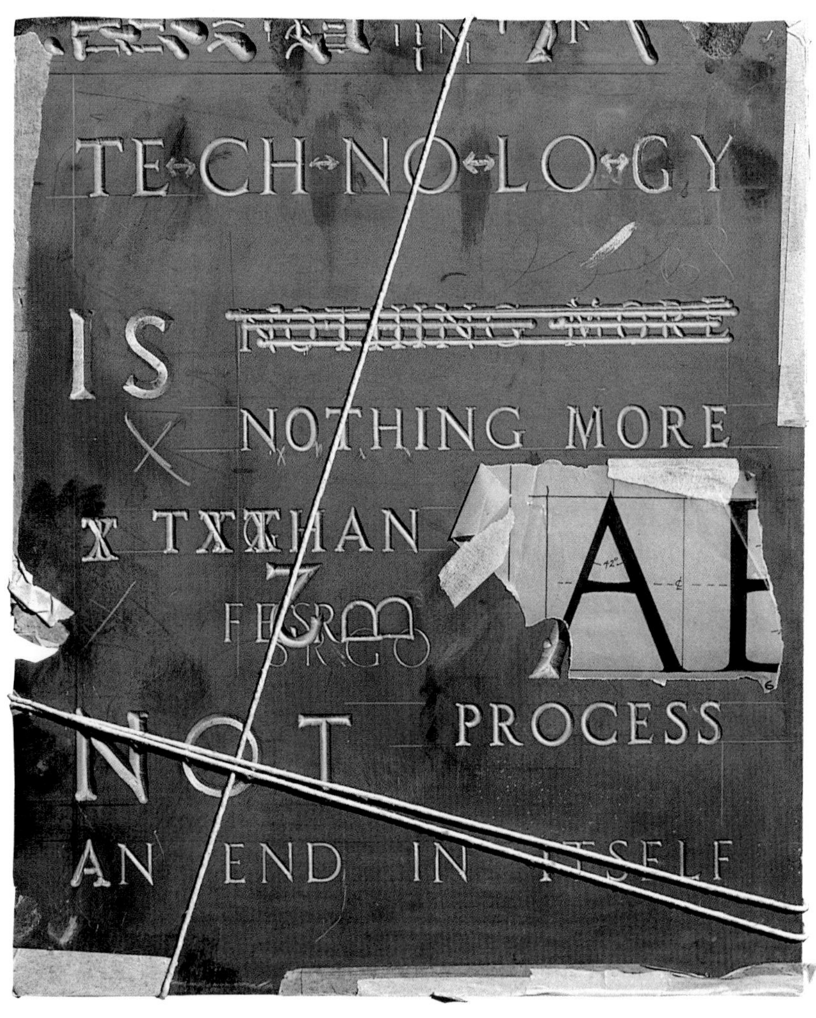

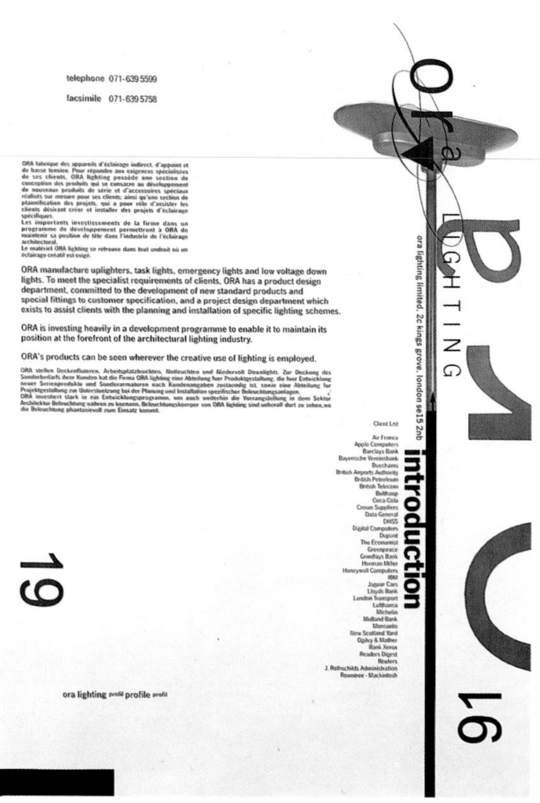

left: Promotional poster. Ora Lighting, UK, 1991
Design **Russell Warren-Fisher**

below: *Next Directory 7*. Section divider. Next, UK, 1991
opposite: *Next Directory 8*. Cover. Next, UK, 1991
Design **Why Not Associates**

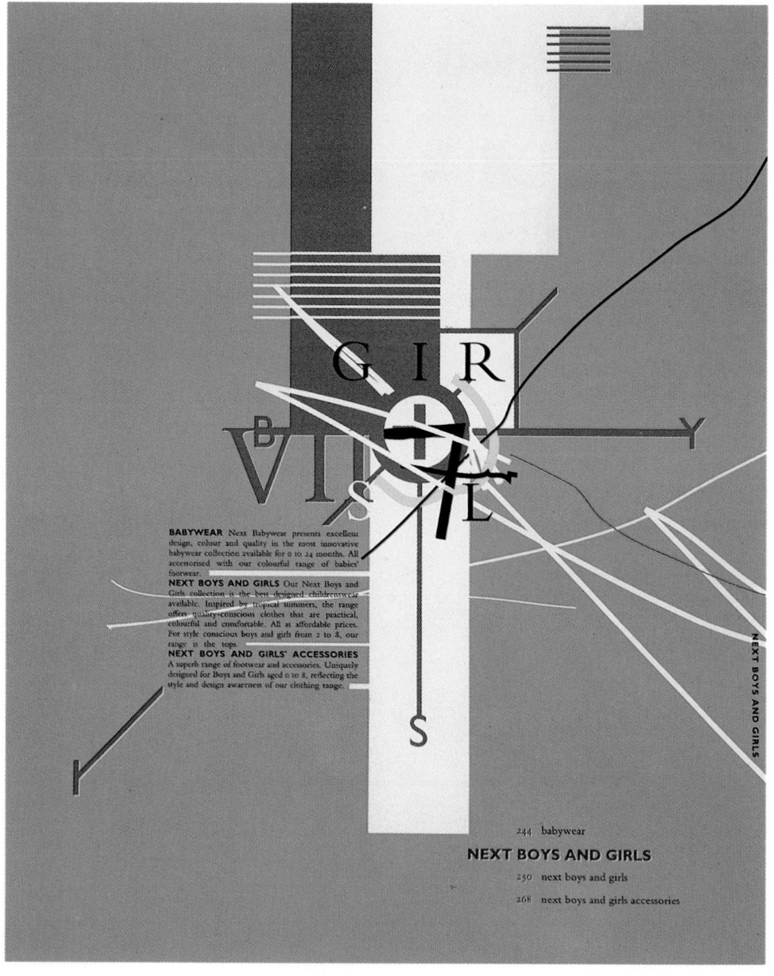

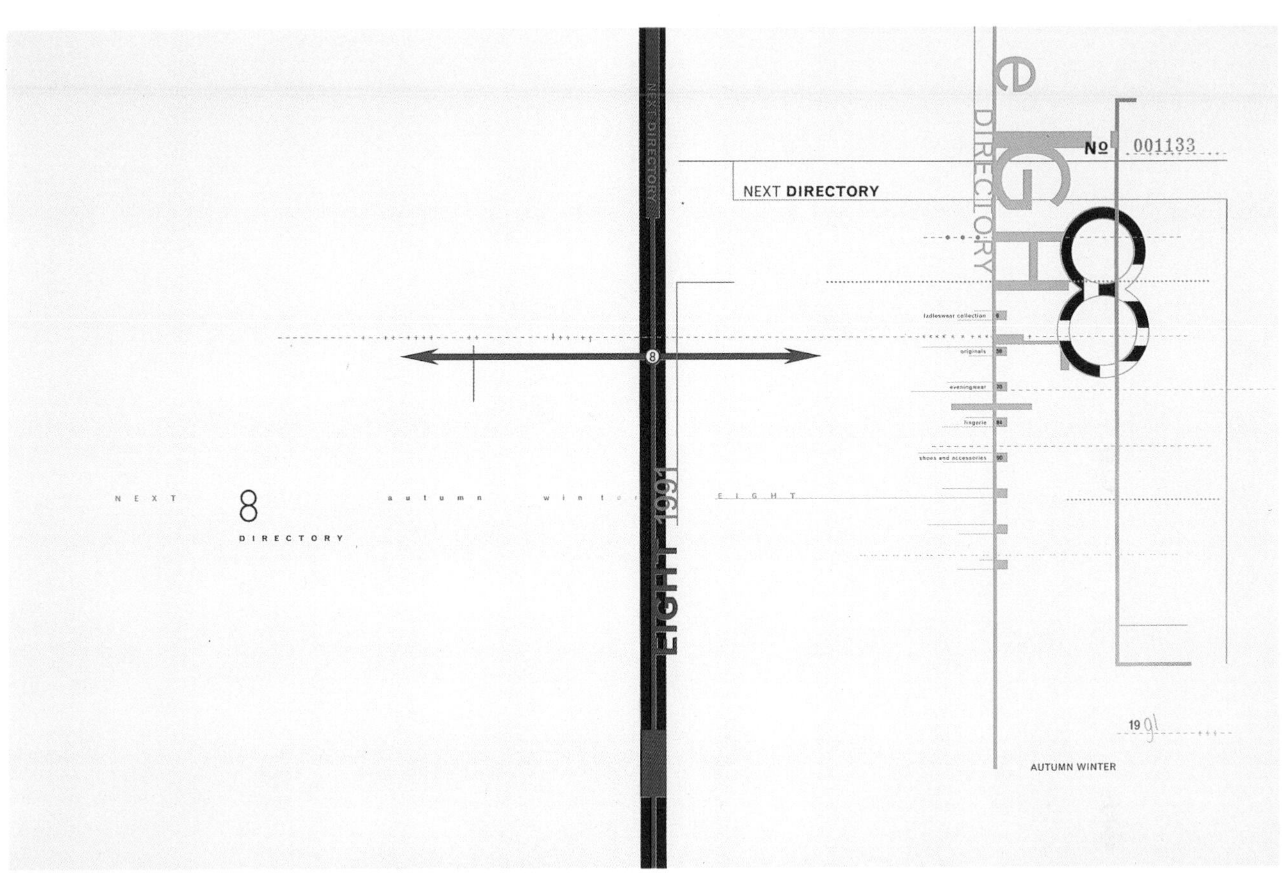
NEXT DIRECTORY
EIGHT 1991
NEXT
8
DIRECTORY
autumn winter
EIGHT
No 001133
NEXT DIRECTORY
eIGHT
DIRECTORY
8
ladieswear collection
originals
eveningwear
lingerie
shoes and accessories
1991
AUTUMN WINTER

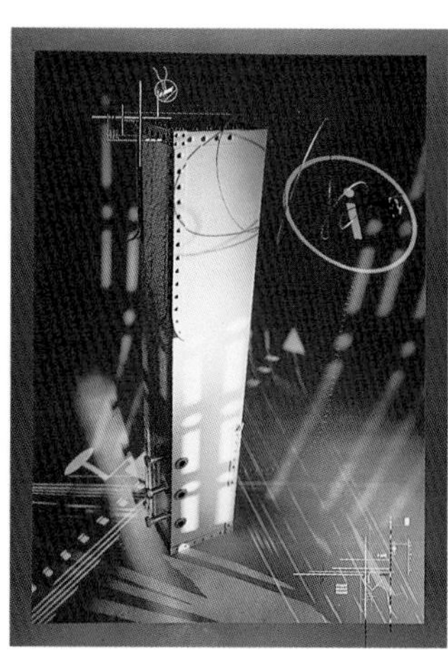

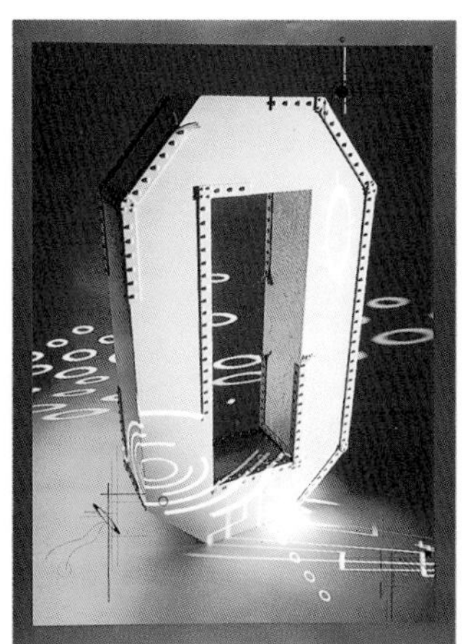

Advertising campaign posters
Smirnoff vodka, UK, 1990
Design **Why Not Associates**
Photography: Why Not Associates,
Rocco Redondo
Agency: Young & Rubicam

Les arts plastiques (The visual arts). Press kit cover. Ministry of Culture, France, 1989. Design Philippe Apeloig

opposite:
Tabbles of Bower. Poster. Cranbrook Academy of Art, USA, 1991
Design Lisa Langhoff Vorhees

Jennifer Bloomer University of Florida College of Architecture

Swanson Fund Lecture

10 December 1990 Monday 7:30 pm
CAA De Salle Auditorium

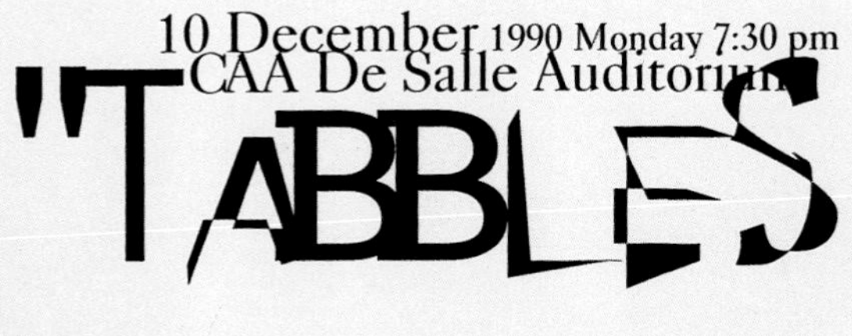

O

Cranbrook Academy of Art Bloomfield Hills Michigan

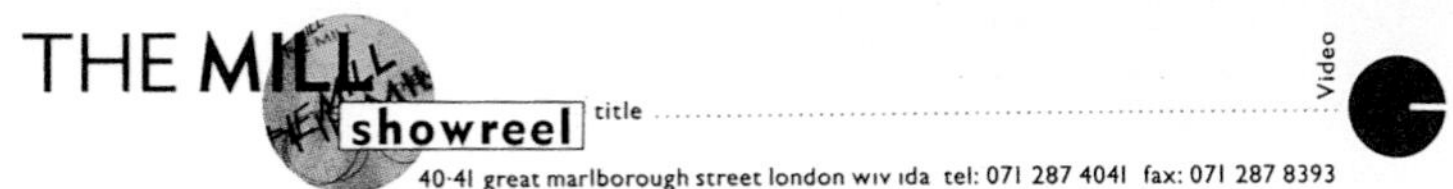

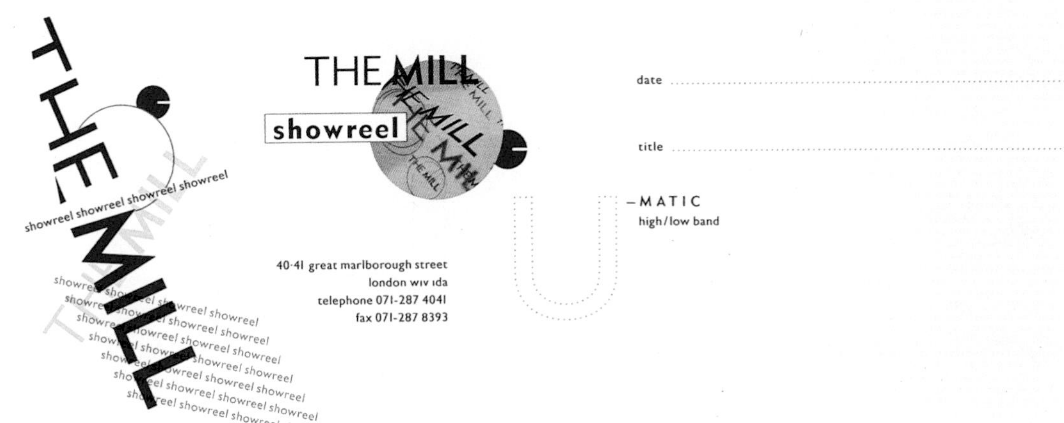

–MATIC
high/low band

title

40·41 great marlborough street london w1v 1da tel: 071 287 4041 fax: 071 287 8393

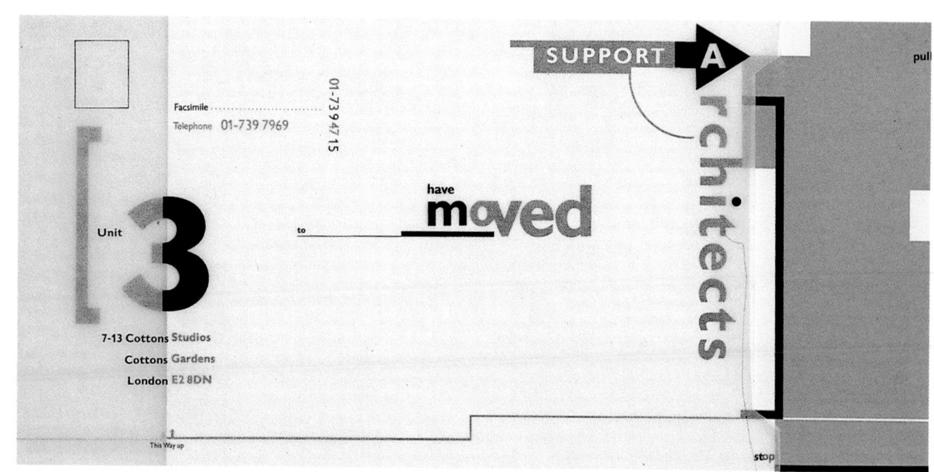

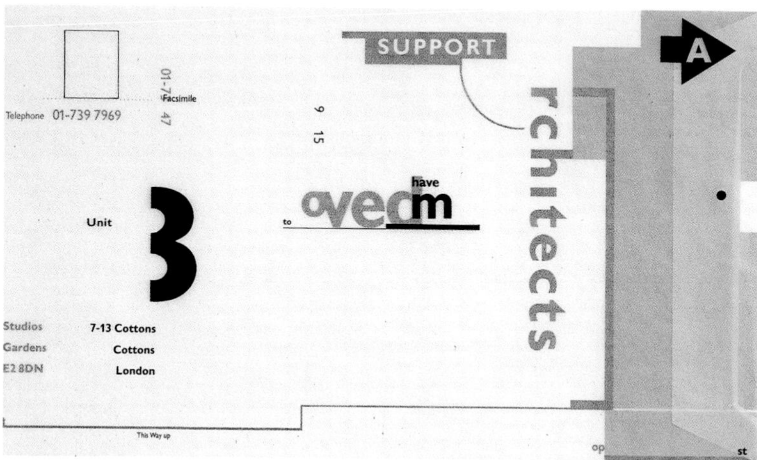

opposite:
Showreel labels. The Mill, UK, 1991
Design Siobhan Keaney

Moving card.
Support Architects, UK, 1989
Design Russell Warren-Fisher

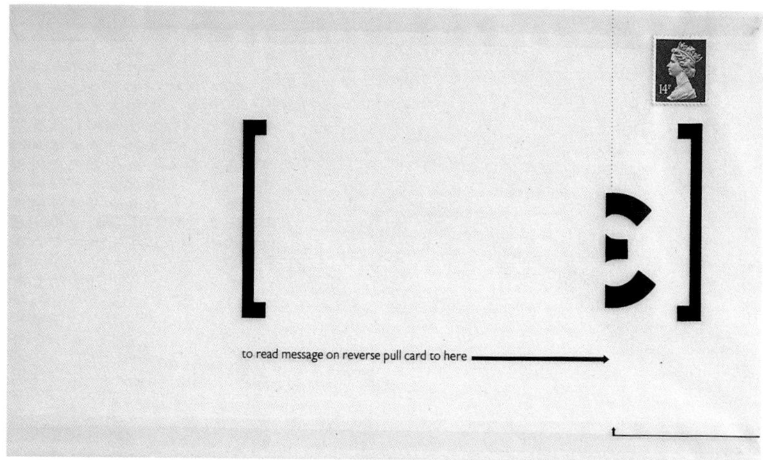

EMIGRE

THE FOLLOWING PAGES CONTAIN EXPLICIT LANGUAGE AND GRAPHIC SCENES. VIEWER DISCRETION ADVISED

ice

Perhaps at the beginn

time and the invisible

a seamless

twin makers of distan

wordlessne

drunk

s that eve

inuous.

The first light sobered

of the far, the past,

rage

PLEASE, DO THIS A

te without

give birth to ancestors

before

the wanted

realms of reams

delineating the distinction between

are syncopated thunderclaps

are bolts of lightening celebrating the indisputable decisiveness of gravity

the internal organs of the collective inhabitants within the forest

their teapo

that dissipate

of joy and rage (their stench hovers in clouds

jungle endangered & potent

#12.5.4

NG, THE

opposite page:
Emigre. Magazine cover. Emigre Graphics, USA, 1989
Design Allen Hori
Warren Lehrer
Phil Zimmerman
Rudy VanderLans

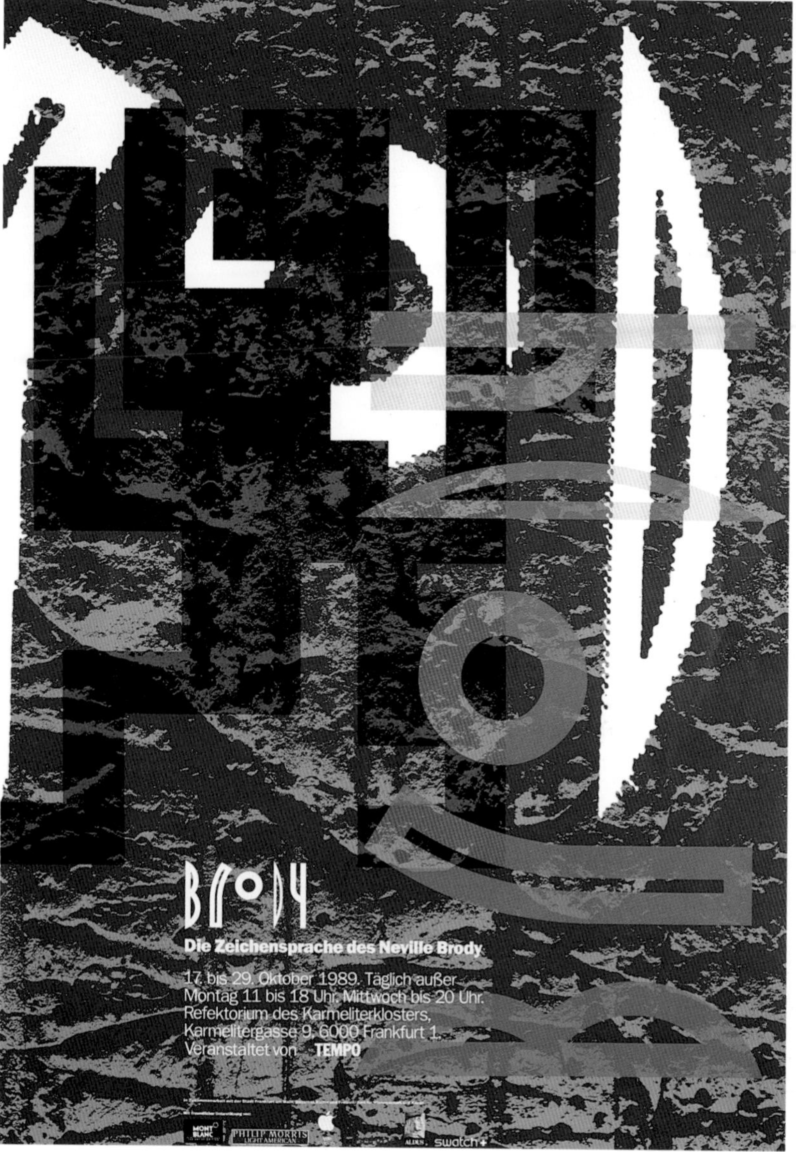

above:
Brody. Exhibition poster
Tempo magazine, Germany, 1989-90

left:
A. Type catalogue divider
FontShop, Germany, 1990
Design Neville Brody

Markus Eichenberger. Poster
Het Apollohuis, The Netherlands, 1991
Design Tom Homburg, Kees Wagenaars Opera

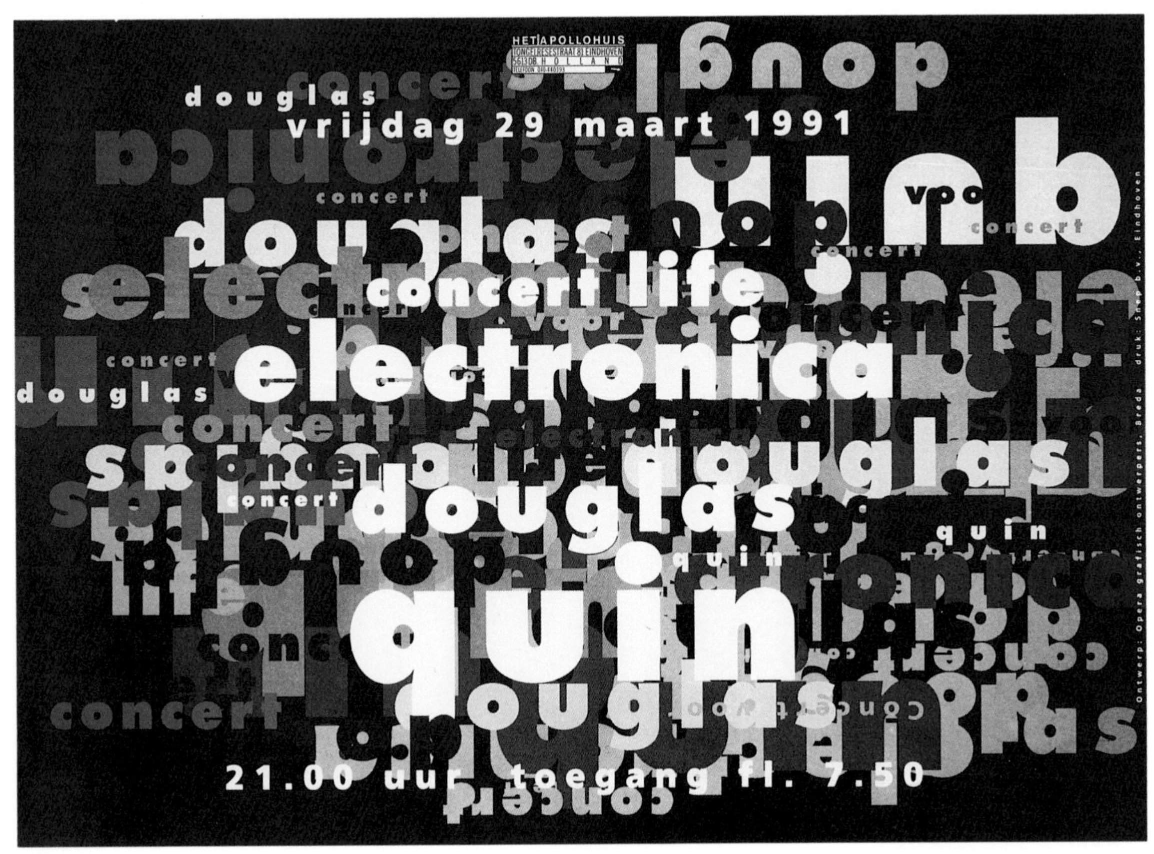

Douglas Quin. Poster. Het Apollohuis,
The Netherlands, 1991
Design Tom Homburg, Kees Wagenaars Opera

van 31 oktober tot 5 december: concerten en performances op woensdagmiddag (en op zondag 9 december): 15.30uur

van 8 november tot 13 december: filmvertoningen, concert op donderdagmiddag, 14.00uur (op 20 | 12: 13.00uur)

laboratorium plastisch geluid

L P G

light

music

film sound

motion

programma aula lezingen

Jan Boerman electronische bandcomposities
31 oktober

Huba de Graaff elektro-instrumentaal Korenicken
7 november

LIGHT

Fred Kolman audiovisuele performance Kolman's Kube
14 november

BMB con. Justin Bennett, Roelf Toxopeus, Wikke 't Hooft performance
21 november

MUSIC

Daniel Brandt performance + toelichting You Control the Audio
28 november

Frank Baldé elektro-instrumentaal
5 december 14.00uur

FILM

Joel Ryan elektro-instrumentaal
5 december

Michael Barker, Jan Boerman, Fred Kolman Multiple Electronic Presentation
9 december

SOUND

Regen Joris Ivens; Hanns Eisler (1932) NL

8 november

Nieuwe gronden Joris Ivens; Hanns Eisler (1934) NL

De 400 miljoen Joris Ivens; Hanns Eisler (1938) USA
toelichting: Gilius van Bergeijk

Entr'acte René Clair; Erik Satie (1934)

15 november

Ballet Mécanique Fernand Léger; George Antheil (1924)

Retour à la raison Man Ray (1923)

Anemic cinema Marcel Duchamp (1926)

Opus I-IV Walter Ruttman (1921-1927)

Begone dull care Norman McLaren; Oskar Peterson (1949)

Entuziazm Dziga Vertov (1930)

22 november

concert door Norbert Möslang en Andy Guhl bij:

The man with the movie camera Dziga Vertov (1929)

Electronische muziektechnieken bij film in de 60-er jaren
lezing door Rick Raaijmakers

29 november

Muziek en films van Mauricio Kagel
lezing door Frans van Rossum

6 december

De meester en de reus Johan van der Keuken; Willem Breuker (1980)

13 december

De Tijd Johan van der Keuken; Louis Andriessen (1984)
toelichting: Johan van der Keuken

Home of the brave Laurie Anderson (1988)

20 december

Kiss napoleon goodbye Babeth van Loo en Lydia Lunch (1990)

N.B. aanvangstijd 13.00uur!

Concerten en manifestaties in het Haags Gemeentemuseum, Stadhouderslaan 40:
toegangsprijs ƒ10, CJP ƒ7,50.

musica electronica

Michael Barker [coördinatie]

docenten

Frank Baldé · Konrad Boehmer · Jan Boerman

Ernst Bonis · Daniel Brandt · Onno Mensink

Dick Raaijmakers

10.00 - 12.30uur en 14.00 - 16.30uur
ƒ255 toehoorders
ƒ160 museumvrienden

MOTION

31 oktober
7 november
14 november
21 november
28 november
5 december
12 december
19 december

film en muziek

Babeth M. van Loo [coördinatie]

docenten

Gilius van Bergeijk · Johan van der Keuken

Dick Raaijmakers · Frans van Rossum

14.00 - 16.30uur

ƒ110 toehoorders
ƒ70 museumvrienden

8 november
15 november
22 november
29 november
6 december
13 december
20 december

De lezingen en bijbehorende concerten, installaties, etc. worden georganiseerd door de Interfaculteit voor Beeld en Geluid van de Koninklijke Hogeschool Den Haag en Ooyevaer Desk.

Met dank aan de Gemeente Den Haag.

Plastic Labyrinth
ontwerp Allen Hori at Studio Dumbar zeefdruk Imaba

Laboratorium plastisch geluid (Laboratory of plastic sound). Poster
Ooyevaer Desk, The Netherlands, 1990. Design Allen Hori Studio Dumbar

5 MAY / JUNE

NEWWRITING @ the DETROIT INSTITUTE of ARTS

LINES

PAUL AUSTER

Facing the Music (Station Hill Press)
The Invention of Solitude (Avon Books)
City of Glass (Sun & Moon Press)
Editor of *The Random House Book of Twentieth Century French Poetry*

&

Robert Hass

Field Guide (Yale University Press)
Praise (Ecco Press)
Twentieth Century Pleasures (Ecco Press)
Co-translator of Czeslaw Milosz's *The Separate Notebooks* (Ecco Press)

3:00 pm
Discussion:
Poetry and Prose: Why Both?
General Admission: $1.00
(book signing follows in Museum Shop)

7:30 pm
Readings-Holley Room
General Admission: $3.00

5/9

National Writers Series

Michigan Writers Series

GloriaDyc

5·26

- *Journal of a Woman Almost thirty* (Glass Bell Press)
- Editor of *Moving Out:* Feminist Literary and Arts Journal
- Recipient of a Hopwood Award for fiction

3:00 pm Reading-Holley Room
General Admission: $1.00
(book-signing follows)

12 1 2

PRESENTO

lines

on

National Writers Series

6/6

patricia JONES

- *Mythologizing Always* (Telephone Books)
- Co-editor of *Ordinary Women,* an anthology of New York women poets
- Program Coordinator of The Poetry Project (New York)

3:00 PM *Informal talk:*
"The Poet Looks at Fiction"
Holley Room
General Admission: $1.00
(book-signing follows)

7:30 PM *Reading—Holley Room*
General Admission: $3.00

Michigan Writers Series

6·16

Sharon Shively

POET AND FOUNDER OF "GORGEOUS CAFETERIA" WITH WORK IN STRAITS AND TELEPHONE

3:00 p.m.
Reading-Holley Room
General Admission: $1.00

For information call LINES: 833-1858

The Michigan Writers Series is made possible by a grant from the Michigan Foundation for the Arts.

The National Writers Series is funded by a grant from the National Endowment for the Arts.

Poetry on the Radio:
DIMENSION Sundays, 11:00 p.m. to 1:00 a.m.
CITY ARTS REVIEW Fridays, 12:00 midnight to 3:00 a.m.
both on wdet

end of transmission

jancourt

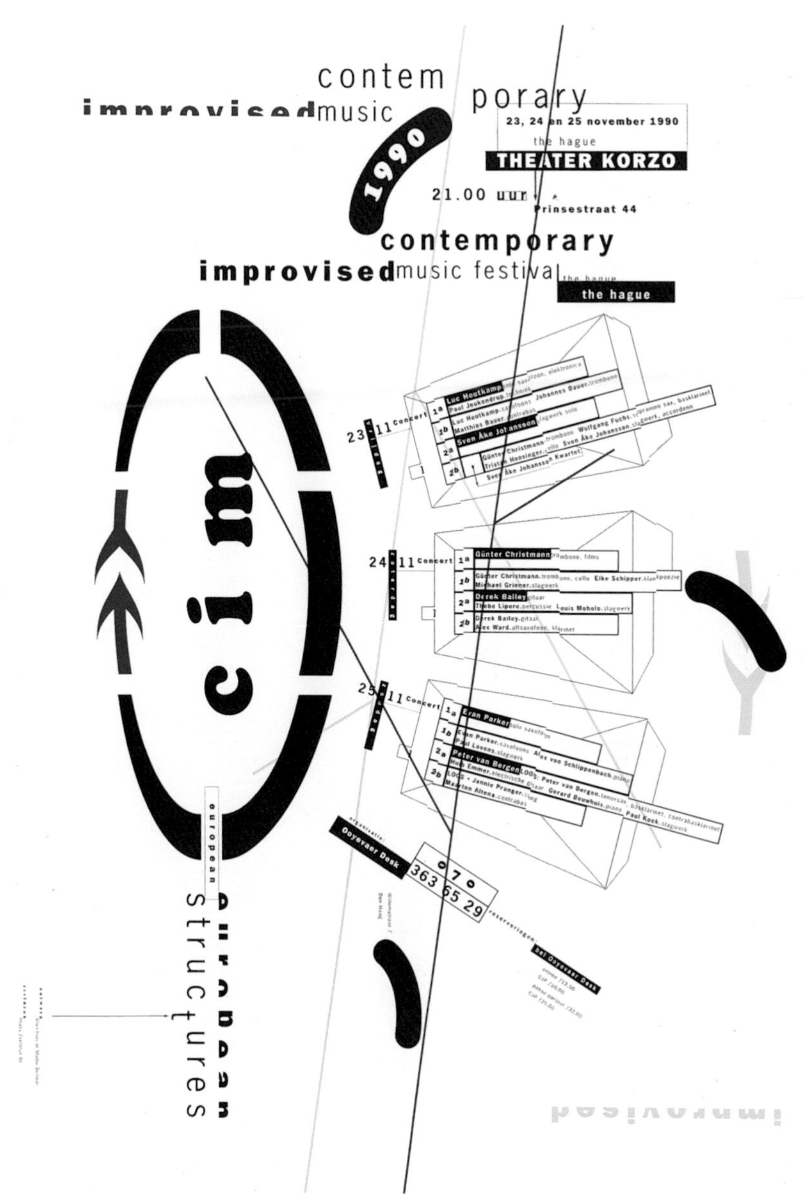

Contemporary improvised music festival. Poster. Ooyevaer Desk, The Netherlands, 1990
Design Allen Hori Studio Dumbar

opposite: *Lines.* Poster. Detroit Institute of Arts, USA, 1985. Design Jan Marcus Jancourt

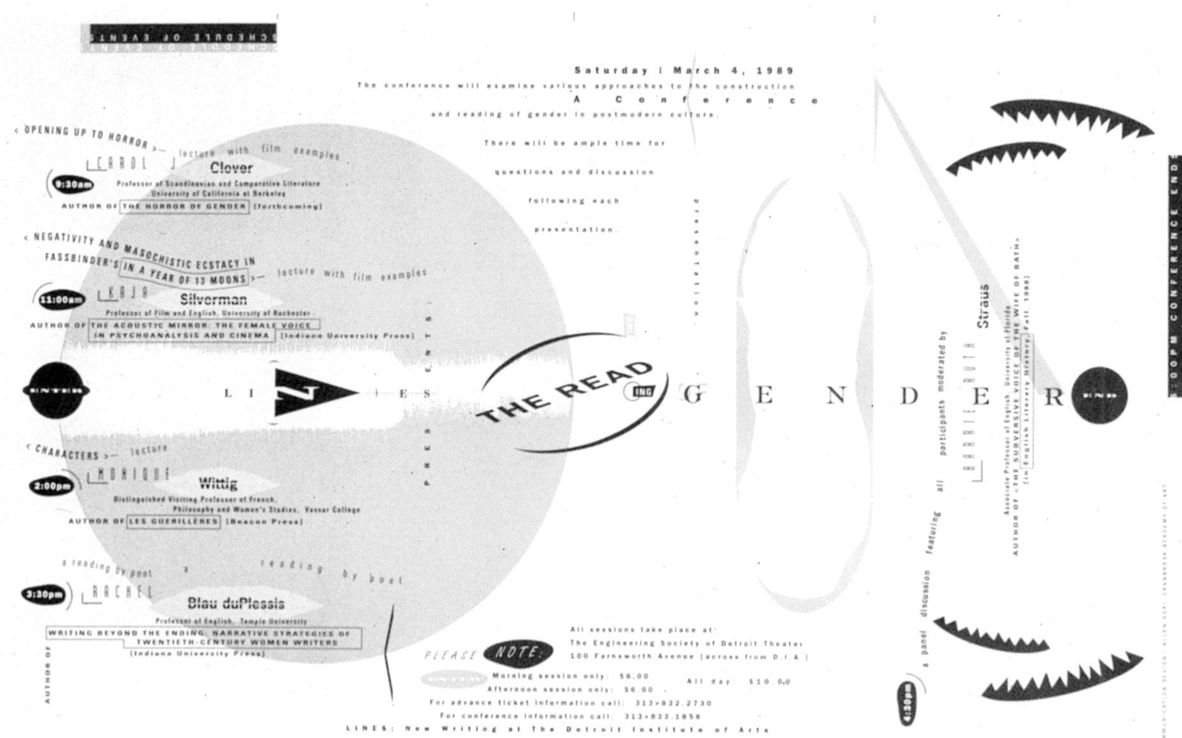

The reading of gender. Poster. Detroit Institute of Arts, USA, 1989

opposite:

Typography as discourse. Poster. American Institute of Graphic Arts Detroit, USA, 1989

Design Allen Hori

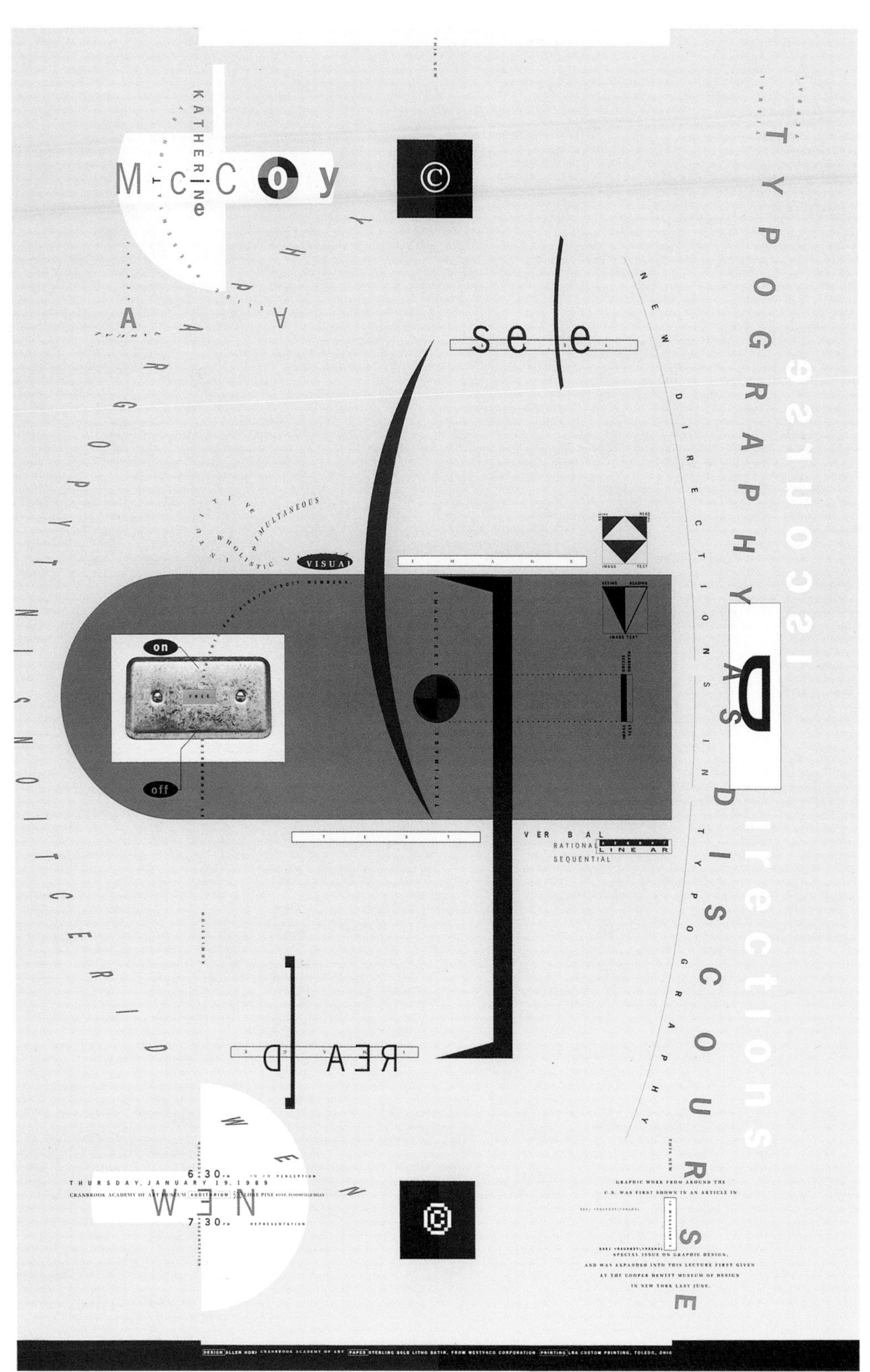

DESIGN ALLEN HORI CRANBROOK ACADEMY OF ART PAPER STERLING GOLD LITHO SATIN, FROM WESTVACO CORPORATION PRINTING LBA CUSTOM PRINTING, TOLEDO, OHIO

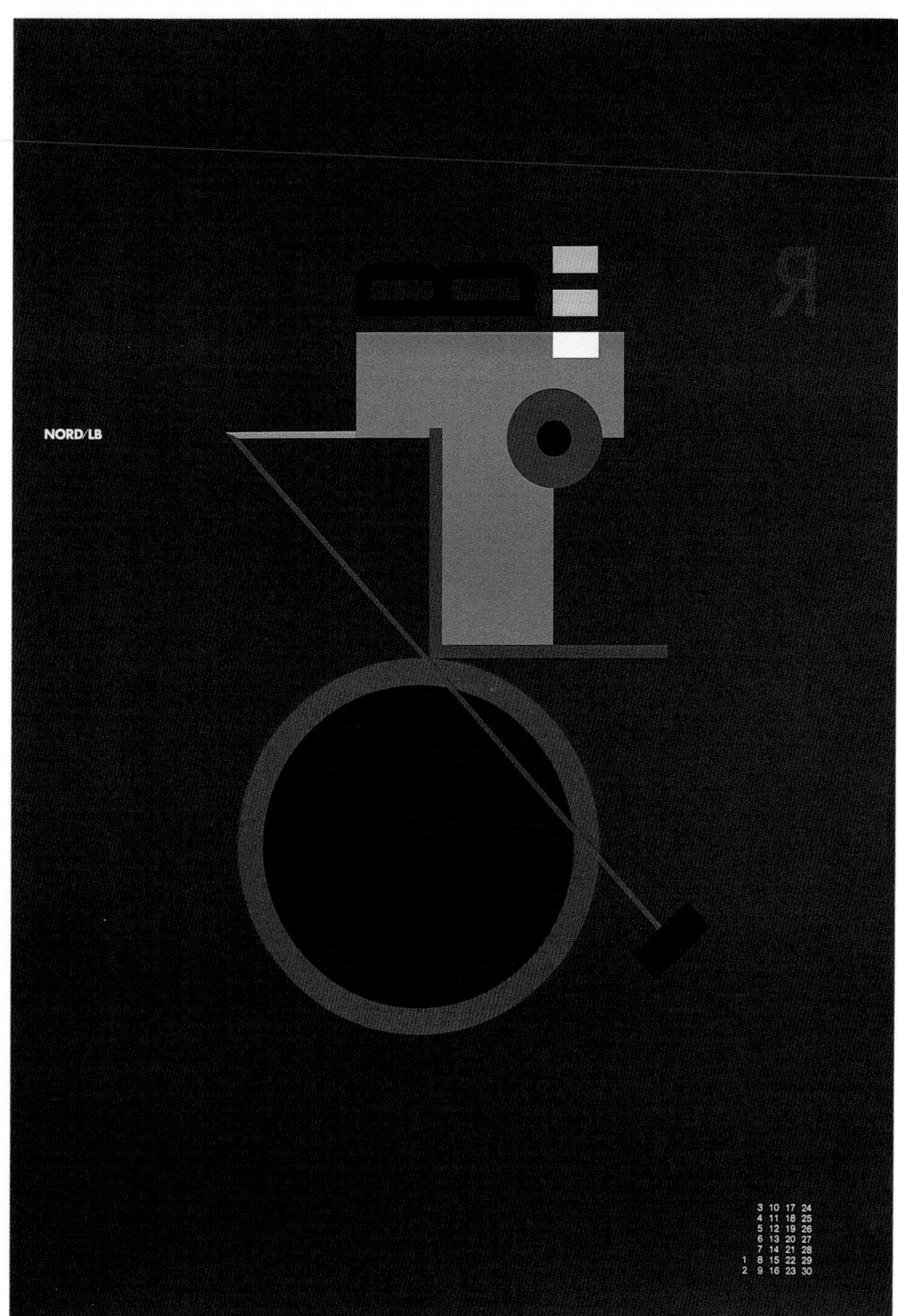

1991 calendar. Poster. Nord/LB, Germany, 1990
Design Nicolaus Ott, Bernard Stein

Beunos Aires. Symposium poster
Internationale Bauausstellung Berlin, Germany, 1984
Design **Nicolaus Ott, Bernard Stein**

Wohnraum Europa. Poster
Berlin city council, Germany, 1988
Design **Nicolaus Ott, Bernard Stein**

I

blow

living

the

in

a

house

down

box

"blow the house down" by **living in a box.** available on 7", 12" and 7" limited edition package.

design: why not associates

Chrysalis

opposite:
Living in a box. Poster
Chrysalis Records, UK, 1989
Design **Why Not Associates**

Tegentonen. Concert poster
Paradiso Amsterdam,
The Netherlands, 1987
Design **Max Kisman**

Diligentia seizoen 1988-89
(Diligentia season 1988-89)
Poster. Kunstring Dilgentia,
The Netherlands, 1988
Design **Robert Nakata** Studio Dumbar

Haçienda seven. Club poster. Factory communications, UK, 1989. Design 8vo

Fuse 1. Promotional poster. FontShop International, UK, 1991. Design Neville Brody

opposite:
Best wishes card.
Festival d'été de Seine-Maritime,
France, 1989
Design Philippe Apeloig

Poster / brochure
Jet Offset,
UK, 1991
Design 8vo

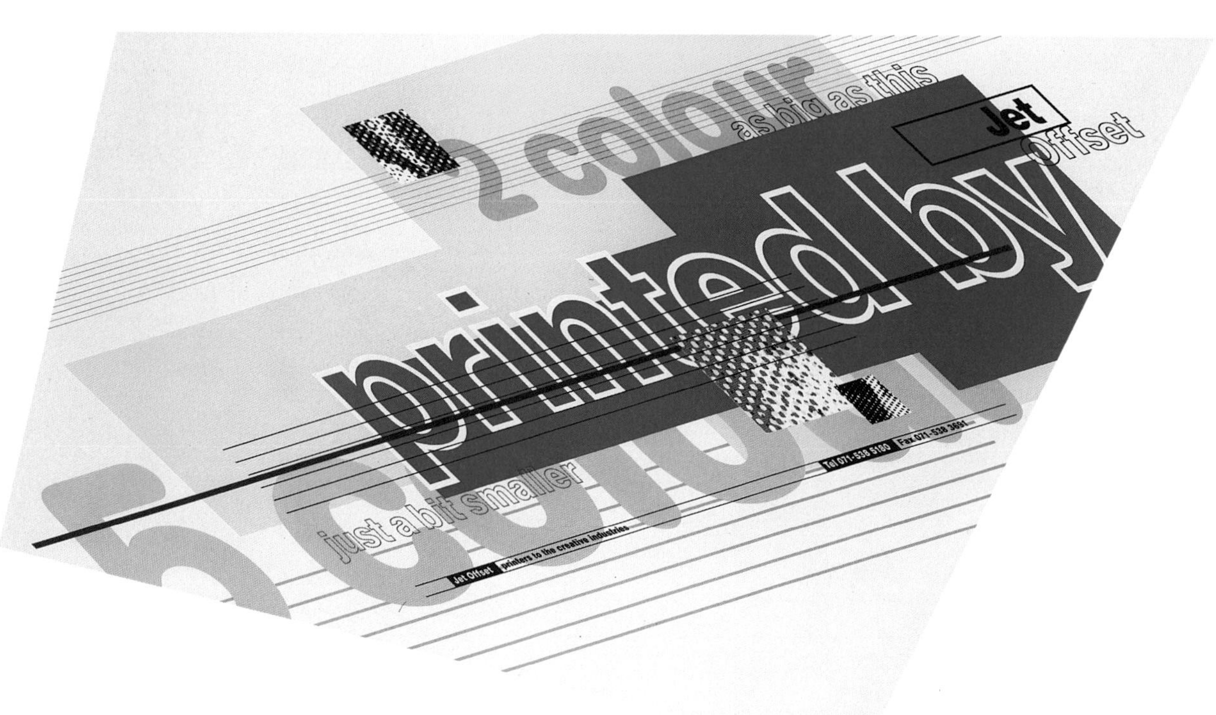

meilleurs vœux
1
9
Festival d'été.
0

Haçienda Nine
21 May 1991
Fac 51

8vo

above:
Haçienda nine. Club poster
Factory Communications,
UK, 1991
Design 8vo

Jujol. Exhibition poster
Spain, 1990
Design Quim Nolla

opposite:
Tegentonen. Concert poster
Paradiso Amsterdam,
The Netherlands, 1991
Design Max Kisman

Paradiso Amsterdam donderdag 21, vrijdag 22 en zaterdag 23 februari 1991
Donderdag 21 februari: Anette Peacock, Terminal Cheese Cake, Cop Shoot Cop, Pain Teens. Vrijdag 22 februari: Simon Turner, Mark Springer, The Cranes, Sagar Radai, Caspar Brötzmann. Zaterdag 23 februari: Surkus, Psychick Warriors Ov Gaia, Jackofficers, The Orb. Entree f12,50 & lidmaatschap per avond. Passepartout f25,- & lidmaatschap. Voorverkoop AUB VVV Nwe Muziekhandel Plaatwerk Get Records Boudisque Raf

Vini Reilly-genius

Poster

Factory Communications,

UK, 1990

Design 8vo

the durutti column

newalbumoutnow

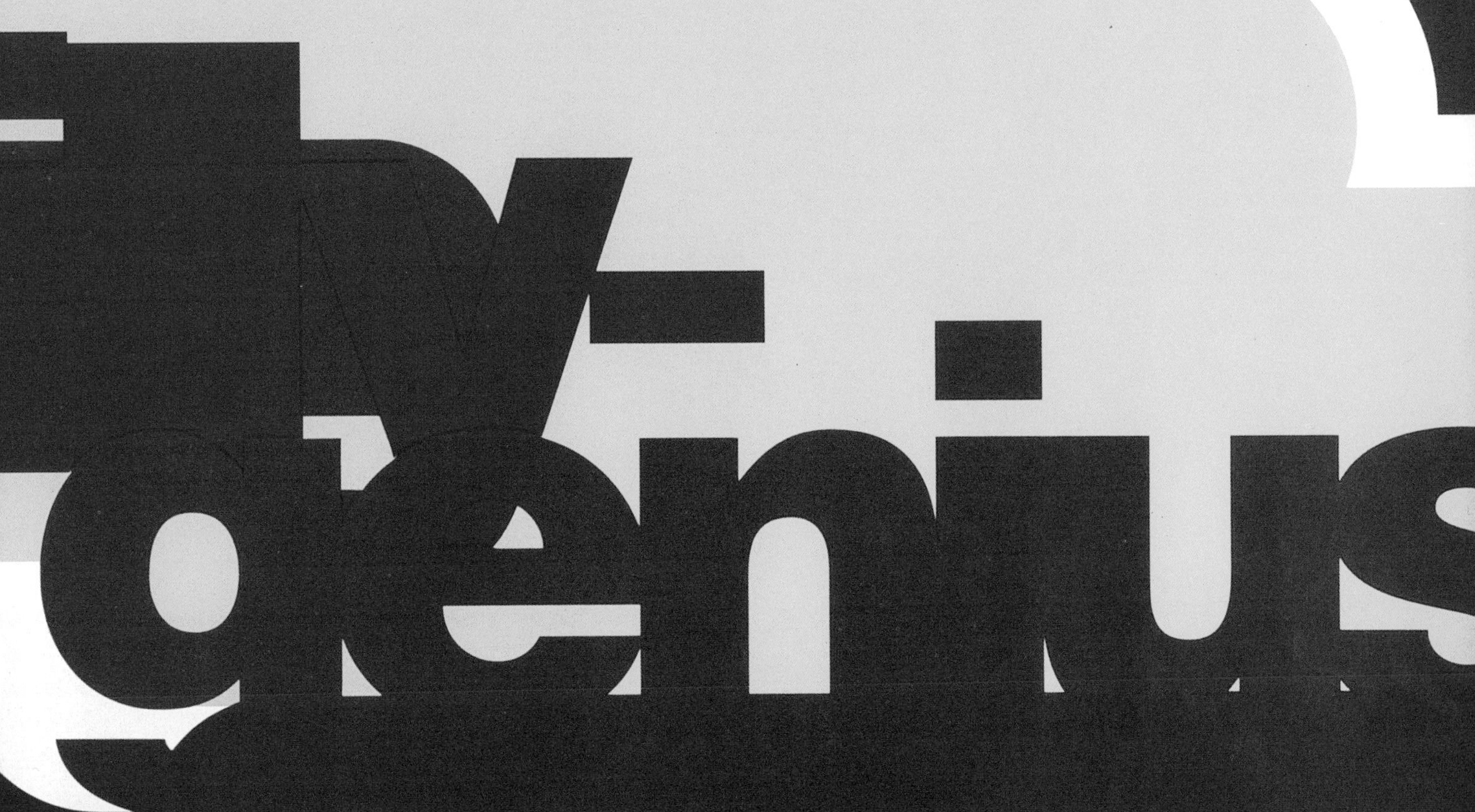

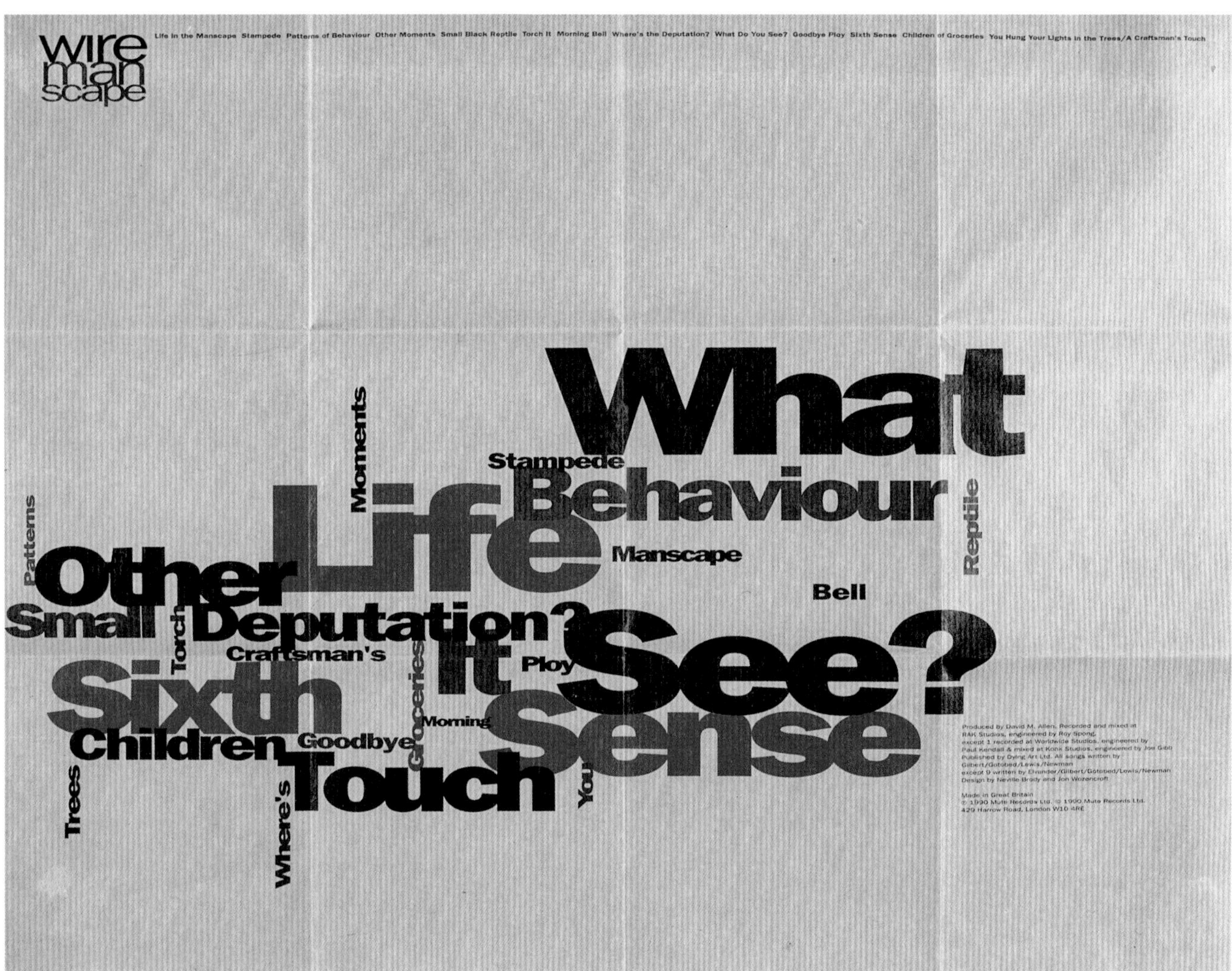

Manscape. CD poster (back). Mute Records, UK, 1990
Design Neville Brody Jon Wozencroft

opposite:
Do you read me? Magazine cover. Emigre Graphics, USA, 1990
Design Rudy VanderLans

this is emigre magazine
EMIGRE
do
number 15, price $7.95
you
[special type issue]
read
max kisman
me
jeffery keedy
karrie jacobs
?
zuzana licko
ellen lupton & j. abbott miller
peter mertens
barry deck

Not just another typesetter

We're not printing a list of faces – it would take too much space and we've no doubt got what you want anyway. If you want to see them, just call for the books that not only give display and text samples for 1350 Berthold faces, but even contain useful information to enable the typographer to make considered judgements about exactly what to specify.

We have the latest Berthold equipment, the star in the typesetting firmament, and we're usually the first in the country to get the newest hardware and software. OK techno freaks, but what does that mean for the designer? Well, it means we're up to the minute technically but not to blind you with science, we understand the technics, you get the job you want – whether you like to be involved with the bits and bytes or just want the end result without knowing how we got there.

If you want to spec 10/11pt and leave the spacing up to us, that's fine, or you can spec everything in millimetres to the nearest 1/100mm and specify exact word and letter spacing to 192 unit increments. **Either way, we understand what designers want. Our finely tuned aesthetics programme makes the most of any typeface – we really are talking accuracy and perfection.**

We call ourselves Magic, because of the tricks we can do for you. We set type, rules, scan logos and artwork, and import images, all in position (forget your wax and scalpel).

We rotate, tint-lay, distort, slant, stretch, outline and overlay

Set complete documents in position with all the text linked to the pagination. Set packaging nets in position and save master nets so you can drop in new copy as required. Then we output to film or bromide to a max image area of 300x750mm. Our film is good enough for the most exacting printer – no grey streaky blacks. And when you specify a 15% tint, that's exactly what you get – every time.

We also have the latest headline distortion equipment (more like a typo manipulation lab). If you thought the Mac was good for effects, wait until you see what this can do.

So what are we doing in darkest Macclesfield? Well actually, it's pretty nice here. And it means you won't be paying big city prices or dealing with big city egos. We are here to help you – we don't view our clients as an inconvenience. You can deal with people on the phone who understand your job, because they are the ones setting it! Not some remote telephone voice always looking for an excuse as to why it's late or too complicated to do. And we can get the stuff back to you fast – overnight by Datapost or courier, often same day by our own courier or Red Star (2 hours from Macclesfield to Euston). Most of our London clients proof-read laser outputs by fax first, so the bromides are right first time.

Magic Computer Graphics Co, Silk Mill, Thorp Street, Off Commercial Road, Macclesfield SK10 1LJ
Contact Granville Sellars
0625 612075

it really is magic

It really is magic. Promotional poster
Magic Computer Graphics Co, UK, 1990
Design 8vo

Cultural identity: or necessity. Symposium poster

Jan van Eyck Academy, The Netherlands, 1991

Design **Ko Sliggers**

e

HASH

exclamation double prime HASH

HAS

ampersand single prime (open parentheses, close parentheses) ASTERIX****comma, comma, comma, comma, Hyphen-Period.Solidus/ colonsemicolon Ð⅔Ð¼ffi BACKSLASH. ascii circumflex underscore+ascii tilde~~~daggerdegreecentsterling•daggerdegreecentsterlingdagger§•¶Eszett Diaeresis≠Æ infinity partial differential summation p roductproductproductππππππππ Ordfeminine OrdmasculineOMEGA DELTA dipthong *em* *EN* *EN* *em*

EM *em EN em EN em EN em EM; batman.*

OPEN DOUBLE GUILLEMOT» close double guillemot... Lozenge —fishermans friends—fraction bar:flutter! double double

C

double dagger-----dotless CIRCUMFLEX.

~~breve˘ ring ring, ring ring.DOT ACCENTsingle baseline quote and~~ double baseline quoteLOGICAL NOT$

(o p e n p a r e n t h e s e s , c l o s e p a r e n t h e s e s) ASTERIX****comma, comma, comma, comma, Hyphen-Period.Solidus/ colonsemicolon Ð⅔Ð¼ffi

BACKSLASH

. ascii

circumflex underscore+ascii tilde~~~~daggerdegreecentsterling•daggerdegreecentsterlingdagger§•¶Eszett Diaeresis≠Æ infinity partial differential summation p roductproductproductππππππππ Ordfeminine OrdmasculineOMEGA DELTAdipthong em EN em EN em EM en EM em EN em EN em EN em EM batman ... &

fl Orin

S NEW R NCE NEW

T R A G E

A T T R A C G O N S

A T T R A C T O R S

I A N T EW

THE S I G N S

S G F S S T

S MUSEU M O F R A T A T T

C H A O S YORK

OF TEM P O RAR Y

RS CON CHAOS

Fractured Fairy Tales, Chaotic Regimes

Laura Trippi

> I had this phrase in my head,
> "What? Is this dancing?" "What is this? Dancing?"
> . . . . [T]he only thing left of *The Crucible* had to be the line
> "What is this dancing?" and there had to be a dance.
> —Elizabeth LeCompte

The ideas embedded in the language and images of "chaos science" strike a familiar, strangely seductive chord. Like the shapes and figures of its "fractal" geometry, our daily experience is fragmented; fraught with arbitrary juxtapositions, patterns of perception and social practice are assaulted by an onrush of information. "Reception," Walter Benjamin wrote as early as 1936, is "in a state of distraction, which is increasingly noticeable in all fields of art and is symptomatic of profound changes in apperception. . . ."[1] Faced with the demands of new computer and video technologies, we collectively confront a quantum leap in the state of distraction identified by Benjamin as a corollary of the emergence of film and photography. Leisure time, work, and art, our bodies and so also our selves — all are absorbed into the breathing and buzzing surreality of simulation culture, of global information networks and cybernetic machines.

"Chaos science" is an umbrella term for two related and emerging fields: fractal geometry and the study of complex dynamical systems. If its computer-generated video graphics strike in us a sympathetic chord — images of a randomized geometry and systems in chaotic states — perhaps it is because of our immersion in an atmosphere turbulent with new technologies. The guiding myths and models of modernity have been hopelessly infiltrated and frayed, and even the once invigorating concept of "crisis" itself seems to have collapsed. This is a journey into space — the "phase space" of turbulence and "sensitive dependence"; of "multidimensional degrees of freedom"; of the decay, creation, and random fluctuation of information. It began as an experiment, a gamble, an *essay* in the sense of an attempt or try, a search for the strangely fractured fairy tales of an emerging regime.

Border Regions

Benoit Mandelbrot's compendium and guidebook, *The Fractal Geometry of Nature*, was published in 1983. In 1985, Goethe House New York sponsored the first exhibition of fractal graphics, produced by scientists and offered in unaltered photo-reproductions as art.[2] By the mid-eighties, the shapes and formulas of fractal geometry had begun to appear in the work of practicing artists. But forces other than the discourse of science seem to have prepared the ground for the expropriation of its latest images and ideas.

The term "fractal," a variant of "fractional," points to the idea both of fragmentation and irregularity. An emerging branch of geometry, the study of fractals breaks with the Euclidean tradition of idealized forms. With an infinite nesting of pattern within pattern, repeating across scales, fractal images open onto an area devoid of fixed coordinates. Because the mathematical operations that produce fractal "landscapes" depend on the introduction of chance (random number generation), each repetition of a given pattern asserts a fractional difference from all others. The notion of boundary, too, is confounded. On closer look, the line dividing two regions reveals unexpected complexity. In the literature, this is sometimes expressed as the

Strange attractors: signs of chaos
Exhibition catalogue: cover and pages
The New Museum of Contemporary Art, USA, 1989
Design Marlene McCarty, Tibor Kalman M&Co

WERE YOU AFTER A TENSION
James Welling
BETWEEN
Interviewed by
LEGIBILITY AND ILLEGIBILITY
Laura Trippi
IN THESE PHOTOGRAPHS?

> **JAMES WELLING.** I was trying to work beyond visibility, with notions of sense, sensuality, that which is of the senses.... I was engaged with other topics of which legibility, or representation, always plays a part: hallucinations, extreme mental states, the drawings of psychotics–castles of detail, sensual, non-quotidian, non-representaional. There were ideas about the wild, wilderness, nature, geological formations. Fabulous landscapes. Creating things that involve aspects of fiction or science fiction.

When I was working on the Aluminum Foil photographs, I understood that I was creating a program or a machine to manufacture randomness, a system to make random images. It seemed extremely simple, straightforward, and *economical*, and also yielded all these images. This one piece of metal could be constantly refolded into itself. It was both a physical way to make pictures, and an analogy for other things, like language: the way language uses the same words but is constantly repermuted and reconfigured.

> **LAURA TRIPPI.** I just read a brief essay David Joselit wrote for your show in Vienna, which discusses your recent photographs of buildings by the late 19th-century architect H.H. Richardson. Joselit cites Richardson's aim as that of "disciplining the picturesque." The phrase caught my attention in connection with your Aluminum Foil photographs and the way they sort of traffic in the picturesque or sublime.

> **JW.** I don't think we have feelings of the sublime anymore. It's a historical idea. I think these photographs do evoke a *lost* feeling of the sublime. The sublime I'm interested in is not a landscape, but more like snow on a T.V. screen. It has its own kind of beauty—if you can apply the word "beauty" to it. We're putting 19th-century terms with a mid-20th-century electronic landscape.... But the idea of electronic snow, of raw electronic states, it was a pretty powerful idea. I don't think I've ever really talked about coming out of making video tapes and going into photography. But that was one of the reasons that, when I figured out what I wanted to do with the photograph, I worked the way I worked in the video studio, on a table top, with a tripod, etc.

986-7, James ling produced a ies of "circle intings" that ear a striking esemblance to the "sphere tremas" of Mandelbrot, among the least obviously "fractional" of fractal images, printed in black-and-white in the book (*The Fractal Geometry of Nature*). In Welling's paintings, the massing shapes come across at once as vaguely ominous and profoundly pop, suggestive in this context of a deadpan commentary on the "promiscuity" of fractal graphics (even, more generally, on that f simulation), the ar-contagion of ir allure.

AVITAL RONELL

THE TELE-PHONE BOOK

Technology — Schizophrenia — Electric Speech —

University of Nebraska Press: Lincoln

& London

O mouth!

at the moment" (*W*, 120). At this point, Heidegger appears to rely on a communality of sense, a *sensus communis*, or an essential consensus, into which the unpresent tense of schizophrenic discourse could not, admittedly, be happily entered. However, even in this convocation of something like a contractual agreement of sense, a common contextuality and steadiness of address, Heidegger amends the speaking to include, as an address, the human and the thingly: "That includes fellow men and things, namely, everything that conditions things and determines men. All this is addressed in word, each in its own way, and therefore spoken about and discussed in such a way that the speakers speak to and with one another and to themselves. All the while, what is spoken remains many-sided. Often it is no more than what has been spoken explicitly, and either fades quickly away or else is somehow preserved. What is spoken can have passed by, but it also can have arrived long ago as that which is granted, by which somebody is addressed" (*W*, 120). **The Laingian** reading of Heidegger establishes a dimension which appears to set objections to schizophrenogenic modes of address, to the distortions of the place of sender and recipient toward which Heidegger's thinking may appear to harbor intolerance. Nonetheless even in these passages, the temporal rendering of that which is spoken in addition to the incomparable inclusion of thingly speakers already complicate any itinerary that would seek reliably to reroute schizophrenic Saying from a more normative grasp of language. But the material with which to seek presence of person in the speaking cannot be securely retrieved from any Heideggerian path of language. In "The Way to Language," Heidegger continues in this way, averting the dangers of the straight and narrow:

Everything spoken stems in a variety of ways from the unspoken, whether this be something not yet spoken, or whether it be what must remain unspoken in the sense that it is beyond the reach of speaking. Thus, that which is spoken in various ways begins to appear as if it were cut off from speaking and the speakers, and did not belong to them, while in fact it alone offers to speaking and to the speakers whatever it is they attend to, no matter in what way they stay within what is spoken of the unspoken. (*W*, 120; italics added)

Not long after this reading, which in part corresponds to the descriptive analysis of schizophrenic utterance in Laingguage, Heidegger offers to accentuate the cutting. Analyzing the sign in terms of *secare*, "to cut," he returns to the decisive disconnectedness in all language tracings. The speaking which appears as if disconnected from speaking and the speakers cannot therefore be used to explicate an essential dimension, gleaned from Heidegger, of schizophrenia in its most advanced stages of psychosis—unless, of course, Heidegger were himself to be implicated in the unfolding of a schizophrenogenic understanding of language. This would be going very far, on the other way to language, whose essential signpost reads "Wrong Way, Do Not Enter." **In another** essay, "The Nature of Language," Heidegger has the following to say on the question, raised so often by the doctors, of not being there:

All is way. . . The way allows us to reach what concerns us, in that domain where we are already staying. Why then, one may ask, still find a way to it? Answer: because where we already are, we are in such a way that at the same time we are not there, because we ourselves have not yet properly reached what concerns our being, not even approached it. The way that lets us reach where we already are, differing from all other ways, calls for an escort that runs far ahead. (*W*, 92–93)

165

That which has been with us, the companion, stretches itself apart from us in answer to a call. The escort does not cease to be an escort when a long-distance runner is called for. It is one that reaches the place where we are not but toward which we point. We are where we are in such a way that, at the same time, we are not there. This is where we stay. Heidegger places some words after one that is simple, single, and armed with the antennae of a colon, *Answer:* Why do we care to mention this total response unit?

The telephone book
Title page and book pages
University of Nebraska Press, USA, 1989
Design Richard Eckersley

between two rooms, Bell's voice was vibrating from it, shouting "Ahoy! Ahoy!" "Are you there?" "Do you hear me?" "What's the matter?" . . . Then began the first "long distance" telephone conversation the world has ever known. We recorded it word for word. The croakers made us do that. The common attitude toward any new thing is apt to be pessimistic for the average man thinks that what hasn't been done, can't be done. It was so with the telephone. It seemed a toy to most persons. Some of Bell's friends, although they had heard the thing talk at the laboratory were doubtful as to its practical value, and one of them of a scientific turn of mind told me that he didn't see how the telephone could be accurate enough for practical use for every spoken word has many delicate vibrations to be converted into electrical waves by the telephone and if some of them get lost the message cannot be intelligible. (*A*, 94–95).

The first long-distance electric conversation enveloped language in high-decibel noise; as an acoustic machine it generated solely on good vibes. Ever since Watson had known Bell, he recounts, his habit of celebrating successful experiments by what he called a war dance was respected, and "I had got so expert at it that I could do it as well as he could. That night, when he got back to the laboratory, we forgot there were other people in the house and had a rejoicing that nearly resulted in a catastrophe" (*A*, 95–96).

The morning after: "after a sleepless night, as I started down the stairs to go to Williams' to build some more telephones, I saw our landlady waiting for me at her door with an acid expression on her face" (*A*, 96). as a noise machine it generated solely on good vibes. Ever since Watson had known Bell, he recounts, his habit of celebrating successful experiments by what he called a war dance was respected, and "I had got so expert at it that I could do it as well as he could. That night, when he got back to the laboratory, we forgot there were other people in the house and had a rejoicing that nearly resulted in a catastrophe" (*A*, 95–96).

The morning after: "after a sleepless night, as I started down the stairs to go to Williams' to build some more telephones, I saw our landlady waiting for me at her door with an acid expression on her face" (*A*, 96). The waiting woman at the end of the line, imaged in the liquefying anger of experimental elements, her acid face about to have words. The naughty young man: "My conscience was troubling me and I felt something disagreeable was about to happen. My pretense of great haste did not work for she stopped me and said in an unpleasant voice, 'I don't know what you fellows are doing up in the attic but if you don't stop making so much noise nights and keeping my lodgers awake, you'll have to quit them rooms.' I couldn't say much to calm her. I assured her we would be more careful although for the life of me I didn't see how we could get along with any less noise than we had been making. I couldn't blame her finding fault. She wasn't at all scientific in her tastes and we were not prompt with our rent" (*A*, 96). This is the only time Watson invokes the prerogatives of scientific sensibility, in the key of aesthetified taste, and we would not be wrong to suggest that he spits out the signifier with irony. The noise without which they would not be able to get along presumably resulted from the war dancing, as telephone connections were tried out in other spaces. Yet the inevitability—at however long a distance—of noise as a by-product of this innovation in the speech conveyance has just been announced to the landlady, whose figure is firmly planted to the ground. This may be the birth of

a new noise era

whose contours make Kafka's thin text,

"The Neighbor,"

explode.

The telephone was hardly a beloved or universally celebrated little monster. It inspired fear, playing on fresh forms of anxiety which were to be part of a new package deal of the invisible. This hardly replicates the way Watson puts it, yet he gives abundantly profiled clues to follow. It soon becomes clear that schizophrenia recognizes the telephone as its own, appropriating it as a microphone for the singular emission of its pain. Schizophrenia was magnetized by the telephone the way neurosis rapped on Freud's door. In a fundamental sense, we can say that the first outside call the telephone makes is to schizophrenia—a condition never wholly disconnected from the ever-doubling thing. Watson mounts his case slowly, describing the call of aberrancy first in terms of "embarrassment." Men in particular were uneasy about the thing. For instance: "It also interested me to see how many people were embarrassed when they used the telephone for the first time. One day a prominent lawyer tried the instruments with me. When he heard my voice in the telephone making some simple remark he could only answer after a long embarrassed pause, 'Rig a jig, and away we go'" (*A*, 98). Regression takes hold, the call transfers the speaker to a partial object, a false self caught up in the entanglement of *fort/da*: away we go.

Watson defines essentially two kinds of men that visited the telephone. The first we have just listened to, away he went. The second returns us to a recurrent concern, the consummate knowledge of disconnection that connects the schizophrenic to things and machinery: "Men of quite another stamp from those I have mentioned occasionally" (*A*, 98). Though he is not necessarily

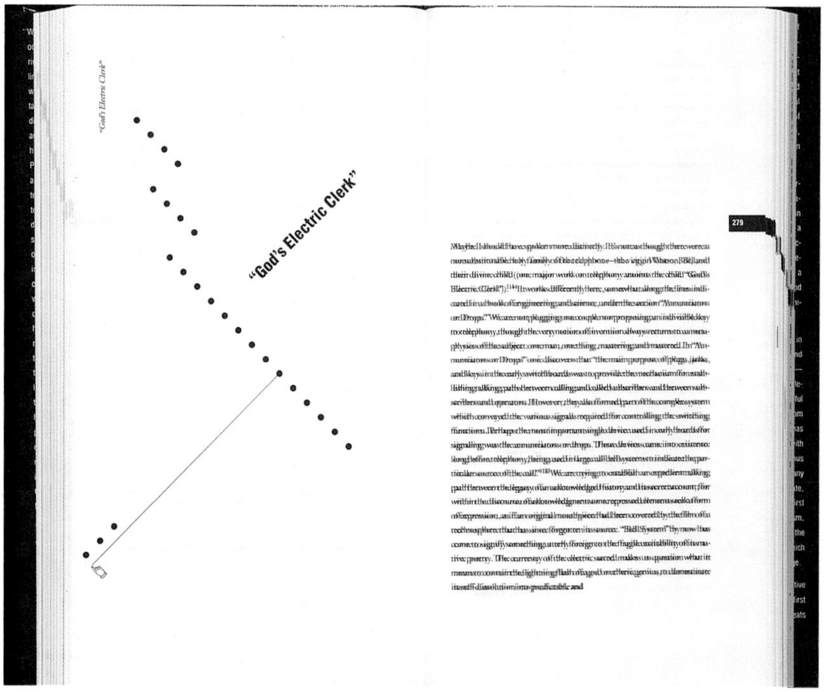

"God's Electric Clerk"

Maybe I should have spoken more distinctly. It's not as though there were a nonassimilable holy family of the telephone—the virgin Watson, Bell, and their divine child (one major work on telephony anoints the child "God's Electric Clerk").[114] It works differently here, somewhat along the lines indicated in a book of engineering and science, under the section "Annunciators on Drops." We are not plugging one couple or proposing an indivisible key to telephony, though the very notion of invention always returns to a metaphysics of the subject: one man, one thing, mastering and mastered. In "Annunciators on Drops" one discovers that "the main purpose of plugs, jacks, and keys in the early switchboards was to provide the mechanism for establishing talking paths between calling and called subscribers and between subscribers and operators. However, they also formed part of the complex system which conveyed the various signals required for controlling the switching functions. Perhaps the most important single device used in early boards for signaling was the annunciator or drop. These devices came into existence long before telephony, being used in large call bell systems to indicate the particular source of the call."[115] We are trying to establish an expedient talking path between the legacy of unacknowledged history and its secret account; for within the discourse of acknowledgment some repressed elements seek a form of expression, as if an original mouthpiece had been covered by the film of a technosphere that has since forgotten its source. "Bell System" by now has come to signify something utterly foreign to the fragile sociability of its narrative poetry. The currency of the electric sacred makes us question what it means to contain the lightning flash of a good electric genius, to domesticate its self-dissolution into predictable and

The BAUHAUS mi
stook legibility for c
ommunication, (it's
a man's world).

Nicolett
e Gray: i
n 1 p.12

'It is not really necessary for the beholder to read, or understand these words. THE WORDS ARE PART OF THE MEDIUM
; what the artist is communicating through the medium is his reaction to, his understanding of these words, which he h
as expressed in the way they are inscribed.'

Six sheets, as if fragments, (keys to a la
rger argument/point of view: wider te
rms of reference lead to a better, more
fully human typography), **in order:-**

1,2,3,4:

LEFT RIGHT

FORGET REMEMBER

SIGHT SOUND

PRINT MANUSCRIPT

INTO THE HOT...

'The system
was basically
very simple. T
he stationer h
eld **a copy of
the book** (exe
mplar) **unbou
nd in** quires o
r **pieces** (peci
e), and hired i
t out to a scri
be piece by pi
ece to copy.'

Richard
Hunt: in
2 p. 202

James S
utton an
d Alan B
artram: i
n 3 p.26

'The Aldine Ro
man is the arche
type of all Old
Face types whic
h during the six
teenth century e
stablished their
ascendancy ove
r gothic throug
hout Europe.'

**'Grotesques
,** which **are cl
oser** in some
ways **to the b
lack letter t
han the nor
mal roman.'**

John Le
wis: in 4
p.46

*The Bauhaus mistook legibility for communicatio
n.* Cover and page from college thesis, UK, 1985
Design Phil Baines

INTO THE HOT...

Ludwig Grote: i 'PROPORTION WAS TO TAKE THE PLACE OF . . FORM
n 9 p.18 hy twice the n ver; discredited. **Broader terms 'All fashion i** Mark E. Smith: o
SYNTHESIS TO REPLACE. . . . . ANALYSIS n 28
umber of sym of reference offer more possi s filched off f
LOGICAL CONSTRUCTION . . LYRICAL SUSPENSION
bols, if half th bilities for finding a rich chaos aggots- then,
MECHANICS . . . . CRAFTSMANSHIP
e number acco , subtle differences, (unity in vari two or more y
COLLECTIVISM . . . . . . INDIVIDUALISM
mplishes the s ety), **an appeal to more of our b** ears later...'
SUCH WERE THE DEMANDS OF DE STIJL.'
ame thing?' eing and an affirmation of our tr **'Rational,** In 30
Herbert B. Oliver: in 29 **'The old ind** ue potential and wealth. **Broade objectiv**
ustrialism r terms of reference as somet e thinking ca
was unconcern **hing to work from,** whatever th **n produce be**
ed with soul or e goal- legibility, clarity or a rich, l **autiful art,** b
spirit: it produc ayered variety- **give typograph** oth fine and a
ed but for mon **y its real kick,** its real utility or it pplied. **What**
ey, colourless g s real wonder, and **it was broad I find depres**
Ivan Illich: in 21 p.13 **'Institutions** create certainties, and taken seriously, certainties
oods that echo **er terms of reference that BA sing is the ex**
deaden the heart and shackle the imagination.'
ed the charact **UHAUS codification stifled. tent to whic**
eristics of any **B**AUHAUS typography came t **h this approa**
nation but our o assume as many gratuitous **ch is misappl**
own. We cease aesthetics as the work it reacted **ied.** In my vie
ed to be. The s against, and the original aims we w the best gr
hekels buried u re soon lost. **Bauhaus disciples** aphic design
s. Our faith is g **ignored many of the questio** comes from p
one in all that & **ns posed, scraped at, or ans** eople trained
we are like a sk **wered on these six sheets; the** in other areas
eleton leaf-plan **y lacked** the **real pioneer spirit** - notably pain
ts pressed in a b **and zest** of El-Lissitsky, Alexand ting and print
ook.' er Rodchenko, Kurt Schwitters or making.'
Piet Zwart; **the cheek** of Dada; **t**
he heat of Hendrik Werkma
n; the **rational historic**
ism of Eric Gill **and**
the **grace** of A
nthony Fr
oshau
g.

overleaf: lan/gua/geb/rea/ksh/ere. Contribution to *Breakthrough* catalogue. Royal College of Art, UK, 1988. Design Phil Baines

lan gua ge|b

SA
"Bridal Bits"
salt sel salz
50
T H O N
s p e c i a l f i l t r e

A dream come true
for 50p
wet & dry
whole cold
wet & wavy

(weave
-on)

sta - sof - fro
ultra sheen afro
sheen
Fantasyclub

18 x 12 x 18
(we

19 x 21 x

Ste
Star

Terry's

T **HE**
P **ANTRY**
PEN

:
:

(weave -on) • • • • • • •

D Share
jucy
mini

16 Ears p ierced
& 12 tun es
4 1 1 8 bankrup t

s e l e c t

Mr. Juicy (**Steve.** Hu bba Bubb

A / P

phil baines words: david blamey. design: phil baines.

rea ks|h ere

Fresh

the critic

ave- on)

ice

's cho

V T **Ne ck**

”

super

”

Big

”

”

op

’

Va-Boy
90p. a pot

gulf

(T
D)

eck

•••••&

wise
182
Yes,
we do!

“99”

knives

Lo		Sunny shoes
M	▓	wide approx
T	□	any case
P	▓	Gary angels
E	▓	Sir sir sir
ut		No eels today

e d

[s

a. Elvis Pr esley; Sam Fox; **Jesu**

publisher: billionth press, 1988. edition, 2000

BRAMEY

Is there If there is, it coul

really a d be just a fashion

swing. After a sea

son of **th** *romantic brushstrokes* a

nd *crayon effects*, some **e ar** thin

g more high-tech m **rang** ay b

e in the air: *a multi-l* **eme** *ayere*

d look of hard type on (. **nt o** *....) vi*

new enthusiasm fo

r typography amo

ng designers? **f co**

deo textures. But what **mpo**

exactly is *typography?* **sed t**

ype.

Graphics World. Magazine cover illustration. Graphics World Publications, UK, 1989. Design Phil Baines

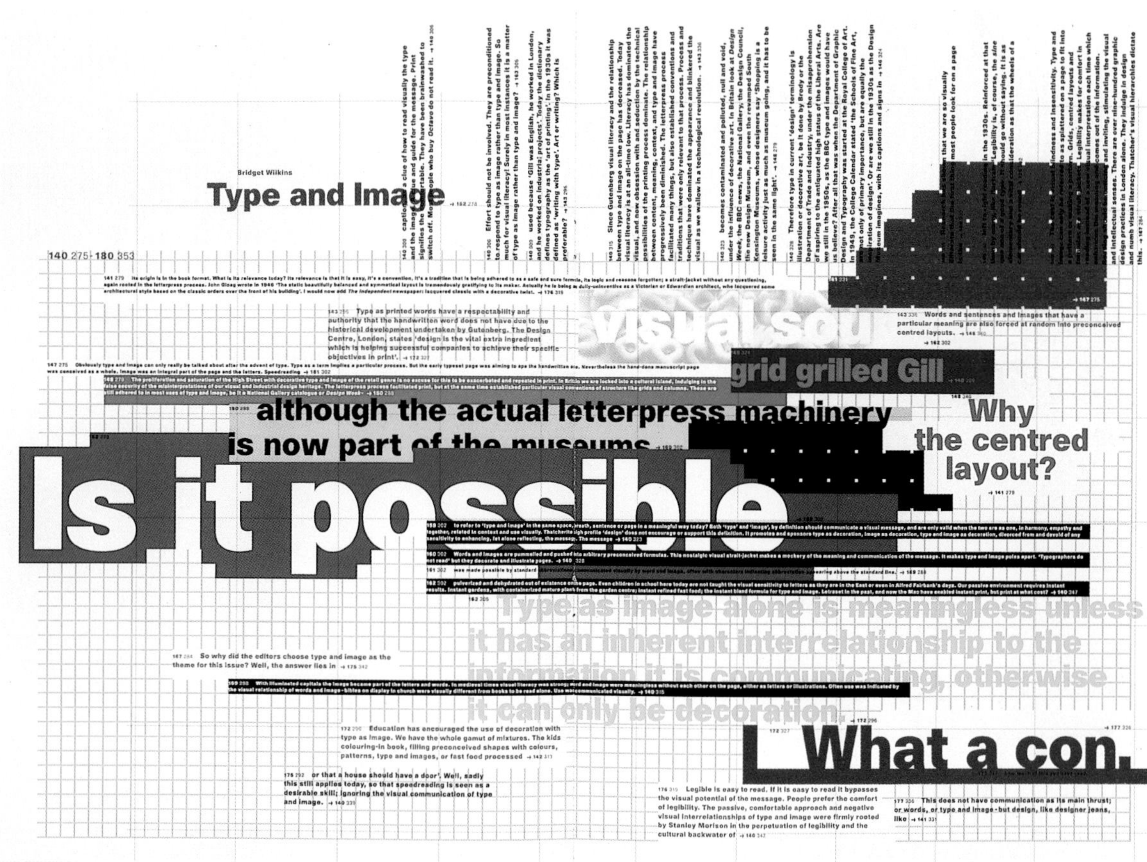

Octavo. Magazine pages. 8vo, UK, 1990 Design 8vo

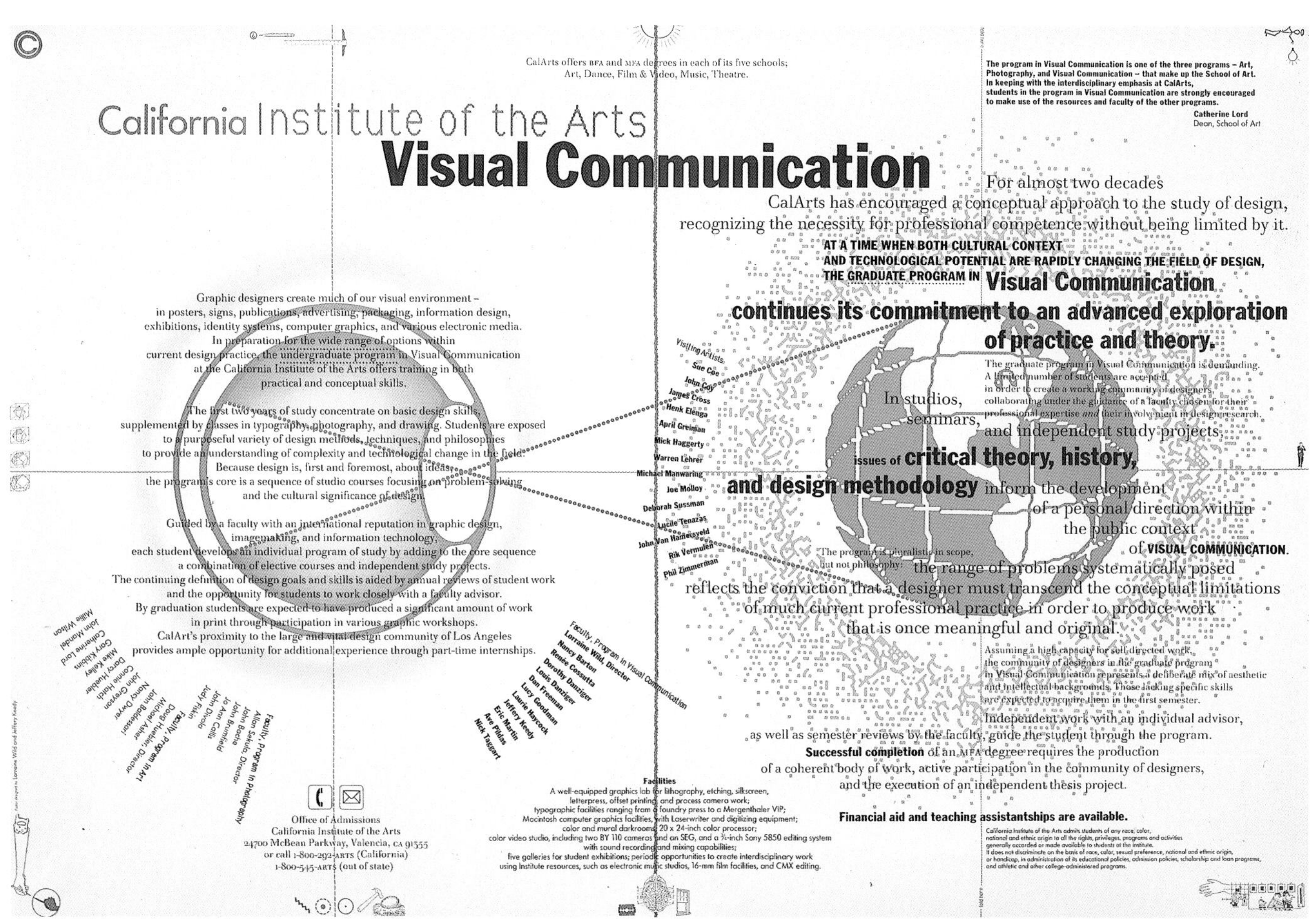

Visual communication. Faculty poster

California Institute of the Arts, USA, 1986

Design Jeffery Keedy, Lorraine Wild

ID "Graphic design" issue. Magazine pages
Design Publications, USA, 1988
Design **David Frej**

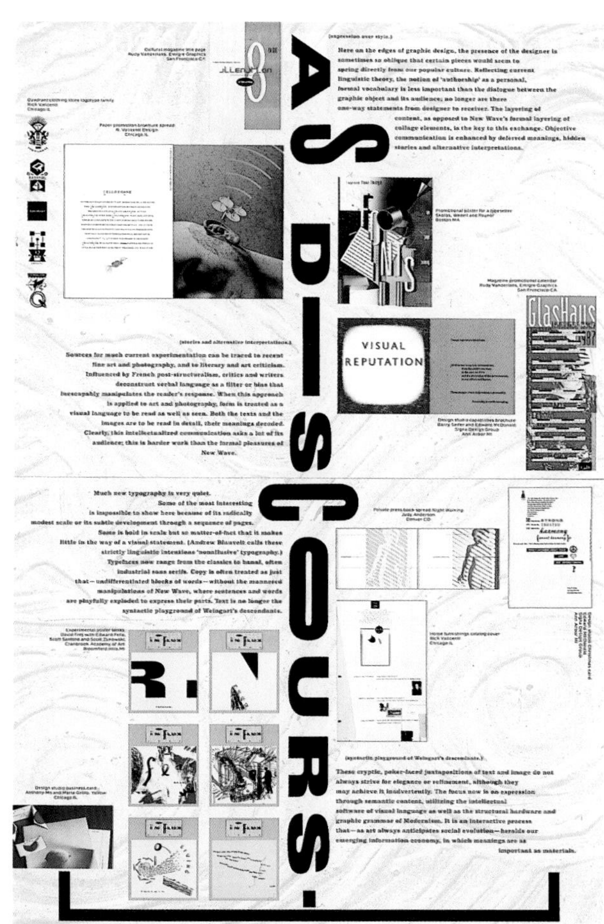

Holland

Windmill Island

Tulip Time

Wooden Shoe Factory

Dutch Village

Michigan

What is the effect of context on the meaning of an image? Today, language and imagery have become enigmas.

Images are something like actors on a historical stage, a history that participates in the stories about our own evolution from creatures 'made in the image' of a creator, to creatures who make themselves and their world in their own image.

Images are not stable or permanent in any metaphysical sense; they are not perceived in the same way by different viewers any more than are dream images. Our senses are windows through which a purposive and acculturated imagination is looking, not a door that swings open to one master key, says E.H. Gombrich. Facts derive their authority in a disorderly and highly political process as constituent parts of a world model that has come to seem natural.

Strange creatures haunt a region at the border between physical and psychological impressions of imagery. Appearances mediate between ourself and reality from the images projected by a skillful actor to those being created for products and personalities in advertising or propaganda.

Optical theory has varied explanations of these intermediate appearances looming between us and the objects we perceive. As in the Platonic doctrine of 'visual fire' and the atomistic theory of *eidola* or *simulacra*, they are understood as material emanations from the objects forcibly impressing themselves on our senses. Some theories actually describe the transmission as moving in the other direction, from our eyes to the objects.

While folk art grew from below, mass culture is imposed from above. Fashioned by business people with the audience as a passive consumer their participation is limited to buying or not buying it. Some ideologically manipulated illusion of taste may equate mass culture with an ideology of false consciousness.

Derrida asserts that when an author is no longer with us, or has lost his authority, the foundation for a sign crumbles and there is no way of stopping an endless chain of signification to follow.

Barthes liked the story of the Argonauts as an allegory of the eminently structural object. The Argonauts were ordered by the Gods to complete a long journey in one and the same ship, the Argo, against certainty of the ships gradual deterioration. During the voyage they slowly replaced each piece of the ship, ending with an entirely new ship without having to alter either its name or form. "By dint of combinations made with one and the same name, nothing is left but the origin: Argo is an object with no other cause than its name, with no other identity than its form."[1]

Twain said that a 'label' is worth more than "a ton of significant expression."[2]

Marx says that what makes a commodity is "at first sight a very trivial thing and easily understood..." it hides in its true nature a twofold veil, the outer a mask of familiarity and naturalness, the inner is an explicit fantasy.

[1]Rosalind E. Krauss, *The Originality of the Avant Garde and Other Modernist Myths* (Cambridge: The MIT Press, 1985), 2-4.

[2]Mark Twain, *Life on the Mississippi*, chap. 44, "City Sights."

"The social character of men's labor appears to them as an objective character stamped upon the product of that labor...the article of commerce. There it is a definate social relation between men, that assumes, in their eyes, the fantastic form of a relation btween things. In the mist-enveloped regions of the religious world, creations of the human mind appear as independant beings endowed with life, entering into relation both with one another and the human race. So it is with the products of men's hands. "This I call fetishism which attaches itself to the products of labor..." producing "material relations between persons and social relations between things."[3] He says that image behind the concept of ideology and commodity is like a *camera obscura*. A machine, thought to produce highly realistic replicas of the visible world, projects shadows: inverted, insubstantial phantoms in darkness. The whole process of production and cosumtion of mass(pseudo) culture may be an all too human readiness for self deception.

[3]Karl Marx, *Capital*, 1:71-72.

Democracy offers freedom to aquire and consume. More consumers in turn create a need for mass commercial entertainment. From the existentialist point of view, man as modern tourist has a prominent component-Pascal's term 'divertissement,' a fundamental element of our existance. It is an escape from the real *'condition d'etre'* with its factual instability supplanting life with difficulties such as anxiety, boredom or worry.[4]

An organized system of mass movement, where leisure is pre-patterned as are travelling conditions, modern tourism levels out the psychological state of travelers. It evokes confidence in the unfamiliar aspects of travel. Compared to the adventurer, who looks for things that are strange, challenging and difficult to assimilate, a so predisposed tourist has expectations based more or less on precise stereotypes. He is certainly not in search of the utterly unknown. The 'attractions' of the place he is visiting have been accurately described to him by a brochure or his travel agent, so he knows fairly well where he will aim his camera.

The demands of numerous consumers induce production with great rapidity. Large quantities of less-perfect commodities and reproductions flood the mareketplace. A popular aquisition of tourists is the souvenir, a memory fetish The only dimension of time lying peacefully is hind us in the past, with its great atmospheric resonance when viewed from the emotional point of view. The past is trapped within the iconic value of the souvenir as the roar of the ocean is imprisoned within a single seashell. How may we see the symbolic value transferred in different forms, materials, and at different sizes and time scaled in entirely different media?

"People want to have fun. A fully concentrated and conscious experience of art is possible only to those whose lives do not put such a strain on them that in their spare time they want relief from both boredom and effort simultaneously."[5]

[4]Ludwig Giesz, "Kitsch-man as tourist," in *Kitsch, the World of Bad Taste*, by Gillo Dorfles (New York: Universe Books, 1969), trans. Studio Vista Ltd., London.

[5]Theodore W Adorno, "On Popular Music," *Studies in Philosophy and Social Science* 9 (1941), 38.

De Zwann. What happens when an object is displaced from its origional purpose, place and time. Does its 'authenticity' in a material sense provide that the values and meanings there embodied in the days of its creators can be interpreted in the same way by those who experience it with a totally different understanding. Does that object still truly reflect Dutch 'tradition' or has its identity now become one facet of our own consumer culture? Perhaps our consciousness is a mirror onto which images of reality are projected. Or is is more aptly true that forms in the world around us are reflections of our own inner consciousness.

Sources

Mitchell, W.J.T., Iconology: Image, Text, Ideology. Chicago: The University of Chicago Press, 1986.

Dorfles, Gillo, Kitsch: The World of Bad Taste. Trans. Studio Vista Limited, London. New York: Universe Books, 1969.

Calinescu, Matei, Faces of Modernity. Bloomington: Indiana University Press, 1977.

Feyerabend, Paul, Against Method: Outline of an Anarchistic Theory of Knowledge. London: New Left Books, 1975.

Visitors' brochures from Holland, Michigan

Emigre. Magazine pages
Emigre Graphics, USA, 1988
Design Lisa Anderson
Cranbrook Academy of Art

Katherine McCoy
Michael McCoy

the new discourse

Art **science**

Nothing pulls you into the territory between art and science quite so quickly as design. It is the borderline where contradictions and tensions exist between the quantifiable and the poetic. It is the field between desire and necessity. Designers thrive in those conditions, moving between land and water. A typical critique at Cranbrook can easily move in a matter of minutes between

Mathematic **poetic**

a discussion of the object as a validation of being to the precise mechanical proposal for actuating the object. The discussion moves from Heidegger to the "strange material of the week" or from Lyotard to printing technologies without missing a beat. The free flow of ideas, and the leaps from the technical to the mythical, stem from the attempt to maintain a studio platform that supports each student's search to

Desire **necessity**

find his or her own voice as a designer. The studio is a hothouse that enables students and faculty to encounter their own visions of the world and act on them — a process that is at times chaotic, conflicting, and occasionally inspiring.

Watching the process of students absorbing new ideas and influences, and the incredible range of interpretations of those ideas into design, is

Mythology **technology**

an annual experience that is always amazing. In recent years, for example, the department has had the experience of watching wood craftsmen metamorphose into high technologists, and graphic designers into software humanists. Yet it all seems consistent. They are bringing a very personal vision to an area that desperately needs it. The messiness of human experi-

Purist **pluralist**

ence is warming up the cold precision of technology to make it livable, and lived in.

Unlike the Bauhaus, Cranbrook never embraced a singular teaching method or philosophy, other than Saarinen's exhortation to each student to find his or her own way, in the company of other artists and designers who were engaged in the same search. The energy at Cranbrook seems to come from the fact of

Individual **communal**

the mutual search, although not the mutual conclusion. If design is about life, why shouldn't it have all the complexity, variety, contradiction, and sublimity of life?

Much of the work done at Cranbrook has been dedicated to changing the status quo. It is polemical, calculated to ruffle designers' feathers. And

Dangerous **rigorous**

Cranbrook design: the new discourse
Book page. Rizzoli, USA, 1990
Design Katherine McCoy
P. Scott Makela, Mary Lou Kroh

Bill Rauhauser

Born: August 14, 1918 Detroit, Michigan

Education: Bachelor Degree, Architecture . . . University of Detroit, 1943

Employment: Professor of Photography, Center for Creative Studies — College of Art and Design, 1970 to present
Visiting Lecturer at University of Michigan, Ann Arbor
1975-76, History of Photography

One Man Exhibitions:
Pierce Street Gallery, Birmingham, Michigan 1982 and 1986
Edwynn Houk Gallery, Chicago, Illinois, 1981
Sara Reynolds Gallery, University of New Mexico, 1978
South Bend Art Center, Indiana, 1966

Selected Exhbitions:
Pierce Street Gallery, Birmingham, Michigan, 1983, 1985, 1986
Saginaw Art Gallery, Saginaw, Michigan, 1985
Pontiac Art Gallery, Pontiac, Michigan, 1985
Detroit Institute of Arts, Detroit, Michigan, 1977, 1983, 1984
Halsted Gallery, Birmingham, Michigan, 1972, 1974, 1982, 1983
The Mill Gallery, Milford, Michigan, 1981
Exhibition for Michigan Artists, Detroit, Michigan, yearly 1944 through 1958
Birmingham Art Center, Birmingham, Michigan, 1965, 1973
Museum of Modern Art, New York, New York, Family of Man Exhibition 1954

Professional Activities:
Numerous Lectures
Workshops

Work in Collections:
Detroit Institute of Arts, Detroit, Michigan
Kresge Foundation, Troy, Michigan
Florence Crittenten Hospital, Troy, Michigan
Walter Rosenblum, New York, New York
David Rottenberg, Chicago, Illinois.
Warren Covell, Bloomfield Hills, Michigan
Morris Baker, Bloomfield Hills, Michigan

Listed In: Archives of American Art

While most of his work derives from the "straight," or, documentary, tradition of photography, Bill Rauhauser has also explored the more manipulative possibilities of the medium. The resulting images have most frequently taken the form of collage.

Rauhauser is a formalist who defines works of art as ". . . primary objects and not cultural by-products or spin-offs of reality." While he believes that the creative element lies in both conception and execution of the work, Rauhauser's recent photographs manifest his increasing interest in aesthetic quality. "More and more," he states, "I am coming to believe that something to be looked at should be attractive."

In this series, the artist restructures each image. The resulting ambiguity invites speculation beyond a mere reading of the facts presented.

Mary McNichols
Professor of Art History
Center for Creative Studies

Statement

In the "Restructured Series" I have attempted to de-emphasize the importance of photographic seeing and reduce the transient element. Selection of subject matter is based not on what it is but rather on what it might become. The shift is from statement to suggestion.

Bill Rauhauser

Checklist of the Exhibition

Number, Title, Year, Size, Medium.

1. *Restructured photographs*, 1985, 14½"x12" Silverprint
2. *Restructured photographs*, 1985, 14½"x12" Silverprint
3. *Restructured photographs*, 1985, 14½"x12" Silverprint
4. *Restructured photographs*, 1985, 14½"x12" Silverprint
5. *Restructured photographs*, 1985, 14½"x12" Silverprint
6. *Restructured photographs*, 1985, 14½"x12" Silverprint
7. *Restructured photographs*, 1985, 14½"x12" Silverprint
8. *Restructured photographs*, 1985, 14½"x12" Silverprint
9. *Restructured photographs*, 1985, 14½"x12" Silverprint
10. *Restructured photographs*, 1985, 14½"x12" Silverprint
11. *Restructured photographs*, 1985, 14½"x12" Silverprint
12. *Restructured photographs*, 1985, 14½"x12" Silverprint
13. *Restructured photographs*, 1985, 13"x26" Silverprint

1. *Still Life*, 1986, 14½"x18½" Silverprint
2. *Still Life*, 1986, 14½"x18½" Silverprint
3. *Still Life*, 1986, 14½"x18½" Silverprint
4. *Still Life*, 1986, 14½"x18½" Silverprint
5. *Still Life*, 1986, 14½"x18½" Silverprint

The market presents Phillip Fike, Bill Rauhauser. Exhibition catalogue
Detroit Artists Market, USA, 1987
Design Edward Fella

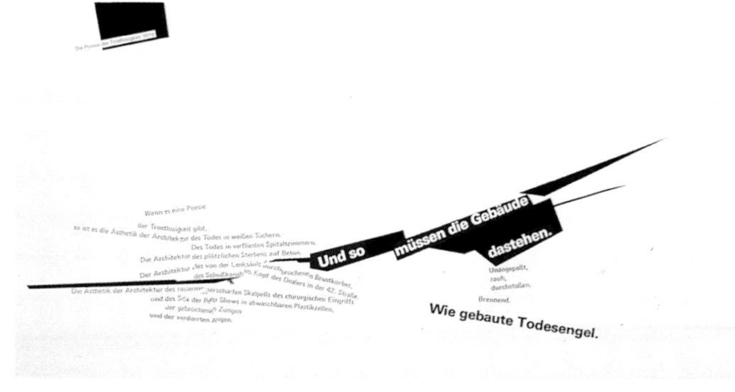

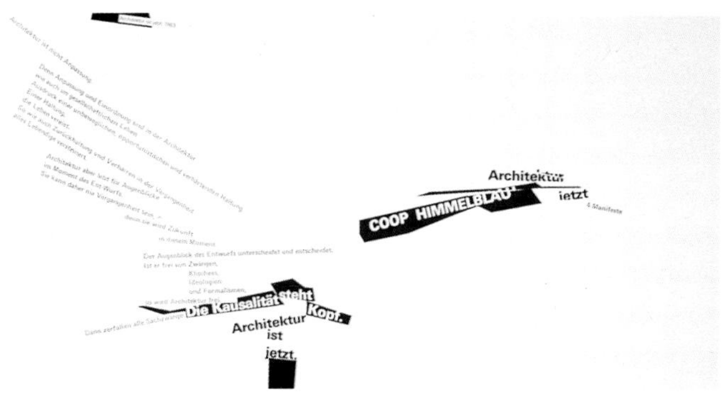

Book pages. Coop Himmelblau, Germany, 1989
Design **Friedhelm Grabowski**
Hochschule für Gestaltung
Offenbach

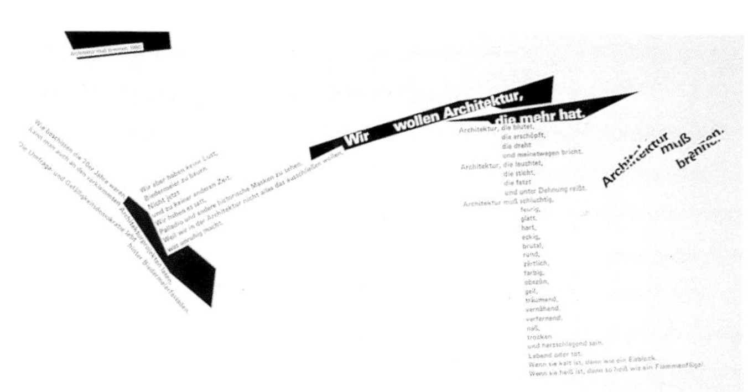

The Spirit of The New Office

The Individual matters as well as the Corporation:
there will be greater choice in style, environment and arrangement of the workplace for ordinary office users.

Der Einzelne ist genau so wichtig wie das Unternehmen:
Auch der einfache Büromensch wird Stil, Einteilung und Umgebung seines Arbeitsplatzes wählen können.

L'individu est aussi important que l'entreprise:

L'esprit créative compte le plus:

Der Geist des Büros von morgen:

Das Büro ist ein Computer:

Le bureau est l'ordinateur:

The office is the computer:
servicing the electronic workstation will be the greatest design challenge.

Software is the key to change:
the management of office space and amenities will have as much impact on the quality of working life as the physical fabric of the office.

Software ist der Schlüssel zur Veränderung:
Raumgrösse, Komfort und ihre Zuordnung werden für die Qualität des Arbeitslebens die gleiche Bedeutung haben wie die Art des Bürobaus.

Le logiciel est la clef du changement:

L'esprit du nouveau bureau

Neun bis Fünf stirbt aus:
Der Arbeitstag wird ausgedehnt und variiert. Jeder wird mehr Freiheit haben, um dann und dort zu arbeiten, wo er es will.

Nine to five is dead:
the office day will extend but also become more varied.
Everyone will have far greater freedom to work where they like, when they like.

Le neuf à cinq est mort:

Le changement est sans pitié:

Change is remorseless:
common to all organizations will be constant physical reorganization and adjustment.

Der Wandel ist erbarmungslos:
Gemeinsam wird allen Organisationen nur noch die Reorganisation, der ständige Um- und Anbau sein.

Support is the heart of the workplace:
group resources such as meeting rooms, libraries, audio visual display, restaurants will make offices more like clubs than paper factories.

Creativity is what matters most:
offices will be designed to stimulate ideas, not just get the administration out of the way.

Le coeur du travail est dans l'environnement:

Das Herz des Arbeitsplatzes schlägt im Umfeld:
Konferenzräume, Bibliotheken, elektronische Schautafeln, Restaurants-all diese Gemeinschaftsanlagen werde wichtiger.
Büros ähneln dann eher Clubs als Papierfabriken.

Es kommt nur auf die Kreativität an:
Büros werden dann entworfen, um Ideen auf die Welt zu bringen. Und nicht mehr, um die Verwaltung zu verstecken.

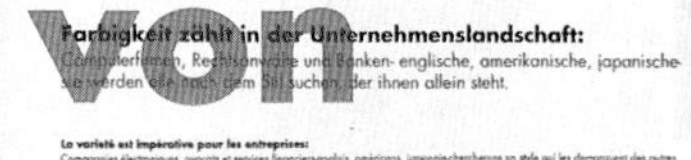

Farbigkeit zählt in der Unternehmenslandschaft:

von Francis Duffy

La variété est impérative pour les entreprises:

Variety matters in different kinds of organizations:
lawyers, computer companies or financial services;
British, American or Japanese will want to find their own style that suits them best.

The consumer is king:
more powerful, better educated and wealthier consumers will expect better quality, more interesting, more beautiful workplaces.

Der Verbraucher ist König:
Endlich werden auch die Verbraucher mächtiger, gesünder und gebildeter sein.
Sie erwarten bessere, schönere und interessantere Arbeitsplätze.

11

Le consommateur est roi:

Workspirit. Magazine pages
Vitra, Germany, 1988
Design April Greiman

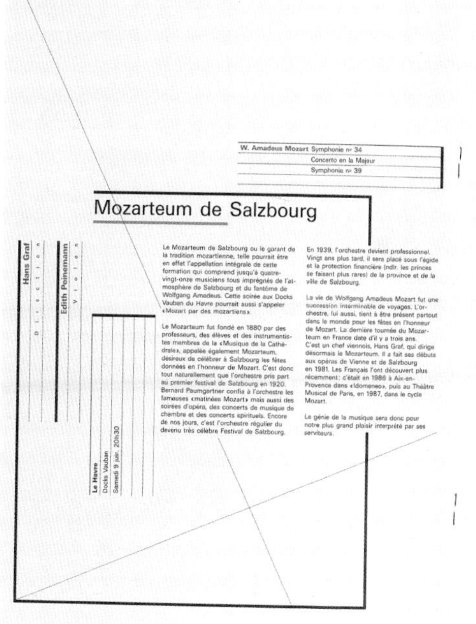

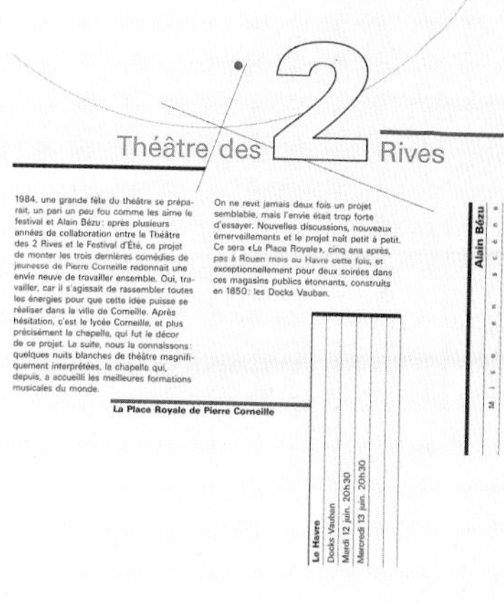

Festival d'été. Programme pages
Festival d'été de Seine-Maritime, France, 1990
Design **Philippe Apeloig**

The new urban landscape. Book contents pages
Olympia & York Companies/Drenttel Doyle. USA, 1988
Design **Drenttel Doyle Partners**

Participating Artists 6
Acknowledgments 8
Introduction 10 By Anita Contini
The New Urban Landscape: Spectators in a Visionary City 18 By Richard Martin
The New Urban Landscape: Public Art for Private Eyes? 24 By Nancy Princenthal
A Photographic Essay 26 By David McGlynn

CITY TAKES: TEN ESSAYS ON THE NEW URBAN LANDSCAPE 35
Douglas Blau 36 Rosetta Brooks 48
Bruce Ferguson 40 Adam Gopnik 42

TABLE *of* CONTENTS

Elizabeth Hardwick 44 Dave Hickey 45
Sanford Kwinter 46 Herbert Muschamp 48
Mark J. Plotkin 50 Mark Richard 52

Olympia & York Arts & Events Program
Anita Contini, Director
Melissa Coley, Manager
Andrzej Drews, Design Consultant

Exhibition/Education Committee
Gary Garrels
Barbara Jakobson
Peter Nagy
Lisa Phillips
Valerie Smith
Philip Yenawine

Exhibition and Catalogue Coordination
Livet Reichard Company, Inc.
Ann Philbin, Coordinator
Anne Blair Wrinkle, Research

Board of Advisors
David Childs
Mildred Friedman
Frank Gehry
Richard Koshalek
Richard Martin
Cesar Pelli
Andrée Putman

Catalogue Concept, Design, and Editorial Consultation
Drenttel Doyle Partners

Catalogue Editor
Richard Martin

Installation Design Concept
David Childs
Frank Gehry
Audrey Matlock

THE EXHIBITION: TWENTY-EIGHT WORKS ABOUT THE NEW URBAN LANDSCAPE 55
Vito Acconci 56 Dennis Adams/Andrea
Blum 58 Kim Adams 60 Judith Barry 62
Alan Belcher 64 Dan Graham 66 Susan
Hiller 68 Hodgetts + Fung 70 Henry
Jesionka 72 Kristin Jones and Andrew
Ginzel 74 Michael Kalil 76 Kawamata 78
Jon Kessler 80 Kunst Brothers 82
Justen Ladda 84 Morphosis 86 Matt
Mullican 88 Jean Nouvel 90
Joel Otterson 92 Nam June Paik 94
Liz Phillips 96 Robert Price 98 Martha
Schwartz 100 Haim Steinbach 102
Mierle Laderman Ukeles 104 Jacques
Vieille 106 Richard Wentworth 108
Stephen Willats 110 MICA-TV 112

Explanatory Notes 114 By Philip Yenawine
Seven Photographs 118 By Elizabeth Zeschin
Contributors Biographies 124

This catalogue documents the exhibition The New Urban Landscape *held at The World Financial Center, Battery Park City, New York, from October 14 through December 31, 1988, sponsored by Olympia & York Companies (U.S.A.).*

This exhibition was a part of the program to celebrate the opening of the the public spaces at The World Financial Center.

The New Urban Landscape Copyright 1989 Olympia & York Companies (U.S.A.). All rights reserved.
The contents of this book may not be reproduced without the written permission of the publishers.
Printed in the United States of America.
Published 1990 by Olympia & York Companies (U.S.A.) and Drenttel Doyle Partners.
Library of Congress Catalogue Card Number: 89-063218
ISBN: 0-9624916-0-8
Distributed by Rizzoli International Publications, Inc.
300 Park Avenue South, New York, New York 10010

Gegen die Konventionen

Against conventions

Daniel Z.: Ihr repräsentiert – mindestens gegenüber "emigre" – die junge Schweizer Grafik. Oder genauer: Die junge Zürcher Grafik. Das Gemeinsame unter euch, so scheint mir, ist das Gestalten wider die Konvention. **Roland:** Konventionen zu überwinden ist schon gut. Aber: Es ist gefährlich, eine visuelle Sprache zu gebrauchen, die letztendlich nur von einem kleinen Kreis Gleichgesinnter oder gar nur noch vom Gestalter selbst verstanden wird. **Daniel Z.:** Wenn es gefährlich ist: Warum machst du es dann? **Roland:** Es gibt verschiedene Ebenen, mit Konventionen zu arbeiten. Wie es auch unterschiedliche Formen gibt, Konventionen zu verweigern oder neue Wege einzuschlagen. Im bildsprachlichen Bereich kann die Konvention im Sinne der Umkehrung, der Satire, der bewussten Vereinnahmung angegangen werden. Daneben gibt es grosse Berührungsflächen, Grenzland sozusagen, zwischen konventioneller Gestaltung und individuellem Anspruch. Wenn ich sage, die individuelle Abweichung von der Konvention könne gefährlich sein, dann will ich damit nicht die Konventionen als unüberwindliche Sprachvoraussetzungen verteidigen. Es geht mir nur darum, das Dogma des Unkonventionellen, Individualistischen gleichermassen in Frage zu stellen. Mir persönlich steht eine dissidente, subkulturelle oder wie auch immer genannte Bildsprache sicher näher als der visuelle Zirkus des spätkapitalistischen Realismus. **Daniel Z.:** Was macht denn die visuelle Verständlichkeit aus? **Polly:** Oft ist die Botschaft eines "normalen" Plakates völlig unverständlich, doch es gibt einen Code zur Verständlichkeit, zum Illusionären, zum Bild, ja sogar zum Ungestalteten, eine allgemeine Glaubwürdigkeit. **Roland:** Ja, dort, wo mit Konventionen gearbeitet wird, gibt es diese Übereinkunft. Dort funktioniert es. **Polly:** Scheinbar, ja. Deshalb ist es auch gefährlich. Doch – und das ist wohl eine Gemeinsamkeit von uns hier an diesem Tisch – wir sind alle sehr vorsichtig mit dieser scheinbaren Übereinkunft. Das Abbild einer schönen, heilen Naturlandschaft zum Beispiel, die dafür wirbt, für deren Schutz abstimmen zu gehen, weckt in dir das Gefühl, du seist wirklich dort.

Daniel Z: ***You represent – at least for Emigre – young Swiss graphic design. Or, to be precise, young Zurich graphic design. What you have in common, it appears, is design that goes against the grain of convention.*** *Roland:* ***It's all very well to kick against conventions, but it's dangerous to use a visual language that is finally only understood by a small circle of likeminded people – or even only by designers themselves.*** *Daniel Z:* ***If it's dangerous, why do it?*** *Roland:* ***There are several levels of working in line with conventions. In the same way that there are various ways to go against them and pursue a new direction. In visual language, conventions can be approached in a sense of reversal, or satire. Besides that there are large areas of contact border zones – so to speak, between conventional design and individual claims. When I say individual deviation from convention may be dangerous, I don't mean to defend conventions as an insurmountable prerequisite of language. To me it's only a matter of questioning the dogma of the unconventional and the individualistic. A dissident, subcultural – or whatever you like to call this visual language – is certainly nearer to me personally than a visual circus of late-capitalistic realism.*** *Daniel Z:* ***So what in fact is visual understanding?*** *Polly:* ***Often the message of the "normal" poster is completely incomprehensible, but there is a code to the understandable, to the illusionary, to the picture, even to the undesigned – a general credibility.*** *Roland:* ***That's right. Wherever one deals with conventions there is this tacit understanding. That's where it functions.*** *Polly:* ***It would seem so. That's why it's also dangerous. And yet – and this is something all of us round this table have in common – we're all very careful with this apparent understanding. The image of a beautiful intact landscape, for instance, is used to advertise its protection and arouses in you the feeling that you are really there.***

Wenn wir ein politisches Plakat machen, geht es um den Umstand des Gedruckten: Du stehst vor einem Plakat, das nichts anderes sein will als ein Plakat und das dich zu etwas auffordert. Es erzählt dir genau das, was gedruckt ist, und nicht mehr. Richard: Ihr habt aufklärerische Absichten. Ich nicht. Mir geht es weder darum, eine eindeutige Botschaft rüberzubringen, noch darum, "verstanden" zu werden. Ich erwarte gar nicht, so verstanden zu werden, wie ich meine visuelle Botschaft verstehe. Daniel Z.: Aber ist es nicht deine Aufgabe als Gestalter, Botschaften verständlich zu machen? Richard: Meine Aufgabe ist es, Wirkung zu erzeugen. Du kannst nicht genau definieren, was und wie der Betrachter deine visuelle Botschaft aufnimmt. Dafür gibt es eine unendliche Anzahl möglicher Betrachtungsweisen. Das einzige, was ich als Gestalter machen kann, ist, den Empfänger meiner Botschaft zu animieren: Er selbst soll aktiv werden, sich auseinandersetzen und die visuelle Botschaft für sich selbst reproduzieren. Mir geht es also mehr darum, Wirkung zu erzeugen, als den Leuten etwas beibringen zu wollen.

A U F L E H N U N G

Daniel V.: Das Problem ist, dass Bilder auf der symbolischen Ebene gelesen werden, nicht auf der konkreten Ebene des Bildgegenstandes. Richard: Wo liegt denn da ein Problem? Daniel V.: Die grosse Bildflut kommt von der andern Seite und besetzt die Sprache. Es entsteht Popularität über ein allgemeines Bildverständnis. Wenn du dem eine Leseart gegenüberstellen willst, die emanzipatorisch ist, dann wirst du schnell zum Einzelgänger. Daniel Z.: Was ist das, Gestaltung, die emanzipatorisches Lesen ermöglicht? Daniel V.: Mehr Wahrheit. Polly: Unsere Arbeiten könnte man sehr leicht verstehen, wenn man sie nicht immer symbolisch lesen wollte. Daniel Z.: Warum lehnt ihr euch gegen diese Art der Betrachtung auf? Polly: Weil die Bildflut unserer Zeit totalitär wirkt; eine Wirkung, die durch den Unwillen oder die Unfähigkeit entsteht, die Bilder auf einer anderen Ebene reden zu lassen als auf der lediglich unterschwelligen – sprich unterbewussten –, eine Bildproduktion in einem undurchdringlichen Gewirr von unreflektiert reproduzierten Wünschen und Zwängen. Unsere Arbeit besteht darin, da irgendwelche Lücken aufzutun, Lücken, in denen du die Füsse wieder auf den Boden kriegst, in denen noch nicht alles zugepflastert ist mit vorgekauten Bildern.

Whenever we design a political poster, it's a matter of what is actually printed. You stand in front of a poster that is nothing else but a poster, and that challenges you to act in a certain way. It tells you exactly what is printed, and nothing more.

R i c h a r d : You want to elucidate. I don't. To me it's neither a question of bringing across a significant message, nor of being "understood". I don't expect to be understood in the way that I myself understand my visual message.

D a n i e l Z . : But isn't it precisely your job as designer to make messages understood?

R i c h a r d : My task is to generate an effect. You can't define what exactly, or how the viewer will take in your visual message. There are an endless number of possible ways of looking at it. The only thing I can do as designer is to animate the person through my message. He himself should act, should analyze, and reproduce the visual message for himself. So for me it's more a matter of generating an effect than wanting to teach the viewer anything.

R E B E L L I O N

D a n i e l V . : The problem is that pictures are interpreted on the symbolic level and not on the factual level of the picture's subject matter.

R i c h a r d : So what's the problem?

D a n i e l V : The great image flood comes from the other side and takes over the language. Popularity is created via a universal understanding of images. If you want to be emancipated and strike against the printed word then you'll quickly become a loner.

D a n i e l Z . : What then is design that makes emancipated reading possible?

D a n i e l V . : More truth.

P o l l y : Our work could be easily understood if one didn't always want to interpret it symbolically.

D a n i e l Z . : Why do you rebel against this kind of viewing?

P o l l y : Because the image flood of our time seems totalitarian. It is an effect due to the reluctance – or incapability – to interpret images on any other level than on the subliminal, or unconscious level. A production of images in an impenetrable array of wishes and constraints. Our work is to open up gaps. Spaces in which you get your feet back on the floor. Where not everything is plastered over with pre-digested images.

DARUM
auch ist für uns de r TEXT sehr wichtig
und die Typographie

That's why text and typography are very important to us. Daniel Z: That may be your personal preference – and I have nothing against the verbal as such – but why can't you counteract this by means of images? Polly: Because images are so charged, because the interpretation of images is done through language rules that are alien to the visual. Roland: Written language makes a higher demand for truth than visual language does. It's more authoritarian. Anyhow, viewed from a totally social aspect – in relation to design – I see it differently. Closeness and distance. Daniel Z: Peter, what's your deeper motivation when you design a concert poster? Peter: There is a fundamental difference for me whether I design a political poster or a concert poster. A concert poster makes hardly any demands. Plus, nobody tells me what to do. With you it's different. You probably have to battle through your concept... but for me it's to design, to deliver and to get it printed. I guess you have all to engage in deep discussions with the client. I don't have to do that. Daniel Z: But you have clients too who have their own ideas. Can you serve them up whatever you like? Peter: It doesn't mean that I design in a vacuum. My discussion with the client takes place on another level that I find more important. It means, for instance, that when I work for RecRec (an independent record label) I am not designing for just any client who I now and again call on and present my work. For me it's important that I have a close contact with the client. At RecRec I had my workplace in the same room and I was present at many meetings (generally when problems about the business were discussed, not about graphic matters) and I lived together with some of these poeple. At that time contact with the client was more intensive than it is now. I realize today that I have lost this physical contact and that this also is expressed in my work. Nowadays I get to know the people for whom I work only

Daniel Z.: Nun, vielleicht mag das eure persönliche Vorliebe sein und ich habe nichts gegen Schrift an sich doch warum kann man dem nicht mittels Bildern entgegenwirken?
Polly: Weil Bilder so besetzt sind, weil das Lesen von Bildern über bildferne Sprachregelungen abläuft.
Roland: Sprache hat einen höheren Wahrheitsanspruch als das Bild, sie ist autoritärer; jedenfalls gesamtgesellschaftlich betrachtet... in Bezug auf Gestaltung sehe ich das schon anders...

WHEN I ACUTALLY WORK FOR

NÄHE
und distanz

Daniel Z.: Peter, wenn du nun ein Konzertplakat machst, was ist dann deine tiefere Motivation?
Peter: Für mich ist da ein grundsätzlicher Unterschied, ob ich ein politisches Plakat mache oder ein Konzertplakat. Ein Konzertplakat hat kaum irgendwelche Ansprüche. Zudem redet mir keiner drein. Das ist wohl bei euch anders, ihr müsst vermutlich euer Konzept durchboxen... bei mir wird gemacht, geliefert und gedruckt. Ich stelle mir vor, dass ihr euch sehr stark mit dem Kunden auseinander setzen müsst, das muss ich nicht.
Daniel Z.: Aber auch du hast doch Auftraggeber, die ihre eigenen Vorstellungen haben. Kannst Du denen vorsetzen, was du willst?
Peter: Das heisst nicht, dass ich im luftleeren Raum gestalte. Meine Auseinandersetzung mit dem «Kunden» findet auf einer anderen Ebene statt, die ich eigentlich wichtiger finde. Das heisst z.B., wenn ich für RecRec (alternatives Plattenlabel) arbeite, so gestalte ich nicht für irgend einen Kunden, bei dem ich ab und zu vorbeigehe und meine Ideen oder Arbeiten präsentiere. Für mich ist wichtig, dass ich einen näheren Kontakt zum «Kunden» habe. Bei RecRec hatte ich mein Arbeitsplatz im gleichen Raum, war bei vielen Sitzungen dabei (wo allgemein über die Problem des Betriebs diskutiert wird, nicht nur über grafische Belange) und wohnte mit einigen dieser Leute» zusammen. Damals war der Kontakt zum «Kunden» intensiver als heute. Ich merke heute, dass ich diesen körperlichen Kontakt verliere und sich das auch in meinen Arbeiten niederschlägt. Heute lerne ich die Leute, für die ich arbeite, oft erst durch die Zusammenarbeit kennen.

them

Das ist für mich nicht ganz einfach. Ich finde es ist wesentlich einfacher und ehrlicher, FreundeInnen ein grafisches Aussehen zu geben, als irgendwelchen "fremden" Leuten, die mir womöglich noch unsympathisch sind. In grossen Agenturen und mit big Auftraggebern geht das soweit, dass der/die GrafikerIn nicht mal mehr direkt mit dem Kunden Kontakt hat, sondern dass es für diese Aufgabe eine/n KontakterIn gibt.

Peter: Ich sage nicht, die Auseinandersetzung mit dem Kunden sei mir unwichtig. Aber sie wirkt sich nicht wesentlich auf das Resultat aus.

Daniel Z.: Reicht dir die Nähe zum Auftraggeber, Peter, um ein Konzertplakat zu machen. Oder brauchst du dafür zuerst ein Konzept?

Peter: Also, wie ich Plakate mache: Ich kenn die Musik, blättere Magazine durch, kopiere ein paar Bilder und fange an. Ich überlege mir nicht vorher, was ist das, was sollte eigentlich da drauf. Für ein politisches Plakat würde ich das tun. Ich würde ganz anders drangehen, mir überlegen, was es aussagen soll etc.... wahrscheinlich würde ich gar kein politisches Plakat machen. Wenn ich all diese Plakate anschaue, da gibt es selten etwas, was mir gefällt, auch von den Linken nicht. Das ist für mich ein Grund, zu sagen, für die würde ich nicht arbeiten. Die interessiert das sowieso nicht, was ich mache, also käme das sowieso nie in Frage. Hier ist es schwierig, Experimente zu machen.

Roland: Das seh ich ähnlich. Für mich spielt es keine Rolle, wofür Gestaltung steht, ob für das Opernhaus, die Rockmusik, das Gestaltungsmuseum oder Citroën: viel wichtiger ist es, in welcher Beziehung der/die GestalterIn innerhalb des Prozesses zum Kunden steht. Dort unterscheiden sich jene GestalterInnen, die ein Plakat für eine Rockband erarbeiten, zu deren Musik sie einen eindeutigen Bezug haben, deutlich von jenen, welche nur die Aufgabe haben, die Verkaufszahlen zu erhöhen.

Richard: Dass ein Kunde praktisch aus der gleichen Lebenswelt kommt wie ich, ist für mich nicht wichtig. Wichtig ist mir, dass ich mich in ihn hineindenken kann und dass ich akzeptieren kann, was er macht. Um zu verstehen, wer er ist und was er will, ist es oft besser, etwas Distanz zu haben. Die gleiche Distanz etwa, die der Psychoanalytiker zu seinem Patienten hat.

Polly: Die kulturelle Differenz zum Kunden wirkt sich oft produktiv aus. Das treibt dich zu etwas an, das du sonst nicht müsstest.

This is not very easy for me. I find it's basically more simple and honest to do graphic design for people I know than for strangers who would quite likely be unsympathetic to me. In large agencies and with big clients the graphic designer no longer has any direct contact with the client. Somebody is engaged specifically for the job of making the contacts. Richard: The fact that a client comes from practically the same background as I do is not important. What is important is that I am able to think on his/her wavelength and that I can accept what he/she does. It is often much better to gain some distance to understand who he and what she wants - about the same distance a psychoanalyst has from his/her patient. Daniel Z: Is the nearness to your client sufficient. Or do you need a concept first, when you design a concert poster, Peter? Peter: Well, I do posters this way: I know the music, I leaf through magazines, copy a few pictures - and start. I don't first stop to consider what it is or what should actually be set down. For a political poster I would approach the task in a different way. I would first consider what the message had to be, etc. ... I would probably not do a political poster at all. When I look at all these posters, there is seldom anything that I like - not even those coming from the left. This is sufficient reason for me not to work for them. They're not interested in what I'm doing anyhow, so it's out of the question. It is difficult to experiment in this field. Roland: I see it the same way. It is unimportant to me what the design is for - whether for the opera house, rock music, the museum of design or Citroën. It's far more important what the relationship is between the designer and the client during the design process. This is the point where those designers who make a poster for a rock band, to whose music they are clearly addicted, differ from those whose task is simply to increase sales figures. Peter: I'm not saying that discussions with the client are unimportant to me. But that they have no significant effect on the end result. Polly: The cultural difference to clients often has a productive effect. It spurs you on to do things you otherwise need not do.

opposite: *Emigre* "Heritage" issue
Magazine pages
Emigre Graphics, US, 1990
Design Richard Feurer
Peter Bäder
Polly Bertram & Daniel Volkart
Roland Fischbacher
Margit Kastl-Lustenberger
Daniel Zehntner

Steelworks. Book pages. Why Not Publishing, UK, 1990. Design Why Not Associates

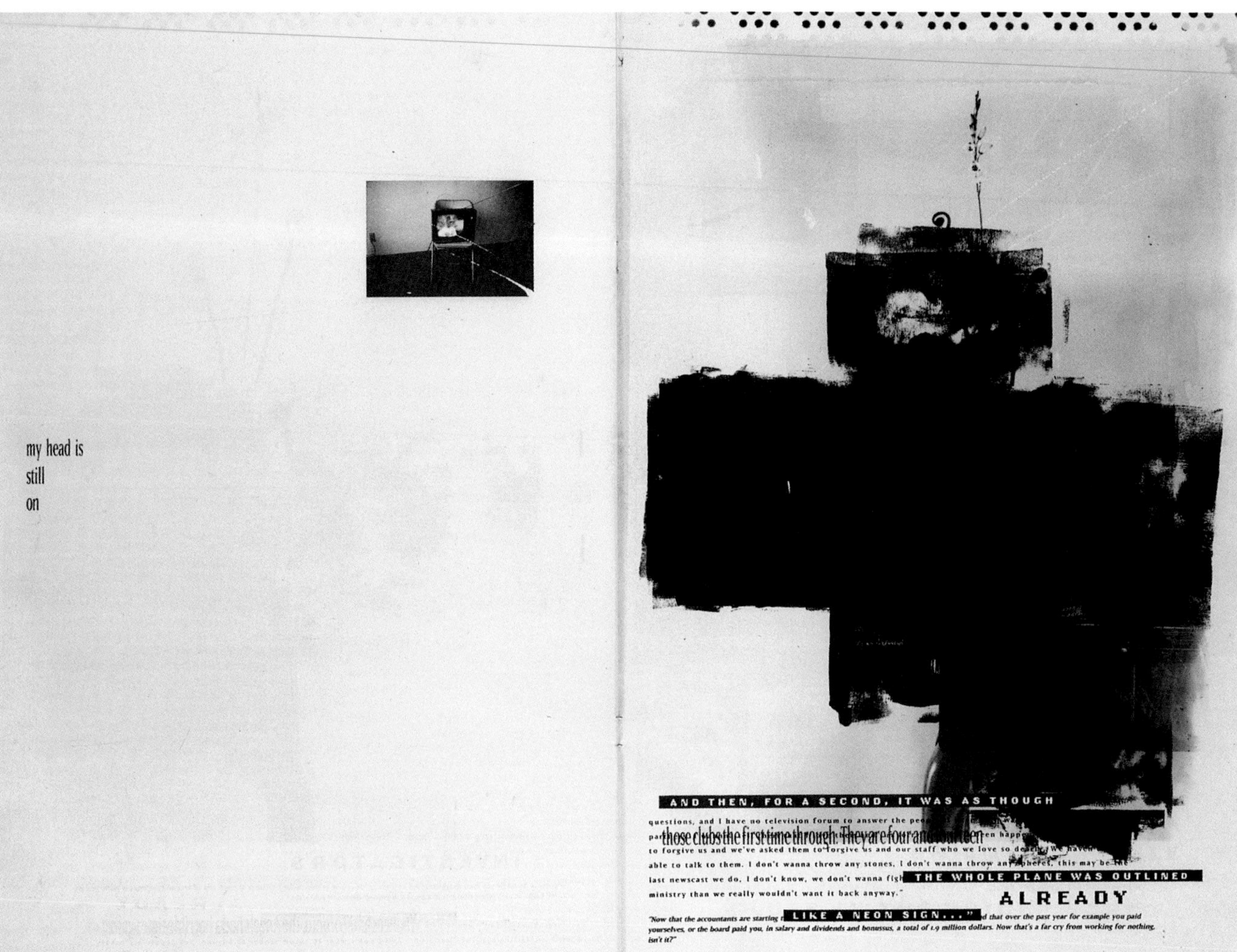

Emigre. Magazine pages
Emigre Graphics, USA, 1987
Design Rudy VanderLans

and
continue
to watch
the movie:
AND DATA TAPES
" I do like to shop, I'm probably well known for my shoppin
"Yes, extravagantly!
cars"?!"
"I don't shop for cars and I don't shop for mink coats! I do
and the ou
help my nerves.
If you are interested in a
news. Right now with America
financing or up to a thousand do
Combine the cash back offer
up to two thousand one hundred eleven
HAMBURGERS, SOMETHING HOT, JUICY, AND SO UTTERLY SIMPLE, THAT YOU CAN
dollars on these best selling pickups.
EAT IT WITH YOUR HANDS. I MEAN I KNOW PEOPLE WHO DON'T EAT BURGERS,
Great value programs also offered on most Big board pickups.
BUT I'M NOT SURE I TRUST THEM."
Take advantage of these savings now!"

April Greiman Continued

that are wonderful and that I need. I'd like to find an economical way to make the paintbox be more **painterly** and maybe be more **ambiguous** in the final result. Sometimes, **accidentally,** this happens because I am new at it, but I don't feel like I'm really controlling that yet. I'm kind of missing that **painterly feeling that you can get on a Mac.** If you airbrush on the Mac, it's so rough that you always get these wonderful **gestures** out of things, because it is making decisions and approximations at every corner! With the graphic paintbox, the resolution is so high that it's all very accurate, there are no visible approximations. **Emigre:** Will the Macintosh contribute to a change in graphic design mostly in the area of production, or will it influence design aesthetics as well? **April:** Both! In principal, I would agree that the Mac saves us time and all that. But what I experience is rather than doing something quickly, we're **looking at more** possibilities. Instead of doing more work we are **seeing more** options. Now we spend **more time visualizing and seeing things,** and before the Mac, we spent more time doing things. You wouldn't look at twelve different sizes of a headline type, because it would involve setting the type and then statting it and you would just say, "Oh come on, I don't have to try this subtler difference." But with the Mac, once the information is stored, you can just look at seventy-two thousand variations. And then the accidents happen and you say, "Oh that's so much better, why don't I go that way?" And then you are off on a whole new idea. This pioneering, **where you don't have an aesthetic yet and you don't have tradition,** is both time-consuming and wonderful. **To feel lost is so great.** There are only a few areas in this very controlled industry that you can feel like that. **Emigre:** Where will these experimentations lead to? **April:** There are two ways that we are pushing this technology. One is by **imitating and speeding up normal processes** of different disciplines, such as production and typesetting. Here, the **technology is a slave** and is simulating what we already know. But I think that, if we all keep going the way we are going and other people jump in, all desperate for **new textures/new languages,** then the other area in which it's going to advance is a **new design language.** Rather than get the language that's built-in to speak to you in English, you say, well, I know it can speak English, it does that very well, but there's also a new language. What do digital words really mean and say? There is a **natural language in that machine** and I am interested in finding out what that is, and where the boundaries are. **Emigre:** How come you haven't done any type design on the Macintosh? **April:** There just isn't enough time to do everything. I am such a fanatic about type, and I am so critical and such a perfectionist about it, and there are so many great typefaces that exist. It would take me a year to come up with anything decent and I just don't have the time. **Emigre:** Do you think that there will be an increase in gimmicks and copying due the Macintosh? **April:** Sure, but that happens with any new technology.

I don't worry too much about that. The Mac's so easy to use. It's going to be very scary. It'll be interesting to see what will happen in another three years or so. Kids know how to use this now and everybody will be **modeming** and using **electronic bulletin boards** and what not. So yes, there'll be a lot of mimicry and copying, but it will make the people with traditional design backgrounds and the people with the high-end equipment who know what they are doing push themselves further. For a while, communications may be really ugly and bad. There are going to be large cor-

Glenn Suokko. Back cover *Emigre* 10.

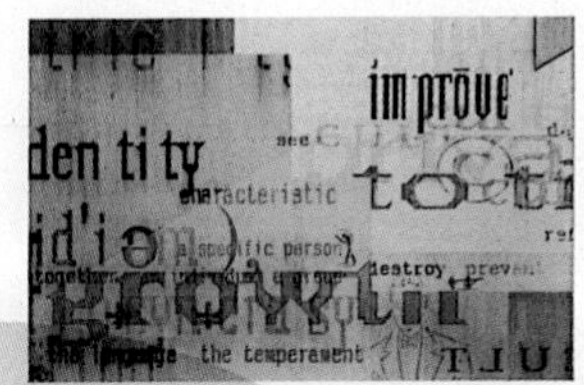

Glenn Suokko. Detail from *Mediate*, a typographic experiment.

Glenn Suokko, Minneapolis, 6/20/90

Emigre: Who had the idea of acquiring Macintosh computers at Cranbrook? The students or the faculty?

Glenn: We were one of the original three design schools chosen for the Apple/Design School Consortium. Apple generously donated both hardware and software to the Cranbrook Design Department and was very helpful in introducing us to this new phenomenon called the Macintosh. Hugh Dubberly from Apple came out for a few days to help set up the network and offered some valuable training seminars. Kathy and Mike McCoy (Co-Chairs, Design Department) were very enthusiastic about the possibilities the computer could offer. Many of my classmates had never used a computer before, so it represented not only a new tool to learn, but a new way of working.

Emigre: Were there specific classes taught on the Macintosh?

Glenn: Cranbrook does not teach any technical skills and the program has no formal instruction. For me, the Macs were a very timely arrival; they arrived the first day of my second year at Cranbrook. Although we had no specific technical training for the Mac, Kathy McCoy assigned design projects that involved using the computer, and just by using it, we quickly learned the technical aspects.

Emigre: What did the assignments involve?

Glenn: These projects were designed to explore the Macintosh as a design tool and to see if it would inspire our own design sensibilities in any new or different ways. My particular group did not have specific design assignments using the computer. However, the first-year graphic designers started the program using them. Projects were designed to incorporate many of the software programs, such as PageMaker and Illustrator. There was one particular typographic assignment that we all did, where I set some type, then laser-scanned it and put it into a paint program, printed it out, statted it, ran it through the waxer and cut up part of it, xeroxed it, photographed it, laser-scanned it again, and basically ran it through all the technology available in the studio to see what would happen. I let the various technologies take over, and through this process, discovered some interesting formal qualities. We were offered complete freedom in these projects and we were never told we had to use the computer exclusively. Using the Mac at Cranbrook was a matter of choice combined with a lot of encouragement. The computer was available to all of us to use and explore in any way we wanted to. We had no technical instruction at all, but we learned how to use the Mac nevertheless. People who can design pick it up rather quickly. Although some of my classmates resisted it totally, other classmates took to it fairly soon and began to use it exclusively.

Emigre: What did the students who resisted it rebel against?

Glenn: I think the feeling was that the Macintosh could not do anything more than we could using traditional design tools.

Emigre: Do you feel you can do more with it than with traditional methods?

Glenn: The Macintosh is an analogue to our traditional design tools. It is a typesetter, drawing board and mayline, pencil and paint brush, sketch pad, and filing cabinet, but it is all located in one tiny electronic box. I must admit I have become completely addicted to using it. The Macintosh is not much different from the design tools we traditionally use, despite its seemingly progressive capabilities. However, it does allow us firsthand control and the opportunity for endless changes and experimentation.

Emigre: I have seen you use it in a very experimental way. When it comes to type, for instance, you have created new letterforms that are more illustration than type. Will you continue these experiments?

Glenn: We have all seen the value of the Mac as a production tool and how easy it is to typeset, construct and output final pages, but there are a lot of undiscovered possibilities the computer suggests. At Cranbrook, Kathy McCoy really pushed us to explore "the other side" of the computer. I became very interested in developing typography as image, which came out of exploring this "other side." At Cranbrook, we tried to push the computer in different ways by using it unconventionally to

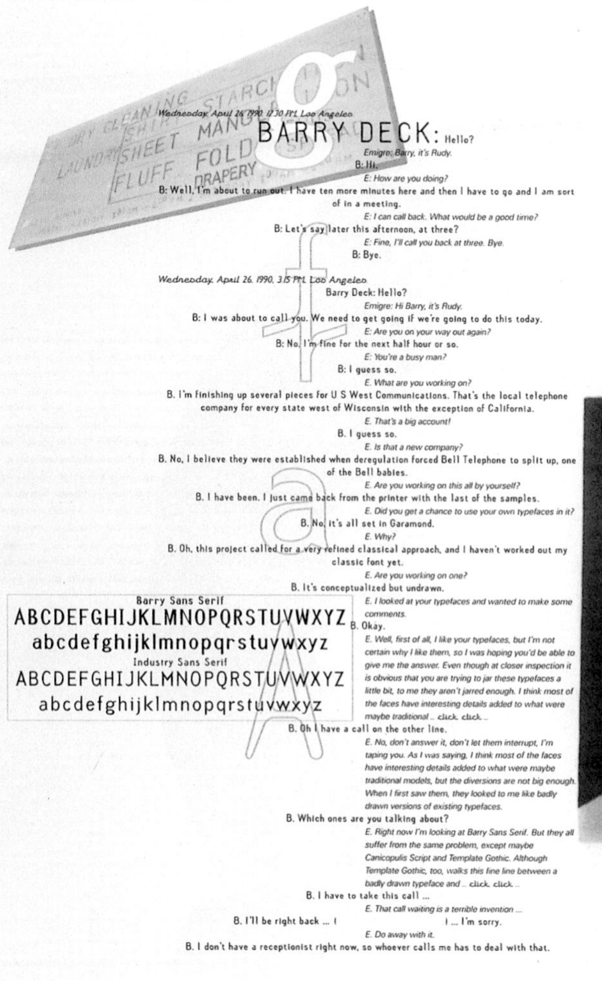

Wednesday. April 26. 1990. 12:30 P.M. Los Angeles

BARRY DECK: Hello?

Emigre: Barry, it's Rudy.

B: Hi.

E: How are you doing?

B: Well, I'm about to run out. I have ten more minutes here and then I have to go and I am sort of in a meeting.

E: I can call back. What would be a good time?

B: Let's say later this afternoon, at three?

E: Fine, I'll call you back at three. Bye.

B: Bye.

Wednesday. April 26. 1990. 3:15 P.M. Los Angeles

Barry Deck: Hello?

Emigre: Hi Barry, it's Rudy.

B: I was about to call you. We need to get going if we're going to do this today.

E: Are you on your way out again?

B: No, I'm fine for the next half hour or so.

E: You're a busy man?

B: I guess so.

E. What are you working on?

B. I'm finishing up several pieces for U S West Communications. That's the local telephone company for every state west of Wisconsin with the exception of California.

E. That's a big account!

B. I guess so.

E. Is that a new company?

B. No, I believe they were established when deregulation forced Bell Telephone to split up, one of the Bell babies.

E. Are you working on this all by yourself?

B. I have been. I just came back from the printer with the last of the samples.

E. Did you get a chance to use your own typefaces in it?

B. No, it's all set in Garamond.

E. Why?

B. Oh, this project called for a very refined classical approach, and I haven't worked out my classic font yet.

E. Are you working on one?

B. It's conceptualized but undrawn.

E. I looked at your typefaces and wanted to make some comments.

B. Okay.

E. Well, first of all, I like your typefaces, but I'm not certain why I like them, so I was hoping you'd be able to give me the answer. Even though at closer inspection it is obvious that you are trying to jar these typefaces a little bit, to me they aren't jarred enough. I think most of the faces have interesting details added to what were maybe traditional ... click. click ...

B. Oh I have a call on the other line.

E. No, don't answer it, don't let them interrupt, I'm taping you. As I was saying, I think most of the faces have interesting details added to what were maybe traditional models, but the diversions are not big enough. When I first saw them, they looked to me like badly drawn versions of existing typefaces.

B. Which ones are you talking about?

E. Right now I'm looking at Barry Sans Serif. But they all suffer from the same problem, except maybe Canicopulis Script and Template Gothic. Although Template Gothic, too, walks this fine line between a badly drawn typeface and ... click. click ...

B. I have to take this call ...

E. That call waiting is a terrible invention ...

B. I'll be right back ... I ... I'm sorry.

E. Do away with it.

B. I don't have a receptionist right now, so whoever calls me has to deal with that.

Barry Sans Serif

ABCDEFGHIJKLMNOPQRSTUVWXYZ
abcdefghijklmnopqrstuvwxyz

Industry Sans Serif

ABCDEFGHIJKLMNOPQRSTUVWXYZ
abcdefghijklmnopqrstuvwxyz

E. Oh. Anyway, in the caps in Template Gothic, it is obvious what you want to accomplish. You have these random thicks and thins. It clearly looks like it's been eaten away by bad reproduction. But that effect is lost in the lower case and the result looks like poor craftsmanship.

B. There are a few things that I tried to accomplish in that particular face. First there is the template reference, which comes partially out of Ed Fella's work, which I'm very much influenced by. It's also an homage to the vernacular. More specifically, there was a sign in the laundromat where I do my laundry. The sign was done with lettering templates and it was exquisite. It had obviously been done by someone who was totally naive. A few months ago, it was replaced with a plastic sign painted by a skilled sign painter. This sign, too, was painted in a naive style, but in another kind of vernacular, the kind that we are more accustomed to seeing these days, so we're not able to fetishize it as easily. I asked them if I could have the old sign, and they gladly handed it over to me. Now it's on the wall in my bedroom.

E. I guess all typeface designers use existing models to style their designs after. Some use old cuts of Garamond and others use laundry signs.

B. I was trying to make it look somewhat as if it had been drawn with a lettering template, but then I also wanted it to look as if it had suffered the distortive ravages of photomechanical reproduction.

E. Why would you want to do that?

B. Well it seems to me that throughout the history of type, type designers have always strived for a certain kind of perfection. Up until today, with some of the recent type designs that I have noticed, things have been getting more and more perfect. I am really interested in type that isn't perfect. Type that reflects more truly the imperfect language of an imperfect world inhabited by imperfect beings.

I am really interested in type that isn't perfect. Type that reflects more truly the imperfect language of an imperfect world inhabited by imperfect beings."

BARTOK
CRUMB
WE ARE WORKING
MONDAY — FRIDAY

BARRY DECK
Contemplating Imperfection With Dead Flowers and Laundry Sign.

E. But traditional typeface designers are imperfect beings, too, and I'm not sure if drawing perfect typefaces was their one and only goal. First and foremost they spend their lifetimes drawing typefaces that they enjoy creating. But they do it with a great deal of respect for well crafted type and they keep in mind that they're doing this as part of a long tradition of people's reading habits, to which they feel a responsibility to conform.

Emigre. Magazine pages. Emigre Graphics, USA, 1989 (opposite), 1990 (above)

Design Rudy VanderLans

edged sounding music. The idea of scanning images is in the same mindset as sampling sounds; the only difference is the medium that you're working in. But both methods make it possible to easily manipulate and collage. Laying out a page is pretty much like laying out a sequence of events that make up a song. They both require discipline, order and planning.

EMIGRE: Do you ever write your music out at all? JAMES: No. I wish I could though, because that way I could work in the car. That way I could drive to work and scribble down ideas.

"The group He Said (Wire's Graham Lewis with Bruce Gilbert) instantly comes to mind, with Towning's monotonic vocals, obsessive drum programs, bizarre tape manipulations, and liberal use of reverb/echo. Some of these tracks actually follow a verse-chorus structure (albeit loosely) with melodic fragments breaking past the mechanical instrumentation on occasion." (Option)

EMIGRE: You can't read or write music? JAMES: NO. EMIGRE: So how do you start a song? JAMES: Mostly trial and error. I usually start with a combination or sequence of notes or some repetitive sample. I can then copy that and change it into a different pitch or tempo, and add more parts to it. Again, it's very much like working on, for instance, a page in Freehand. I do this on an 8-track sequencer/digital synthesizer and a multitude of inexpensive add-on samplers, synthesizers and drum machines. It's not exactly a state-of-the-art setup, but I just keep adding on. I have 8 separate tracks that allow me to record different patterns of sounds simultaneously next to each other. I don't use the drum machines as drum machines. Through the miracle of MIDI (Musical Idiot's Digital Interface), I can play the drum machine noises from the sequencer. That makes it easier to integrate drum noises with other sounds throughout a song. EMIGRE: Do you actually play any other instruments besides keyboards when you are creating these songs? JAMES: No. It's all keyboards. All the "data" is input through a keyboard that's laid out like a piano. The only real contact I have with traditional music-making is those twelve-toned black and white keys. EMIGRE: Do you know how to play the piano, or any other instrument, conventionally? JAMES: No, not conventionally. I have a piano and an old church organ, but I've only sampled and used them as percussion noises or something. (I can play "Chopsticks" and "Heart and Soul" on the piano,) but that's about it. I'm sure that just as a lot of people consider the computer as an invalid way of creating artwork, a lot of musicians consider sequencing as an invalid method of creating music. It's the same argument over and over. Vince Clark once said in an interview something like, "A note is a note, no matter what it's played on." And I agree.

Black catalog cover.

EMIGRE: So you start out with a short pattern. Then what?

JAMES: I start layering, building things on it. I have eight tracks of

Cover Cathode Raymonde cassette.

Postcard announcing the release of the Chatterbox cassette.

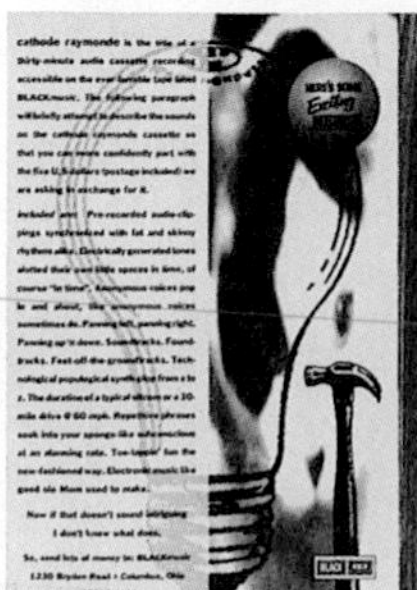

Postcard announcing the release of the Cathode Raymonde cassette.

Cassette cover The Trembling Way / Cathode Raymonde.

analog tape that I can record onto. I usually use five or six of them for music, leaving a few for vocals of some accent dialogue or texture of some kind. I often end up using makeshift guitar pedal effects, noise gates, etc. It gets really frustrating sometimes. Like I said before, my studio is certainly far from being state-of-the-art. EMIGRE: Would your music sound significantly different if you had infinite amounts of money to spend on the equipment? JAMES: It would be better. It would be more complex and more precise and the production would be of a higher quality. EMIGRE: Do you feel that's lacking in your work right now? JAMES: No, not really. I think I've come quite a way since I first started. But there's always a lot to learn. The first keyboard I bought was a sampler, and I just taught myself how to use that. Then I kept developing and building. Every couple of months, I usually buy something new, whether it's a used old drum machine from 1980 or whatever. But in general, I'm quite satisfied with the results, considering the equipment that I have. I'm using each piece of equipment to its fullest potential and each has its own qualities. EMIGRE: If any of the established indie record companies approached you and said, "We'd like to do a record with you, we have a decent budget, now pick a producer," would you be interested? And whom would you pick?

"Towning has quite an ear for sounds and tonalities, flawlessly mixing bass, clavinet, and percussion with droning synth washes, voice and noise." (Option)

JAMES: I think that would be very interesting. There's a lot of producers that I really respect, like Gareth Jones and Flood and John Fryer and Adrian Sherwood. EMIGRE: Basically the same producers Trent Reznor picked for his Nine Inch Nails record. JAMES: Yes, except I would try to keep my music less predictable. EMIGRE: You don't like that record? JAMES: It can't hold my attention very long, unlike Legendary Pink Dots, The The, He Said, or Severed Heads records. But that's just me. EMIGRE: You are, in a sense, your own producer. If you worked with or worked through someone like John Fryer, do you expect that it would change your music? JAMES: I've never worked with a producer, so I'm not sure how much input they would have. I was just looking at it from a standpoint that if someone took what I've recorded, mixed it, and added their little tricks of the trade, it would enhance the end result, and I wouldn't have to deal with the whole mixing thing alone. EMIGRE: So there's still a lot to be learned? JAMES: Oh, yes. And to me the most frustrating part of creating music is either the singing or the mixing. Those are the two most organic processes in recording music. They happen in real time. I find it easy to sit down and program something to a point where it is exact and all I have to do is hit the start button to record it. But then, when I have to mix it, it's an altogether new game. You can do twenty mixes of something and still not get it right.

EMIGRE: What do you think of the rising status of producers? Their credits are getting bigger and bigger and some records sell better because a certain producer has their name on it. JAMES: I don't think their work has changed much. Maybe the world is becoming a bit more receptive to or aware of what they're doing. I know I always look at the producer's name on the back of a record before buying it. Producers do great things with other people's music. What puzzles me is how satisfying can it be to be a producer and not play music yourself? It's like art directors or production persons who don't design anything themselves. If I were a great producer, I'd be out there making my own music. EMIGRE: Well, aren't you? JAMES: Yes, I guess I am. Not a great producer, but at least I'm producing my own music. I could be completely wrong about the role producers have though, they could all be closet rock stars.

EMIGRE: If you had to give up one or the other, which would you choose to do, the graphic design work or the music? JAMES: I like doing both, but I get more out of the music because I find it more difficult to create. I'd love to eventually be able to integrate the two more, maybe through video or computer animation. I'm investigating the creative advantages of sequencing and recording on the Macintosh, and if I decide to go with that,

Mac-animation software will be next.

Emigre. Magazine pages
Emigre Graphics, USA, 1990 (above), 1991 (opposite). Design Rudy VanderLans

A CONVERSATION WITH Edward Fella AND Mr. Keedy

Two flyers for the Forum for Architecture and Urban Design. Left - Ed Fella, Jan 89, right - re-contextualized by Mr. Keedy, July 89.

Mr. Keedy: You were trained as a commercial artist and illustrator and worked in various commercial art studios in Detroit. After 30 years in a successful career, why did you go to school, first at Center for Creative Studies and then to Cranbrook?

Fella: One reason was I had spent all these years in the commercial art business and I never felt I was really "legitimate." So I thought if I went to school, getting a degree would somehow legitimize what I did. By this time, design degrees were quite prevalent in the profession. Another reason was that it would give me the option to teach.

Mr. Keedy: These were not really considerations when you started your career?

Fella: Not at all. I went to Cass Technical High School. I never attended a university. Despite being offered a scholarship when I graduated, I didn't go, because I received such good training as a commercial artist in high school, I entered the art business immediately and became a practicing professional by the time I was nineteen. In the fifties, going to school and having a degree, especially with my Detroit working class background, wasn't that important. Being able to work was. Years later, I came to regret that. By the mid-eighties, I had another opportunity to go to school. My children were grown up, about to leave home to go to college, and I thought, "*Wow*, why don't I do the same thing? Then I won't feel this kind of separation anxiety." I had spent the last fifteen years bringing up my children as a single parent, all while working of course. Which is easy to do in the design/art business, since you make your own time and hours and determine your own income.

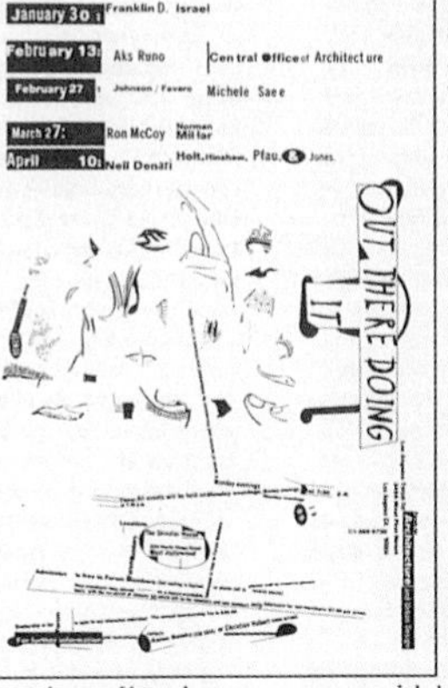

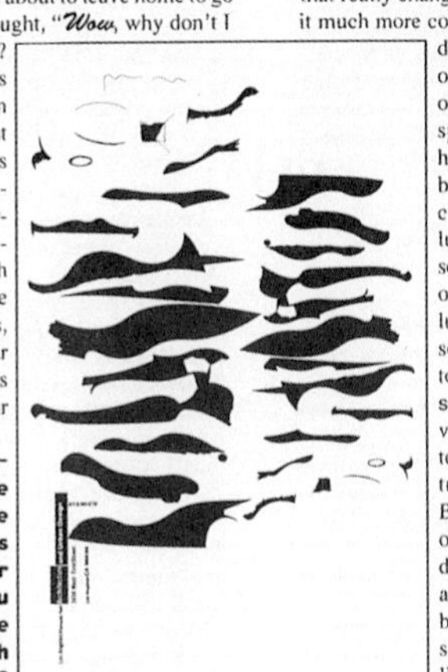

Mr. Keedy: Going to graduate school at the age of 48 was also easier for you because you happened to be friends with Kathy McCoy?

Fella: Right, that was another connection. In the late sixties, I was working as a designer/illustrator at Skidmore Sahratian, a Detroit art studio, when Kathy McCoy was hired on as a designer. She was different from most of the other people I'd known in the art business, because she had actually studied design in college, whereas most of my peers hadn't. Though we were all very successful commercial artists, most of us had either technical high school backgrounds or had come up through the apprentice system, a sort of on-the-job training. Kathy studied industrial design, and then she went on to work as a graphic designer for various corporations. Through her I became more involved in an analytical approach to design than I had ever considered before. This approach was more typical of academic, "pure" graphic design... What I opened up for Kathy, which later fed into the program at Cranbrook, was an understanding and sympathy for the "low end" of commercial art and the vernacular. This happened at the same time as the transition between Modernism and Post-Modernism, and the influence of the Venturi books. In the studio, we commercial designers would kid Kathy about her high design background, and she would kid us back, but we developed a common respect that really changed my own practice and made it much more considered. It helped me put the design part of my own work into a sort of historical perspective, which I hadn't connected before. In commercial art studios, illustrators like myself were very aware of the history of illustration and knew some design history too. I knew the Museum of Modern Art version of the history of design, Futurism, Dada, the Bauhaus. Like a lot of other advertising designers, I wasn't aware of the ideas behind later versions of Modernism, like Swiss Design; I thought it was just another style. It really didn't mean much to us because we weren't corporate designers and we weren't involved in design systems. But we did recognize the stylistic signs of that work. This was in 1969 or 1970.

Mr. Keedy: The vernacular is a very hot issue in graphic design today. However, most graphic designers think and use the vernacular differently from you, since you came out of commercial art.

Fella: I was the vernacular! I was like those people that Robert Venturi wrote about, right? The guys that made the signs in Las Vegas. On a somewhat higher level of course, kind of a mid-level of vernacular. It wasn't the folk vernacular, which commercial artists were very fond of. We all read *GRAPHIS* and articles about various kinds of folk art and signs. Since I was also a decorative illustrator, I was especially interested in things that were crude or naive, unlearned, because that is what decorative illustration took so much inspiration from.

Mr. Keedy: When you entered Cranbrook, and were really immersed in "high design," did it change the way you thought about the vernacular and what it means? You could have just completely dumped the vernacular and become a sophisticated Modernist designer.

Fella: I guess I could have, but I was too cynical for that. I saw this "high end" design being as much a style as the various vernaculars.

Mr. Keedy: So you are interested in them equally then?

Fella: Yes, and one of the things I wanted to bring to "high design" was the vernacular or commercial art, which had had a really bad name, as did advertising, since the sixties. Somehow graphic design was considered to be more pure, despite it's connection to the corporate world. Today, corporate, Swiss (International Style) graphic design has a bad name, like commercial art or advertising design had twenty years ago, which is kind of ironic.

Mr. Keedy: You have a lot of polaroids of signs. And have been collecting examples of the vernacular for a

Type catalogue. The Netherlands, 1990, Design Max Kisman

Beach culture. Magazine pages
Surfer Publications, USA, 1991 (top), 1990 (bottom)
Art director **David Carson**

carmine st.

The year is 1979. And 1942. At a small neighborhood pool in Greenwich Village, a movie crew is time-tripping 30-odd years into the past to film "Raging Bull," the story of boxer Jake LaMotta. A gang of skinny, shirtless kids holler from a rooftop as the cameras follow Robert DeNiro (playing LaMotta). He buys a soda at the concession stand, and sits at a picnic table with the actor playing LaMotta's brother. Around the pool, women in one-piece bathing suits relax in chaise lounges, and local Mafia hoods in tropical shirts play cards. DeNiro has eyes for only one: the platinum blonde who sits at pool's edge, luxuriantly paddling her long legs in the cool water. The camera moves in for a close-up of her legs...and director Martin Scorsese calls,

Beach culture. Magazine pages
Surfer Publications, USA, 1991 (left), 1990 (right)
Art director David Carson

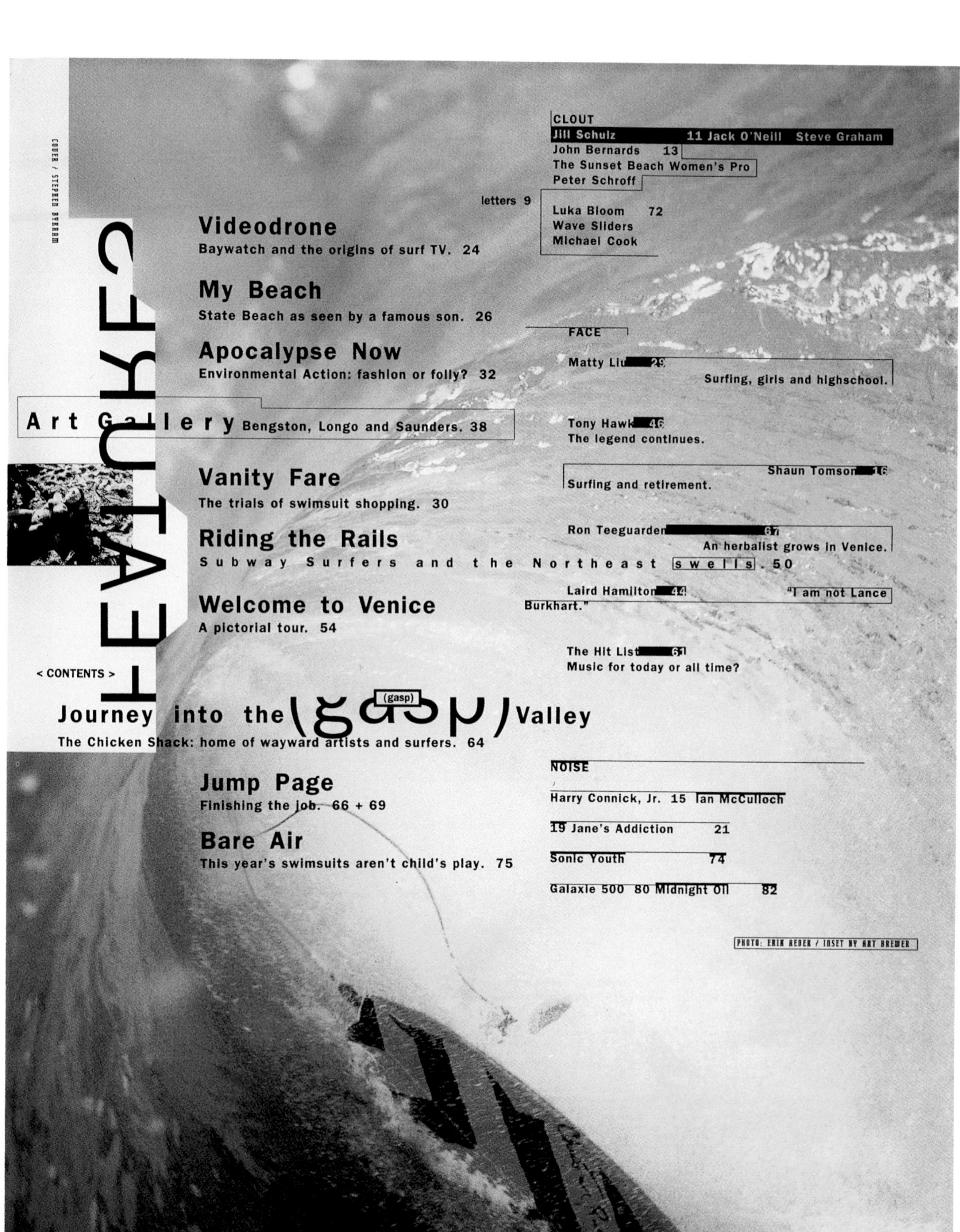

COVER / STEPHEN BYRAM

FEATURES

< CONTENTS >

PHOTO: ERIK AEDER / INSET BY ART BREWER

impure
type
IMM PURE
TYPE
[ver -nak-yoo-

Performance, Muziek,
Installaties.

11 t/m 18 mei 1985

Perfo 3. Poster. Lantaren Venster, The Netherlands, 1985
Design Hard Werken

Doorbraak (Breakthrough). Exhibition poster. Damrak Amsterdam, The Netherlands, 1989
Design: The Thunder Jockeys

intomart
wenst u een *gelukkig*

opposite:

Intomart wenst u een gelukkig 1986 (Intomart wishes you a happy 1986). Best wishes card. Intomart, The Netherlands, 1986
Design: Ton van Bragt, Studio Dumbar
Photography: Lex van Pieterson

European illustration. Book pages. Booth-Clibborn Editions, UK, 1989
Design: The Thunder Jockeys
Photography: Peter Ashworth

introduction

When we first published "European Illustration" back in the early seventies, much of the work we featured was prettily decorative. In the years since then we've seen trends come, & trends go. We had the punk influence. We saw the emergence of savage social comment. Illustrators like Sue Coe and Ian Pollack asked us to look again at the world we live in. Older masters such as Steadman and Scarfe showed us our political masters in the cloaks of bloody satire.

Today there is a new thread running through the tapestry of the media. In Britain – indeed, in much of Western Europe – we live in the best of times. Or so the politicians would have us believe. 'Poverty' has been abolished (though the homeless throng the streets of London by day and night). Affluence is everywhere (though the wasted heaths of Britain's industrial heartland might make a Martian wonder who the wealthy really are). And illustration reflects this.

In the pages of this book you'll see mirrors of our society. Technically much of it is brilliant. Visually much of it stuns the eye. Superficially it is remarkable.

But I wonder, how much of it is a triumph of technique over content? How much of it is simply a reflection of a worryingly empty "Golden Age" whose starkest feature is a kind of inner poverty.

If this is so, it will not be new. Nero's Rome was a magnificent playground. Its luxury and plentitude seemed unassailable. But we know what happened eventually. Very much closer to our own time, the exotic flamboyance of the sixties hid a period of moral lassitude.

I am not saying that it is the job of any illustrator to show us how we should live or teach us how we should think.

But illustration inevitably – and necessarily – reflects the way we are at any one time. And, at the present time, we are in a world where "I consume therefore I am" has become, for some, the norm. Conspicuous glamour is, for many, the only style there is. Even art students wear suits.

And all this is healthy. Society is not a stagnant pond. And if it were, someone would – and should – disturb it from time to time. We do not live in a timeless state, but in one where the timely and topical set the trend.

This edition of European Illustration contains much that is topical, and much that is part of a trend, whether it is a good trend or bad trend it is for you to decide. Next year, no doubt, there may be the emergence of yet another trend. I hope you will be with us to see it.

5

European Illustration

89 – 90

European Illustration

edited by Edward Booth-Clibborn

edite par Edward Booth-Clibborn

herausgegeben von Edward Booth-Clibborn

jury

Michel de Boer

Jerry Hibbert

Mary Lewis

Richard Markell

Bela Stamenkovits

Brian Webb

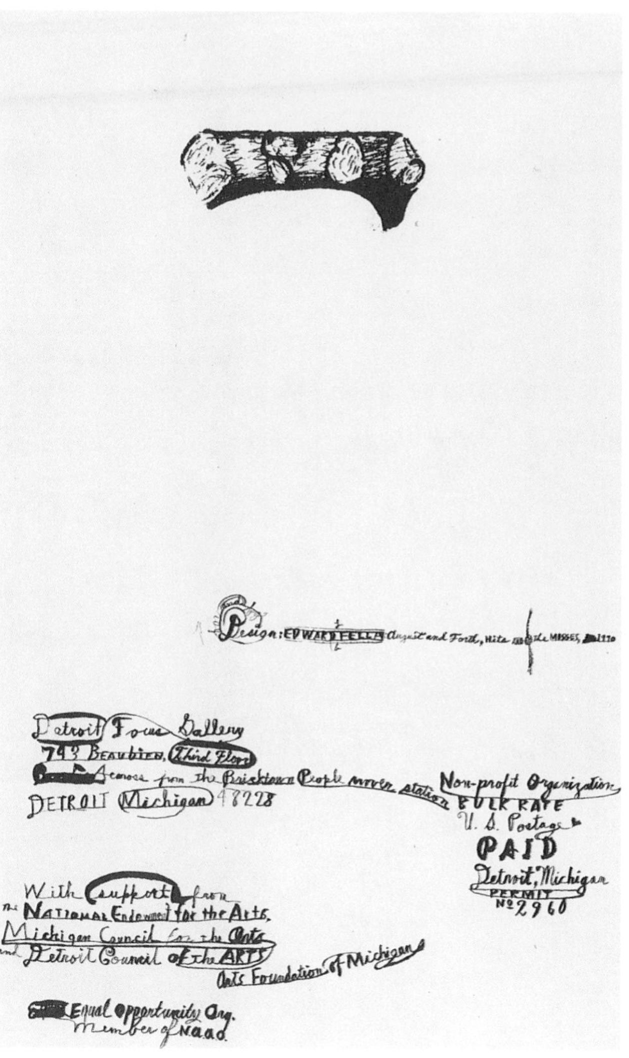

Current work from artists studios
Poster/mailer. Detroit Focus Gallery, USA, 1987. Design Edward Fella

Vickie Arndt/Peter Lenzo
Poster/mailer. Detroit Focus Gallery, USA, 1990. Design Edward Fella

opposite:
European illustration. Book page
Booth-Clibborn Editions, UK, 1989. Design The Thunder Jockeys

Mei programma. Programme poster
Zeebelt theatre, The Netherlands, 1986
Design Linzi Bartolini
Gert Dumbar
Esther Vermeer
Studio Dumbar
Photography: Lex van Pieterson

JAMES SURLS

NOVEMBER 17, 1987 TO JANUARY 24, 1988

recent work

CRANBROOK ACADEMY OF ART MUSEUM

James Surls. Exhibition poster
Cranbrook Academy of Art Museum, USA, 1987
Design David Frej

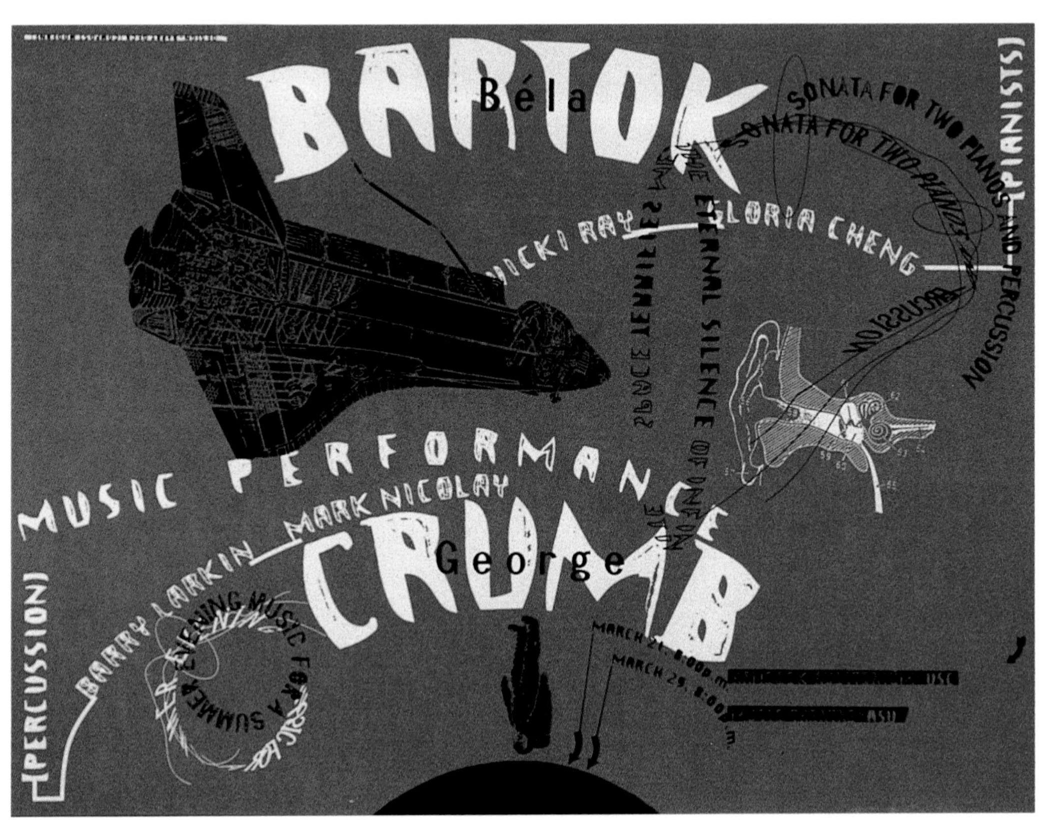

above: Poster. USA, 1989. Design Barry Deck

Nu-bodies. Poster/flyer. Detroit Focus Gallery, USA, 1987. Design Edward Fella 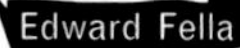

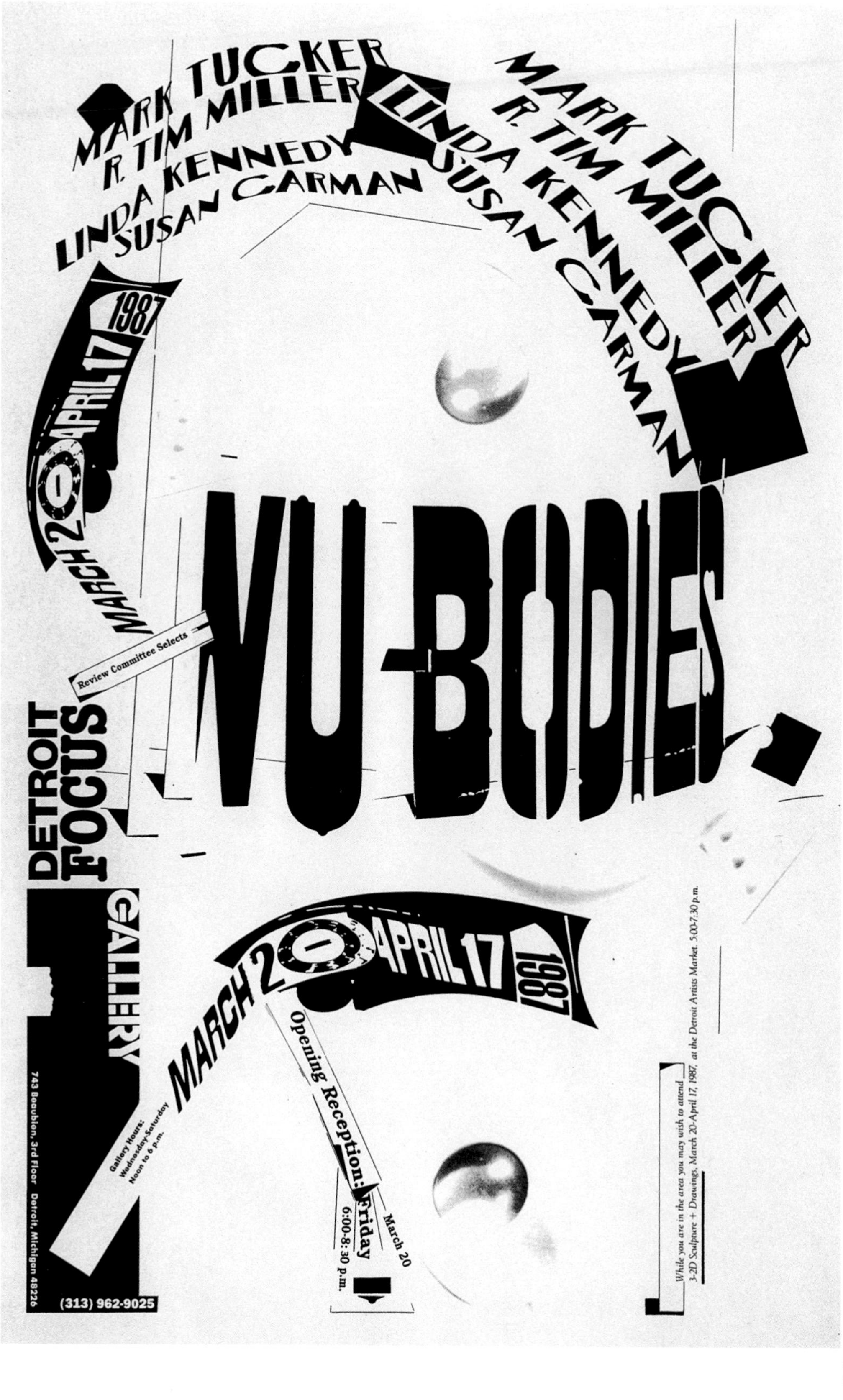

MARK TUCKER
R. TIM MILLER
LINDA KENNEDY
SUSAN CARMAN

MARK TUCKER
R. TIM MILLER
LINDA KENNEDY
SUSAN CARMAN

MARCH 20 – APRIL 17 1987

Review Committee Selects

NU-BODIES

DETROIT FOCUS GALLERY

MARCH 20 – APRIL 17 1987

Opening Reception: Friday March 20 6:00–8:30 p.m.

Gallery Hours: Wednesday–Saturday Noon to 6 p.m.

743 Beaubien, 3rd Floor Detroit, Michigan 48226

(313) 962-9025

While you are in the area you may wish to attend 3-2D Sculpture + Drawings, March 20–April 17, 1987, at the Detroit Artists Market. 5:00–7:30 p.m.

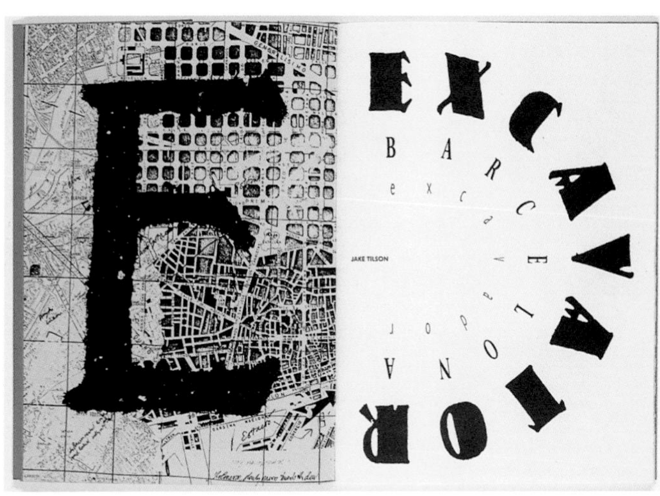

above: Postcard. Artworks, USA, 1988
Design Jeffery Keedy

Excavator-Barcelona-Excavador. Pages from an artist's book. UK, 1986. Design Jake Tilson

opposite: *Continuum.* Poster/mailer
Detroit Focus Gallery, USA, 1990
Design Edward Fella

Reception: FRIDAY, OCT. 12TH, from 5:30–8:30 PM

Oct 12 – NOV. 10th 1990

CONTINUUM

AVERY BOONE

JAMES H. DOZIER

MARIA-THERESA FERNANDES

RUTH LAMPKINS

RICHARD LEWIS

STEVEN MEALY

AARON IBN PORI PITTS

REGINALD GAMMON

ESDRAS M. SANTIAGO

CURATORS

GILDA Snowden

LESTER Johnson

DETROIT FOCUS GALLERY

743 Beaubien 3rd. fl.

DETROIT, MI 48226

tel. (313) 962-9025

hrs: WED-SAT. 12-6 P.M.

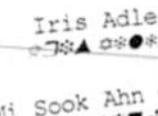

Artemisia Gallery
Chicago Artists Spaces
Poster/mailer
Detroit Focus Gallery, USA, 1987
Design Edward Fella

opposite:
i-D. Magazine pages
Terry Jones/Tony Elliot, UK, 1990
Art director Stephen Male Nice

the i-D Forums

music

Lisa Anderson *(BMG/RCA)*, **Norman Cook** *(Beats International)*, **Dave Dorrell** *(ex- M/A/R/R/S/, DJ, remixer)* **Boy George** *(Jesus Loves You)*, **MC Mell'O'** *(UK rapper)* **and Tony Wilson** *(Factory Records /media mouth)*.

Chaired by John Godfrey

WHAT DO YOU THINK THE BIGGEST PROBLEM FACING THE RECORD INDUSTRY IS NOW?

TONY WILSON Personally, the problem for the British record industry now is breaking the British scene in America.

NORMAN COOK Is it such a big deal?

TONY WILSON Yes, it makes a massive difference.

BOY GEORGE Financially.

TONY WILSON Financially, yeah. It makes an enormous fucking difference financially

BOY GEORGE Is there anyone making money out of dance music in this country?

LISA ANDERSON and ***TONY WILSON*** (in unison): Yes.

TONY WILSON If you get albums out of it - no-one makes money out of dance music per se if it remains 12'' single orientated, only if you have an album going.

DO YOU THINK THE BRITISH SCENE TODAY HAS ANY SIMILARITIES TO THE '60S?

TONY WILSON Yeah, drugs.

NORMAN COOK Is it that simple?

BOY GEORGE I think it is drugs.

DAVE DORRELL Everyone is giving it hippy this and that, but they're all mods really, they should all be wearing straight suits.

TONY WILSON But none of them were born in the '60s. When everyone tried to revive psychedelia, like the Liverpool bands tried to do in '81/'82, it didn't work. It could only really happen again when young people hadn't experienced it. And there's an unselfconsciousness to it now which was never there in the '60s, and that's what makes it new.

BOY GEORGE I think all it is is the drugs that have got a lot of normal kids from the suburbs into music that they probably weren't even into before, there's a lot of people dancing now who weren't into music before.

NORMAN COOK I still don't think they're into music.

TONY WILSON Course they are, course they are, course they are!

NORMAN COOK I think they're into it through fashion.

TONY WILSON Noo!

BOY GEORGE And I think the record companies are just destroying everything.

LISA ANDERSON Here we go, here we go.

BOY GEORGE: They are, they are destroying everything.

LISA ANDERSON Thankyou George.

THE 'SIGN UP ANYTHING FROM MANCHESTER' MENTALITY?

LISA ANDERSON Certainly not.

TONY WILSON We'll sell anything.

LISA ANDERSON I wouldn't sign just anything from Manchester, anyway it's all been signed up.

TONY WILSON If you think it's going to make money, and clearly several people think that the new scene is going to make money...

LISA ANDERSON It's going to make money for someone.

TONY WILSON It's making money already, and as I said, the only problem left is if it breaks in America, cos if it does it will make an awful lot of money for everybody.

DAVE DORRELL Do you think it will?

TONY WILSON Er, 60/40 - about the same odds as keeping the Hacienda open, slightly more than even.

BOY GEORGE I don't know if America's that into it though.

TONY WILSON But it depends if they're going to wake up. ***The kids who were buying Jason and Kylie two years ago are now 11, and 11 year olds are buying Stone Roses, Happy Mondays and the rest of it.*** And if that's happening in Britain, one has to wonder if American kids who are buying New Kids On The Block now, in a year's time they're going to be older and they're going to see this exciting stuff coming out of this country.

NORMAN COOK Well let's face it, if 11 year old English kids can cope with The Happy Mondays, 20 year old Americans must be able to, mustn't they?

LISA ANDERSON: Not necessarily. They're so susceptible to what is sold to them.

NORMAN COOK I reckon Americans are hung up on the whole dream of rock'n'roll, the James Dean element. I don't think they can cope with anything unless it has the essential rock'n'roll ingredient.

I-D THE BIRTHDAY ISSUE 19

the i-D Forums

books

Pete Ayrton *(Serpent's Tail)*, **Michael Bracewell** *(novelist)*, **Christopher Fowler** *(horror writer)*, **Giles O'Brien** *(4th Estate)* **and Mike Phillips** *(crime writer)*.

Chaired by Steve Beard and Jim McClellan

What do you think the Booker Prize represents and is it desirable?

MIKE PHILLIPS: I don't have anything against the Booker Prize. Unfortunately I don't think I'm going to get it. But does it represent a kind of oppressive literary culture? I don't think that it does in itself. I think it reflects a literary culture that comes out of a static notion that the country has of itself, never mind literature. And I think the reason that can be oppressive, if it's oppressive at all, is because we haven't yet begun to reassemble the elements of an English or British identity and understand it. So in a way, the whole superstructure that's represented by the Booker Prize and the publishers and all the rest of it is, in a sense, ***alien*** to lots of people writing now. Because it doesn't share the identity that they're describing and assembling in Britain *now*.

CHRISTOPHER FOWLER It represents a sort of stratified upper middle class, and it's almost a genre in itself, in that you can classify a book as a Booker book. It's almost as if the books are being chosen for the ability to find some permanence in some pantheon of future literature. It seems to be very narrow, and it keeps dangerously away from anything realistic, or too much outside of what the average person who sees the little sticker on the shelves saying 'Booker Prize short-listed', experiences.

MIKE PHILLIPS You can see the style - it's the sort of book that when you open it you think, **Oh shit this is going to be really hard to read.**

GILES O'BRIEN You've got to remember that the reason that money is there is that Booker want to see their name on those nice little printed plaques that go round with the books. Each year it's a completely different set of six judges, mind you these people are chosen cos they represent some kind of literary establishment, and I think they feel a pressure to represent that establishment. But I think they also feel a pressure to produce a popular winner, one that people will actually read and enjoy. And that is because it is a marketing exercise, it's not conceived as a literary exercise, it's very useful for publishers, it's very useful for Booker - although I don't actually know what Booker do other than sponsor the Booker Prize.

MIKE PHILLIPS I'll tell you what Booker has done - **Booker owned my country.** The country where I was born, Guyana, you walk down the high street and everything says Booker, Booker, Booker. I've always found it slightly galling to come here, and to find that Booker is handing out money in this way.

PETE AYRTON To be fair it's changing, and to a certain extent the way it's changing is reflected by the jury and who's chosen, and the things we're doing and other people are publishing. I mean, last year Maggie Gee and Ed White were on the jury, this year Kate Saunderson, and James Kelman was short-listed last year - these are steps forward. You know, one's looking at it as if it's this dead weight that every year comes up with Anita Brookner, which happens some years, but it is changing, and to a large extent it depends on who's in the jury. To what extent they will continue to get interesting and non-mainstream people onto the jury though, one doesn't know, but it's the book trade that is the first to complain. When Keri Hulme won, the New Zealand feminist novelist, it was the book trade who complained cos they couldn't sell the book. The problem is the book shops, not Booker or the people who select the book.

CHRISTOPHER FOWLER So are there some books which the audience would buy if it won the Booker?

GILES O'BRIEN Yeah, it makes a tremendous difference.

PETE AYRTON But I think that one can get too hung up on this thing - obviously it's been good for books, it's been good for writers, it gets TV coverage, it raises the profile of books and makes this country more book conscious, which God knows, you know...

MICHAEL BRACEWELL I agree with Pete, the fact that Kelman and Banville got on the short-list last year - I thought that was very much a step in the right direction. I have this sneaking suspicion that any of us who write couldn't help but feel rather pleased.

PETE AYRTON And everybody's doing it now - *The Sunday Express* have got one, Whitbread have got one - it can't be bad, all these people throwing money at writers.

CHRISTOPHER FOWLER *The Sunday Express* have got one?!

PETE AYRTON Yeah, I think it's the richest, and there's one in Ireland, the Guinness one, which is £50,000.

CHRISTOPHER FOWLER ***I didn't think the people who read The Sunday Express bought books, I thought they watched TV.***

Are genre writers perceived as being on the margins of literature?

Last night a DJ saved my life. Club poster. Parco, Tokyo, 1990

Design Richard Bonner-Morgan, Neil Edwards, Stephen Male Nice

MADSTOCK...

...THE CONTINUING ADVENTURES OF

bubble car fish

lp mc cd
OUT NOW!!!!

'ooh that's
a nice record'

candyflip

Madstock. . . Advertisement. Candyflip, UK, 1990

Side One
Track 1
PWEI IS A FOUR LETTER WORD
(1'12.34/681")
93.3 BPM
PREACHING TO THE PERVERTED
Track 3
WISE UP! SUCKER
(3'17.09/998")
96 BPM
Track 4
SIXTEEN DIFFERENT FLAVOURS OF HELL
(2'03.46/705")
96 BPM
Track 5
INJECT ME
(4'31.45/674")
97 BPM
Track 6
CAN U DIG IT?
(4'32.77/007")
129 BPM
22
Track 7
THE FUSES HAVE BEEN LIT
(4'02.46/946")
120 BPM
PL 74141
0 035627 414114
D:SE F:RC270 UK:HH
All Songs Written by Vestan
All Songs Published by BMG Music Publishing
Produced by
and Engineered by Dave
Assistant Engineer Karl
except: Track
Original Recording Produced by Mr X & Mr
and Engineered by Robin
Additional Production by Mark
Mixed by
Remix Engineered by Dave
and Track
Produced by D. Steele & A.
and Engineered by Robin
and Track
Produced by Robert Gordon for The FON
Mixed by Flood and Engineered by Cenzo
Stun Guitar on Track 2 by Frank
Wild Guitar on Tracks 3, 6 &
by The Buzzard from
Backing Vocals on Track
by Twig The Wonder
Turntables by
Except Tracks 9 & 10 by DJ
The Sleeve Design & The Artwork
This is The Designerstar
Computer Images by Phil
Live Photography by Kevin
Worldwide Representation by Craig
for Chapter 22 Management
6 New Street Warwick CV34 4RX
UK Agent: Paul Boswell for The
370 City Road London EC1
USA Agent: Ian
for Frontier Booking
1776 Broadway New York NY 10019
℗ 1989 BMG Records (UK)
© 1989 BMG Records (UK)
All Trademarks and Logos are
RCA is a Registered Trademark of RCA
Distributed in the UK by BMG
Distribue en Europe par
Vertrieb in Europe durch
A Bertelsmann Music Group
PWEI
RCA
WISE UP!
NOT NOW JAMES WE'RE BUSY 120 BPM
WAKE UP!
HORSESHOE
GAMBLIN
pop
Side Two
Track 8
POISON TO THE MIND
(0'58.88/317")
95 BPM
Side Two
Track 9
DEF. CON. ONE
(4'39.00/001")
96 BPM
Side Two
Track 10
RADIO PWEI
(4'17.93/462")
96 BPM
SHORTWAVE TRANSMISSION ON "UP TO THE MINUTEMAN NINE"
Side Two
Track 12
SATELLITE ECSTATICA
(4'37.36/485")
Side Two
Track 13
NOT NOW JAMES, WE'RE BUSY
(3'08.03/313")
Side Two
Track 14
WAKE UP! TIME TO DIE...
(7'21.87/552")

Wise up sucker. 12" single cover (back)
RCA, UK, 1989
Design Designers Republic

opposite: *This is the day . . . this is the hour . . . this is this!*
Album cover (back). RCA, UK, 1989
Design Designers Republic

EMIGRE

opposite:
Emigre. Magazine cover. Emigre Graphics, USA, 1990
Design Rudy VanderLans

Tegentonen. Concert poster. Paradiso Amsterdam, The Netherlands, 1986
Design Max Kisman

below: *Breakfast Special*
Pages from artist's book. UK, 1989
opposite: *Excavator-Barcelona-Excavador*
Pages from an artist's book. UK, 1986
Design **Jake Tilson**

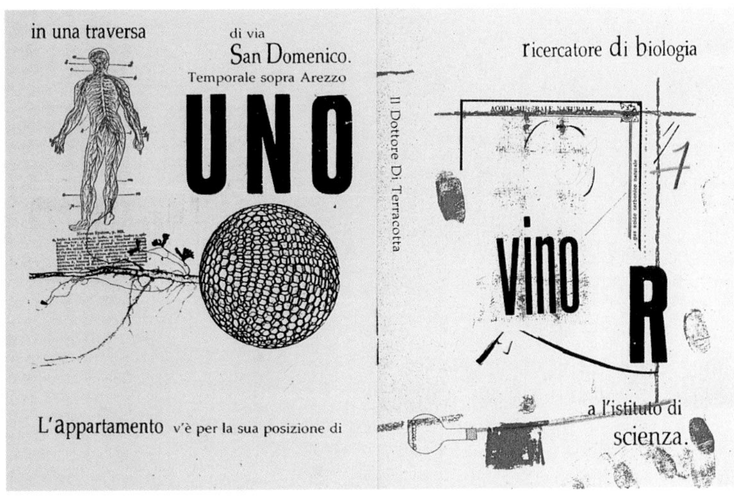

ENTRADA
Núm.
ENTRADA
Núm.
ENTRADA

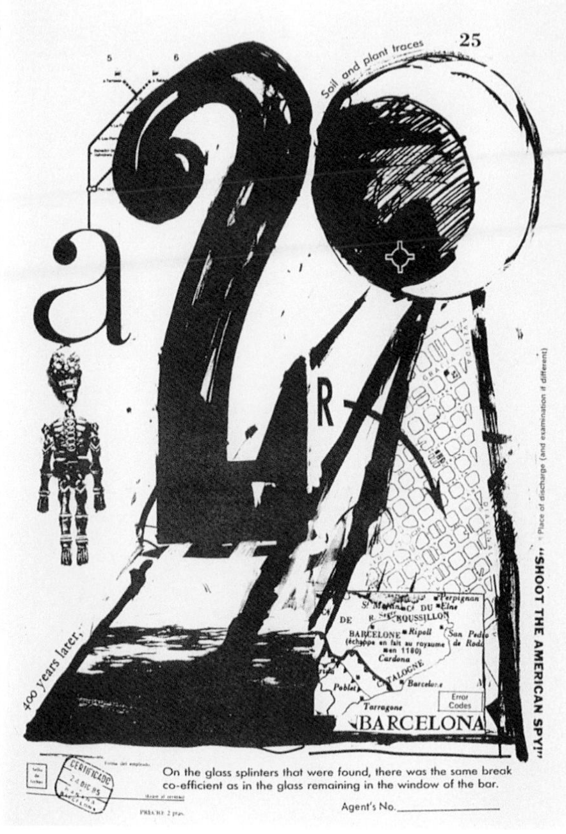
25
Soil and plant traces
a
R
400 years later,
BARCELONA
Error Codes
"SHOOT THE AMERICAN SPY!"
On the glass splinters that were found, there was the same break co-efficient as in the glass remaining in the window of the bar.
Agent's No.

EMIGRE

Design Department

THE MAGAZINE THAT IGNORES BOUNDARIES

PRICE: $7.95

Cranbrook

graphic

design

special

Change

ISSUE

Dutch

Several Designers

opposite:
Emigre. Magazine cover. Emigre Graphics, USA, 1988
Design **Glenn Suokko**

Binary race. Booklet. Emigre Graphics, USA, 1991
Design/photography **Rudy VanderLans**

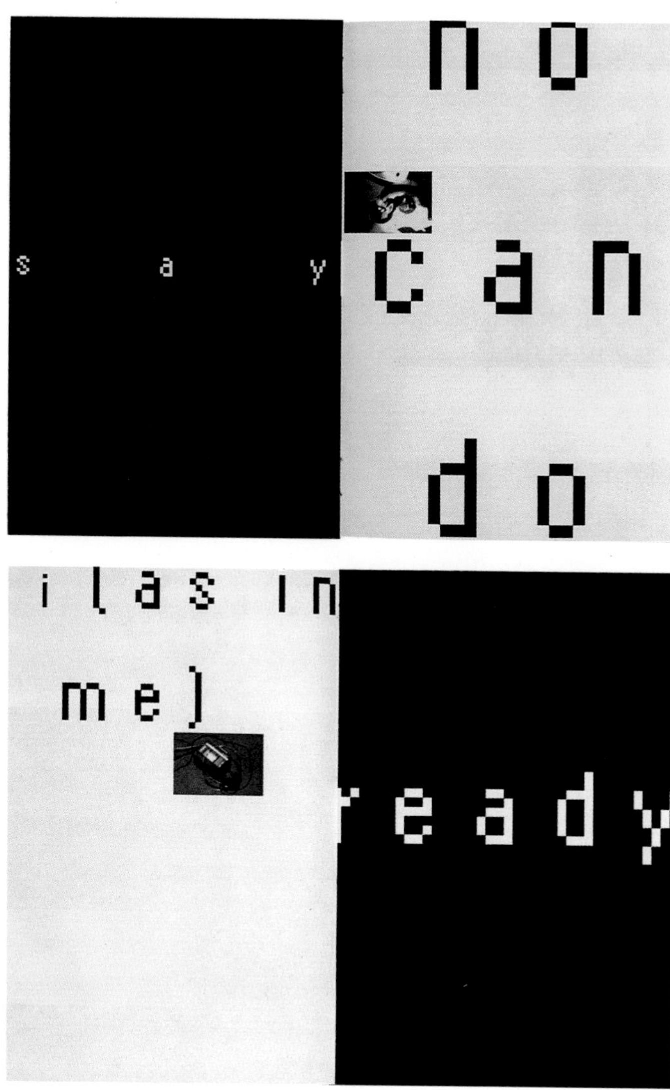

History of design/story of sign. Poster/mailer
American Institute of Graphic Arts Detroit, USA, 1988. Design Edward McDonald

above:
Blaise Bryski. Concert poster. California Institute of the Arts, USA, 1988. Design Barry Deck
below:
Fournier le jeune. Poster. USA, 1985. Design Edward McDonald
Cranbrook Academy of Art

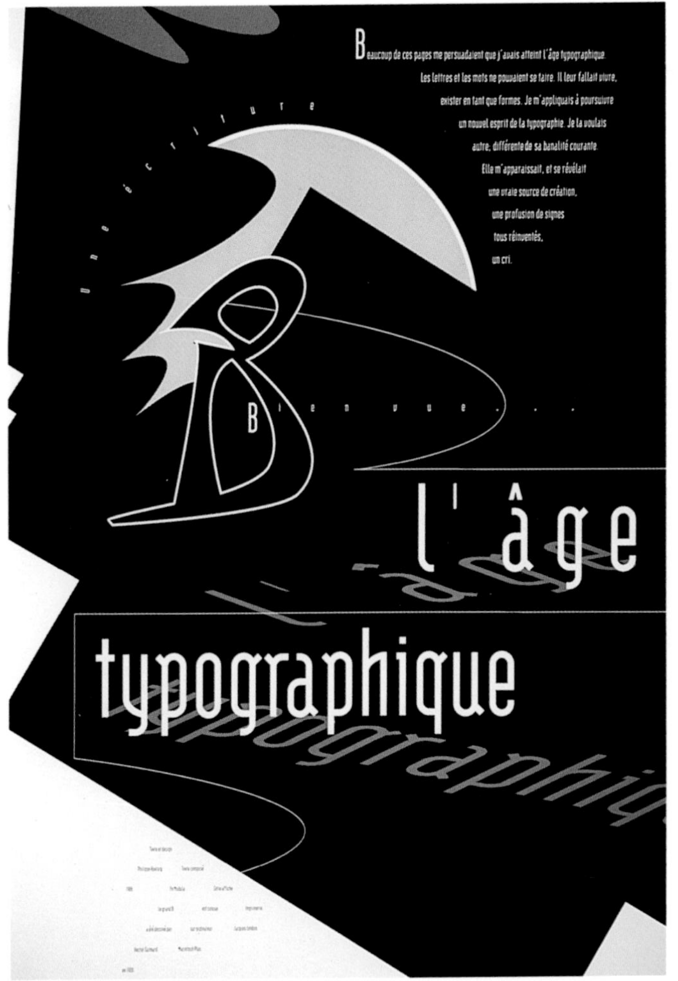

L'âge typographique (The age of typography). Poster. France, 1989

Design Philippe Apeloig

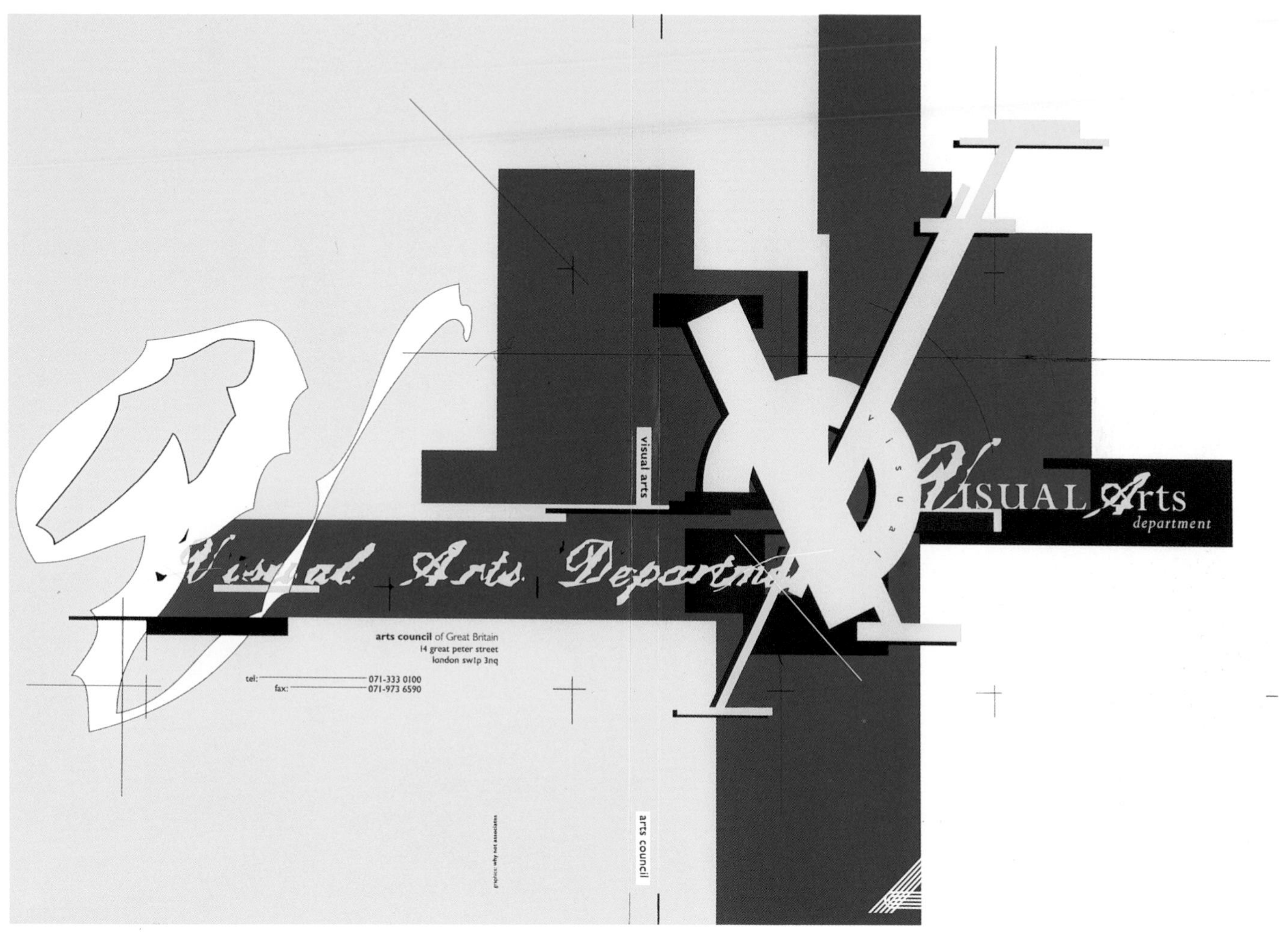

Visual arts department. Folder. Arts Council, UK, 1991

Design Why Not Associates

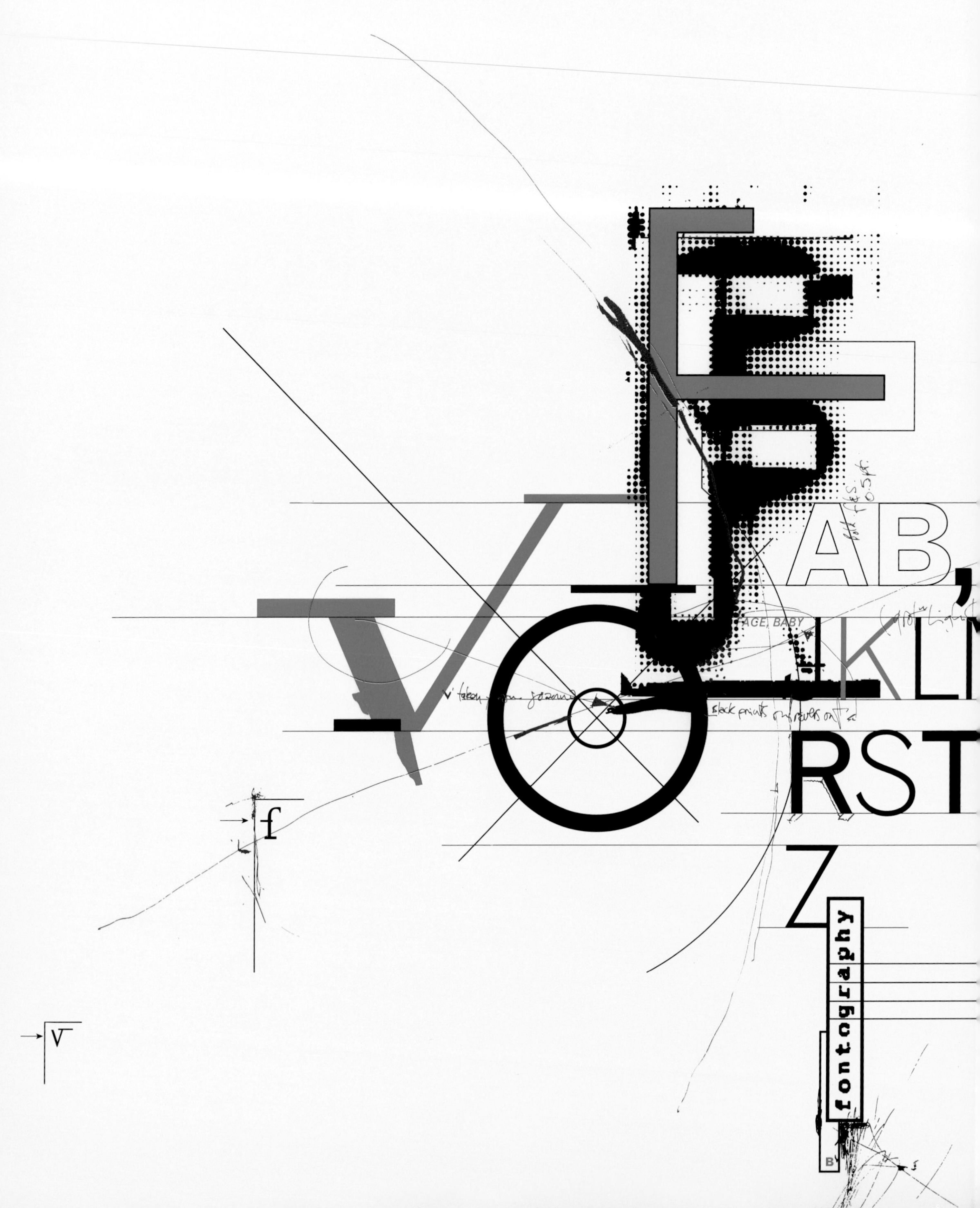

AB,
AGE, BABY
KL
RST
Z
fontography
B
f
V

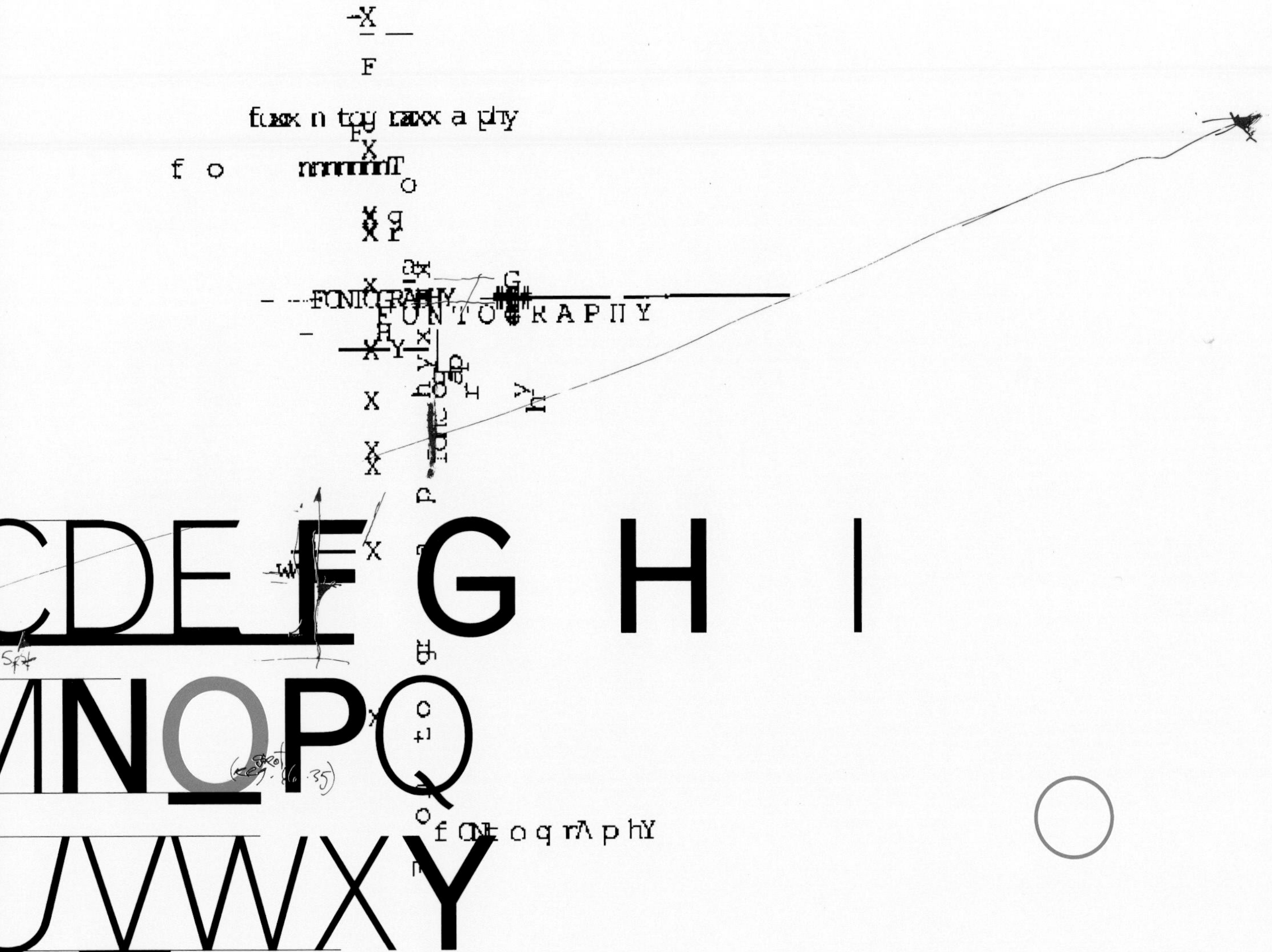

in

A B C D E F G H
a b c d e f g h
I J K L M N O P Q
i j k l m n o p q
R S T U V W X Y Z
r s t u v w x y z
1 2 3 4 5 6 7 8 9 0

Industria Inline. Linotype, UK, 1990
opposite: *Arcadia.* Linotype, UK, 1990
Design Neville Brody

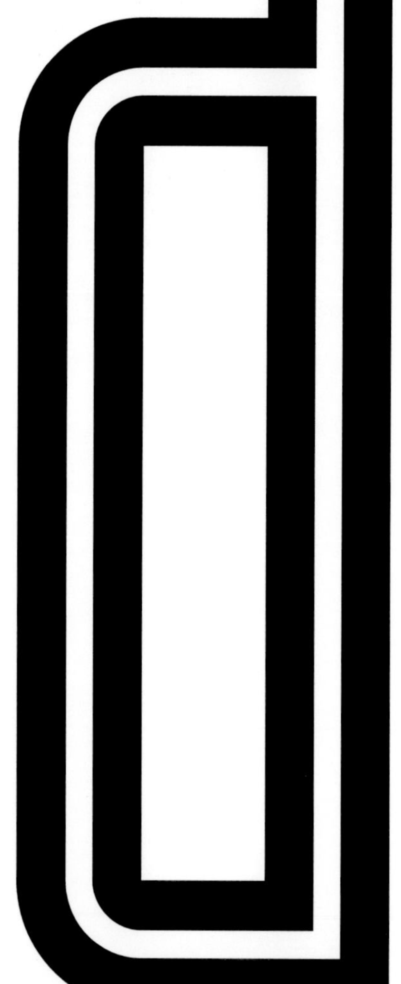

ustria

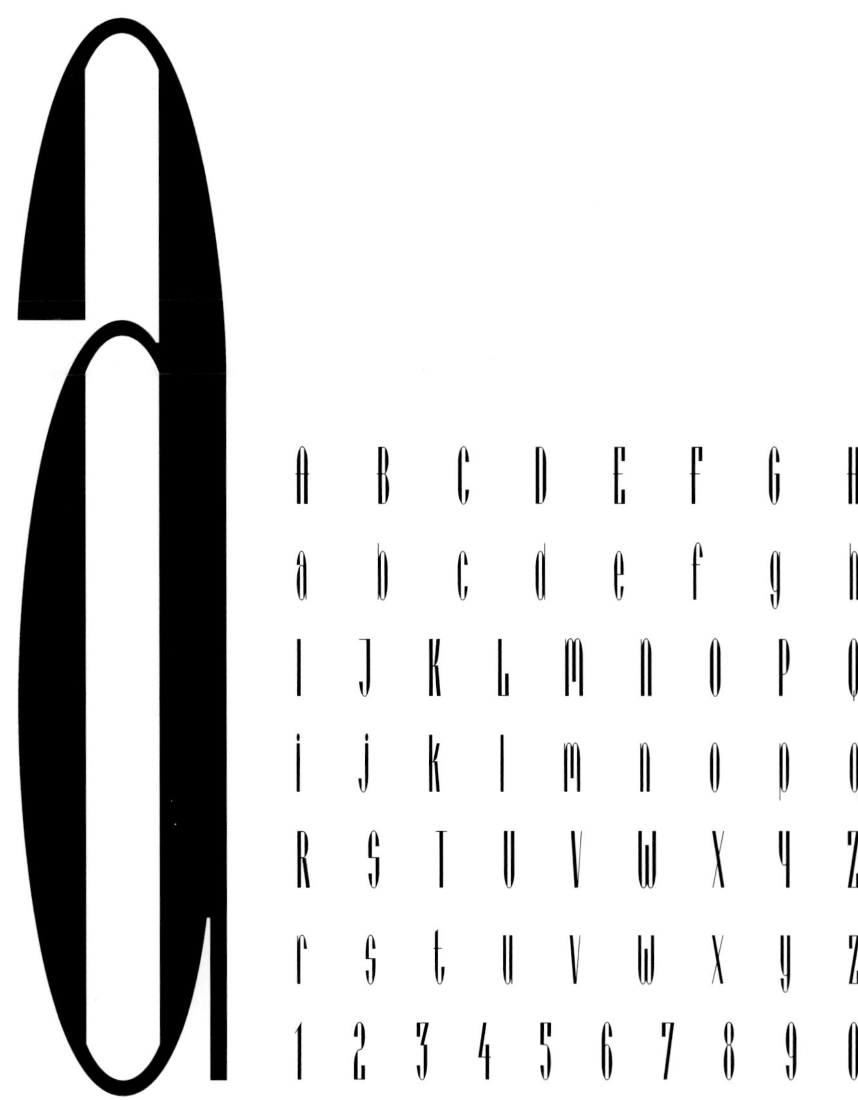
A B C D E F G H
a b c d e f g h
I J K L M N O P Q
i j k l m n o p q
R S T U V W X Y Z
r s t u v w x y z
1 2 3 4 5 6 7 8 9 0

rcadia

Oakland Ten. Emigre Graphics, USA, 1985. Design Zuzana Licko

A B C D E F G H
a b c d e f g h
I J K L M N O P Q
i j k l m n o p q
R S T U V W X Y Z
r s t u v w x y z
1 2 3 4 5 6 7 8 9 0

Matrix Regular. Emigre Graphics, USA, 1986. Design Zuzana Licko

matri x

ABCDEFGH
bcdefgh
IJKLMNOPQ
ijklmnopq
RSTUVWXYZ
stuvwxyz
1234567890

above:
Concert poster. Application of Tegentonen
Paradiso Amsterdam, The Netherlands, 1988

Tegentonen. The Netherlands, 1988-90
Design Max Kisman

Modular Regular. Emigre Graphics, USA, 1985. Design Zuzana Licko

Traveller Regular. The Netherlands, 1991. Design 

A B C D E F G H
a b c d e f g h
I J K L M N O P Q
i j k l m n o p q
R S T U V W X Y Z
r s t u v w x y z
1 2 3 4 5 6 7 8 9 0

traveller

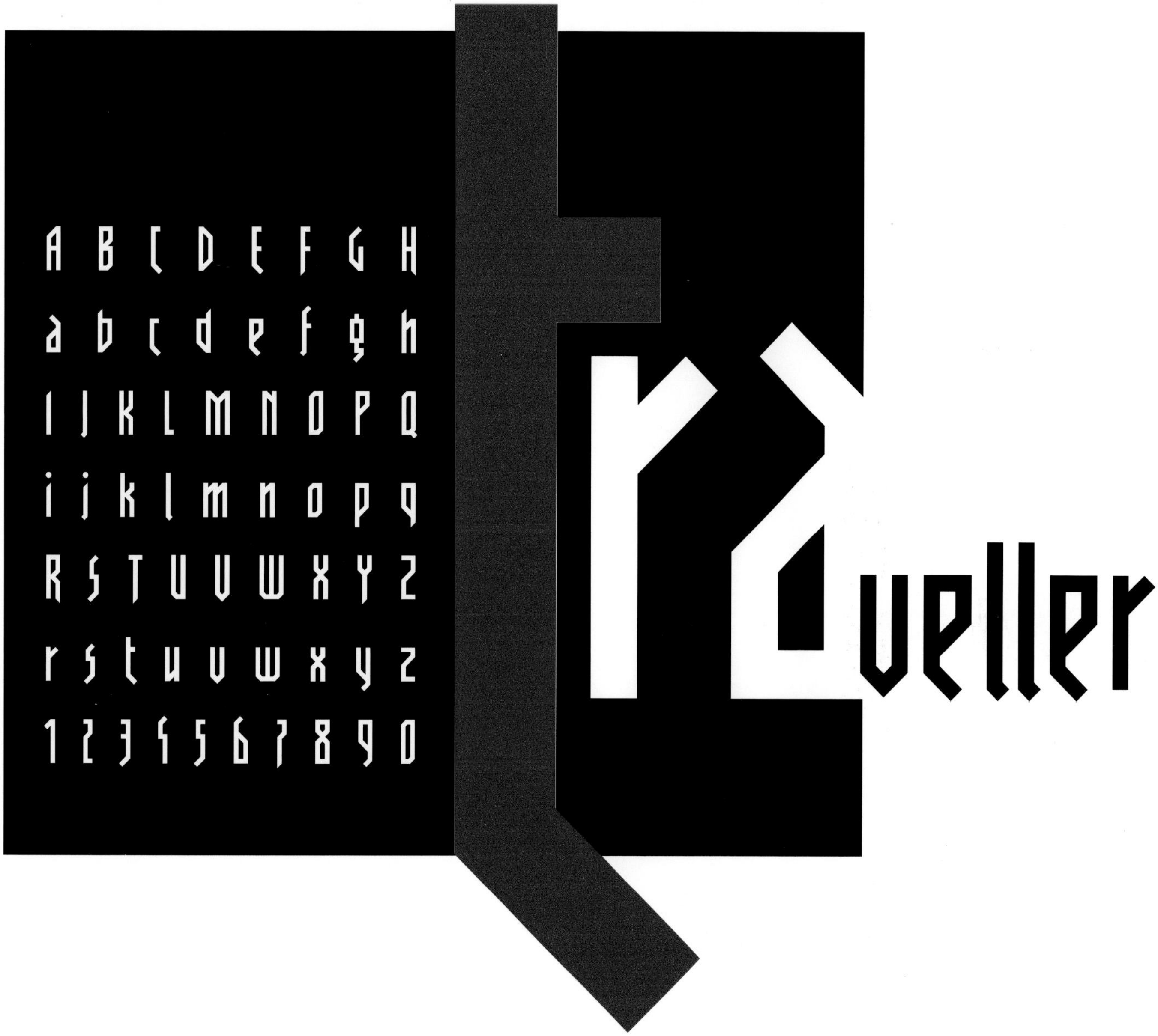

A B C D E F G H

a b c d e f g h

I J K L M N O P Q

i j k l m n o p q

R S T U V W X Y Z

r s t u v w x y z

1 2 3 4 5 6 7 8 9 0

Zwart Vet. The Netherlands, 1987 (capitals), 1990 (lowercase and special characters). Design Max Kisman

Scratch Regular. FontShop "FontFont" series, The Netherlands, 1990. Design Max Kisman

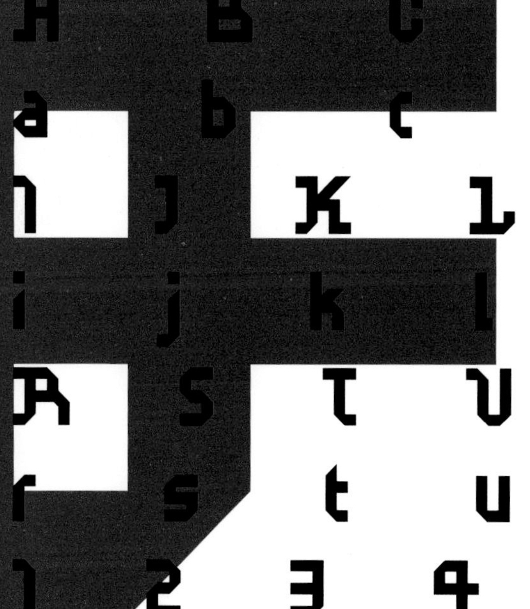

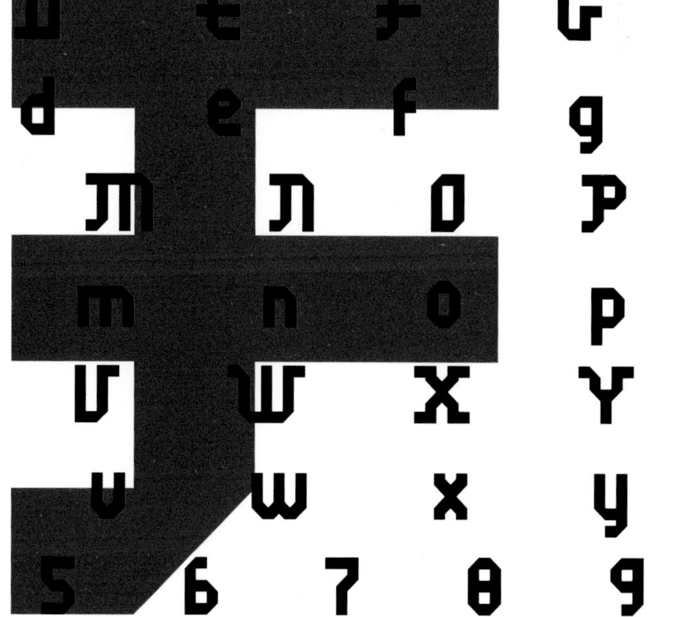

Vortex. FontShop "FontFont" series, The Netherlands, 1990. Design **Max Kisman**

eX

A B C D E F G H
a b c d e f g h
I J K L M N O P Q
i j k l m n o p q
R S T U V W X Y Z
r s t u v w x y z
1 2 3 4 5 6 7 8 9 0

R

l u n a t i

A B C D E F G H
a b c d e f g h
I J K L M N O P Q
i j k l m n o p q
R S T U V W X Y Z
r s t u v w x y z
1 2 3 4 5 6 7 8 9 0

Lunatix Bold. Emigre Graphics, USA, 1988. Design Zuzana Licko

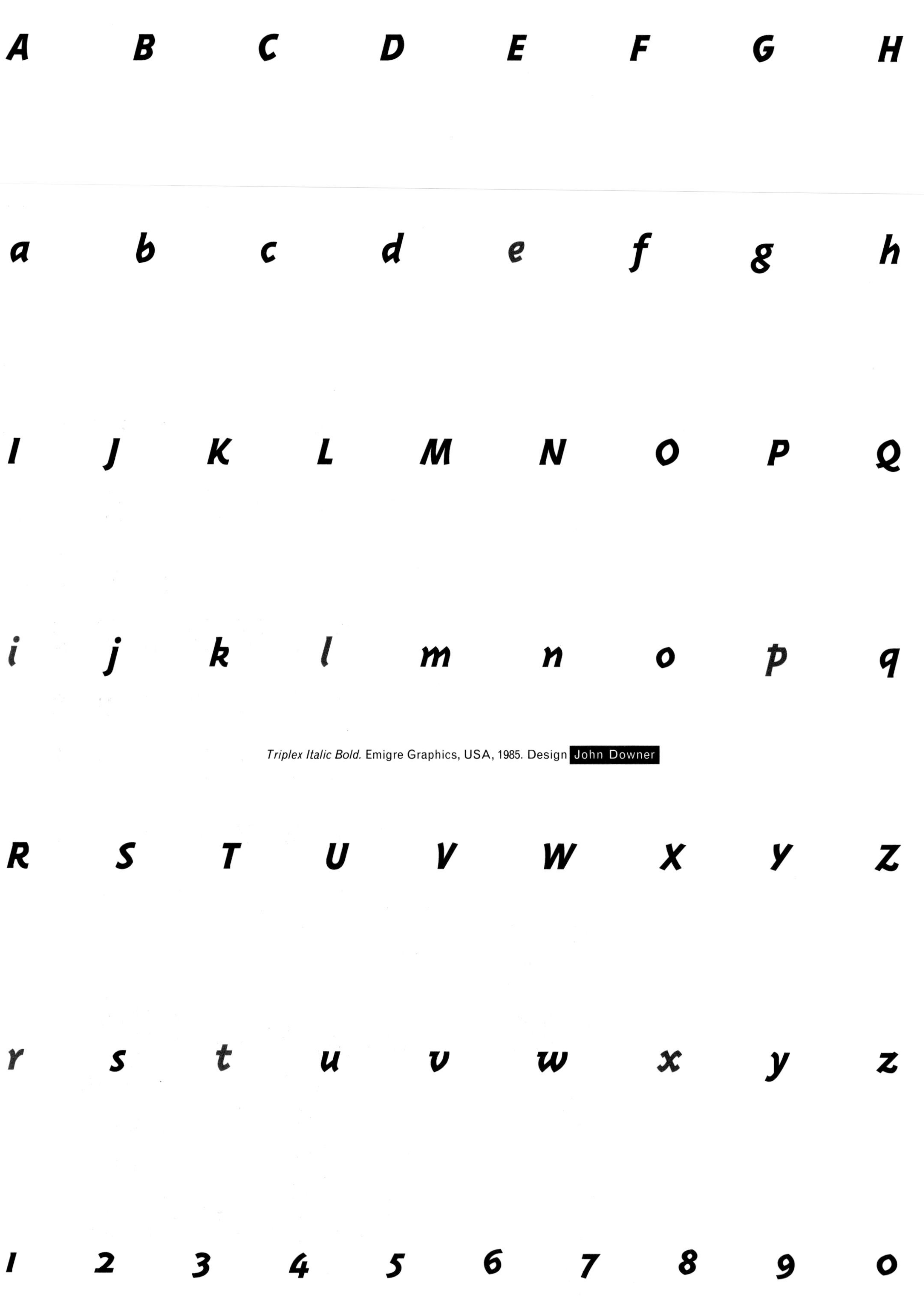

Triplex Italic Bold. Emigre Graphics, USA, 1985. Design **John Downer**

slim

Jacque Slim, Regular and Fat. FontShop, The Netherlands, 1990. Design Max Kisman

A B C D E F G H
a b c d e f g h
I J K L M N O P Q
i j k l m n o p q
R S T U V W X Y Z
r s t u v w x y z
1 2 3 4 5 6 7 8 9 0

regular

Brokenscript Bold. FontShop "FontFont" series, The Netherlands, 1991

Design Just van Rossum

ABCDEFGH
abcdefgh
IJKLMNOPQ
ijklmnopq
RSTUVWXYZ
rstuvwxyz
1234567890

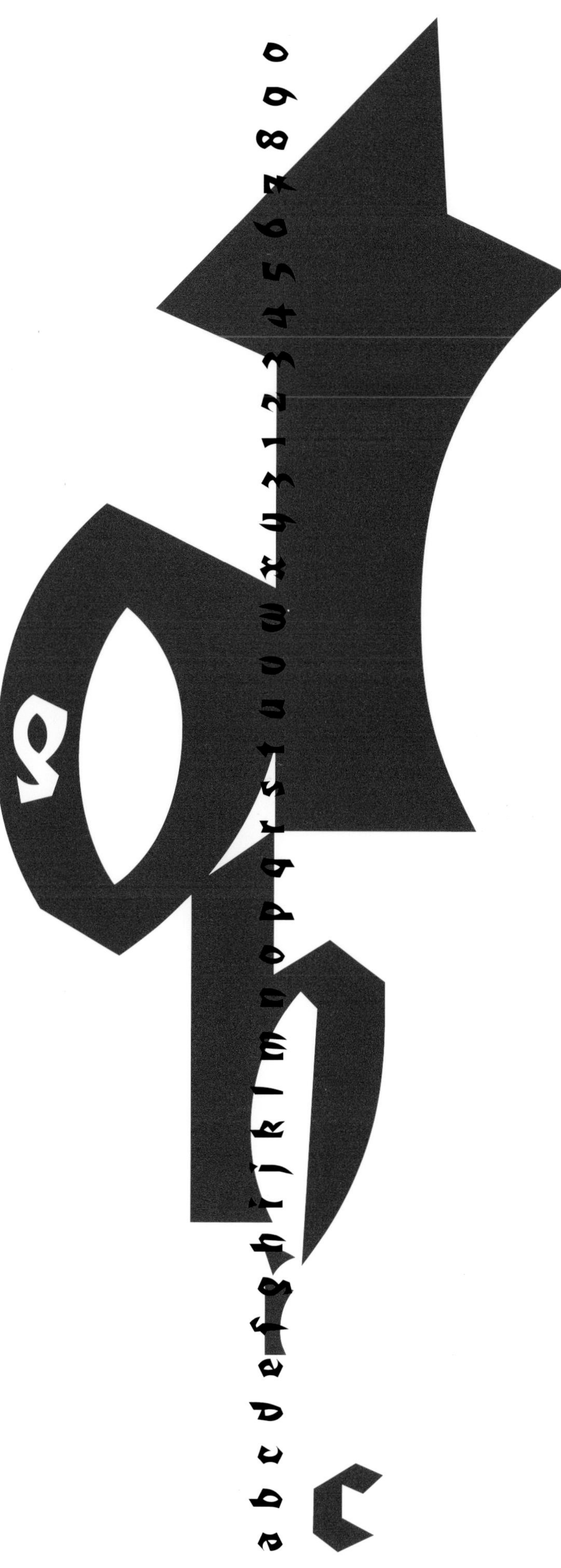

Totally Gothic. Emigre Graphics, USA, 1990
Design Zuzana Licko

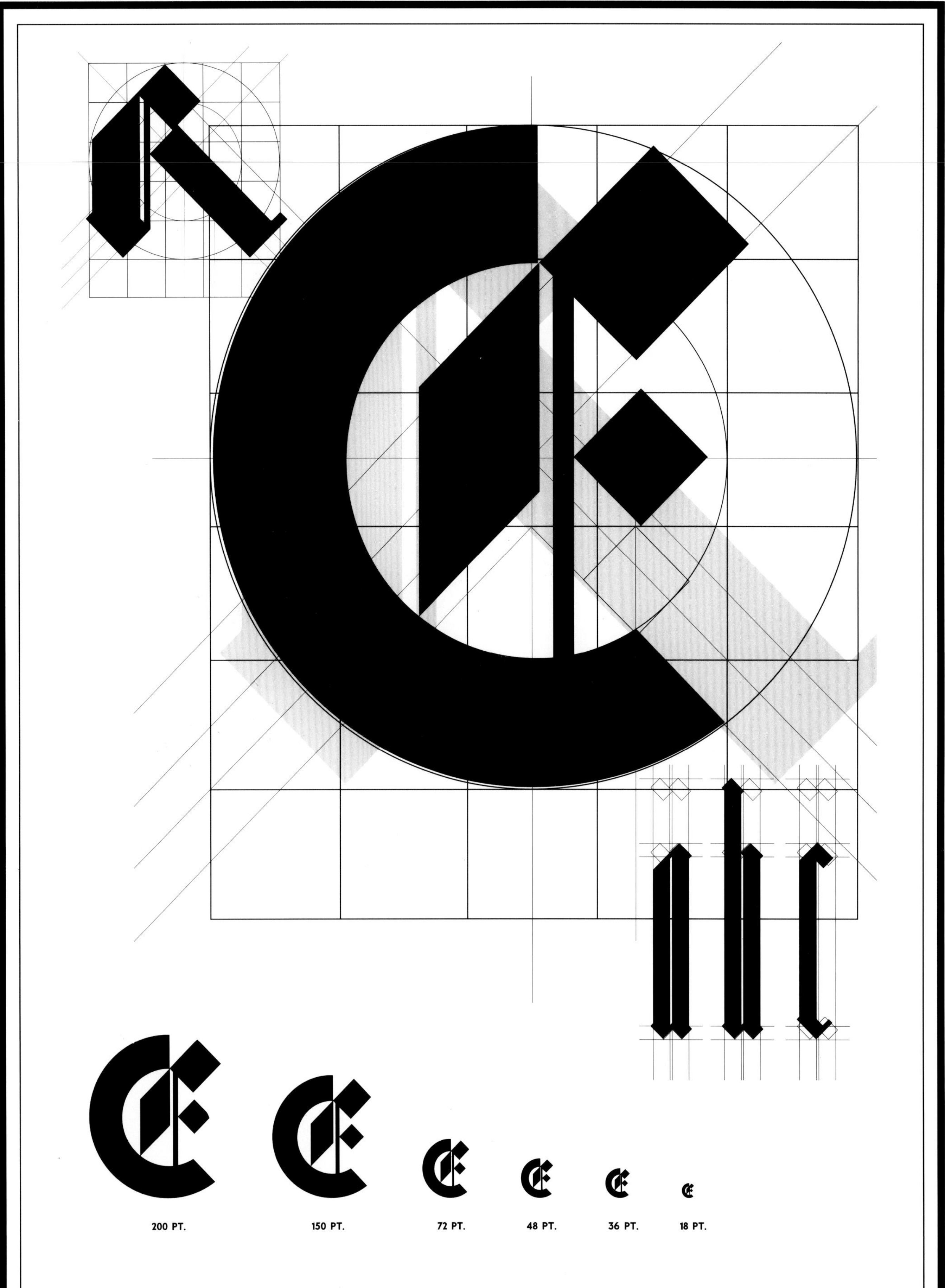
abc
200 PT.
150 PT.
72 PT.
48 PT.
36 PT.
18 PT.

A B C D E F G H I K

L M N O P Q R S

T U V W X Y Z

a b c d e f g h i j k l m n o p q r s t u v w x y z

Spindly Bastard. UK, 1990. Design Jonathan Barnbrook

Posters. Applications of Bastard. UK, 1990
Design Jonathan Barnbrook

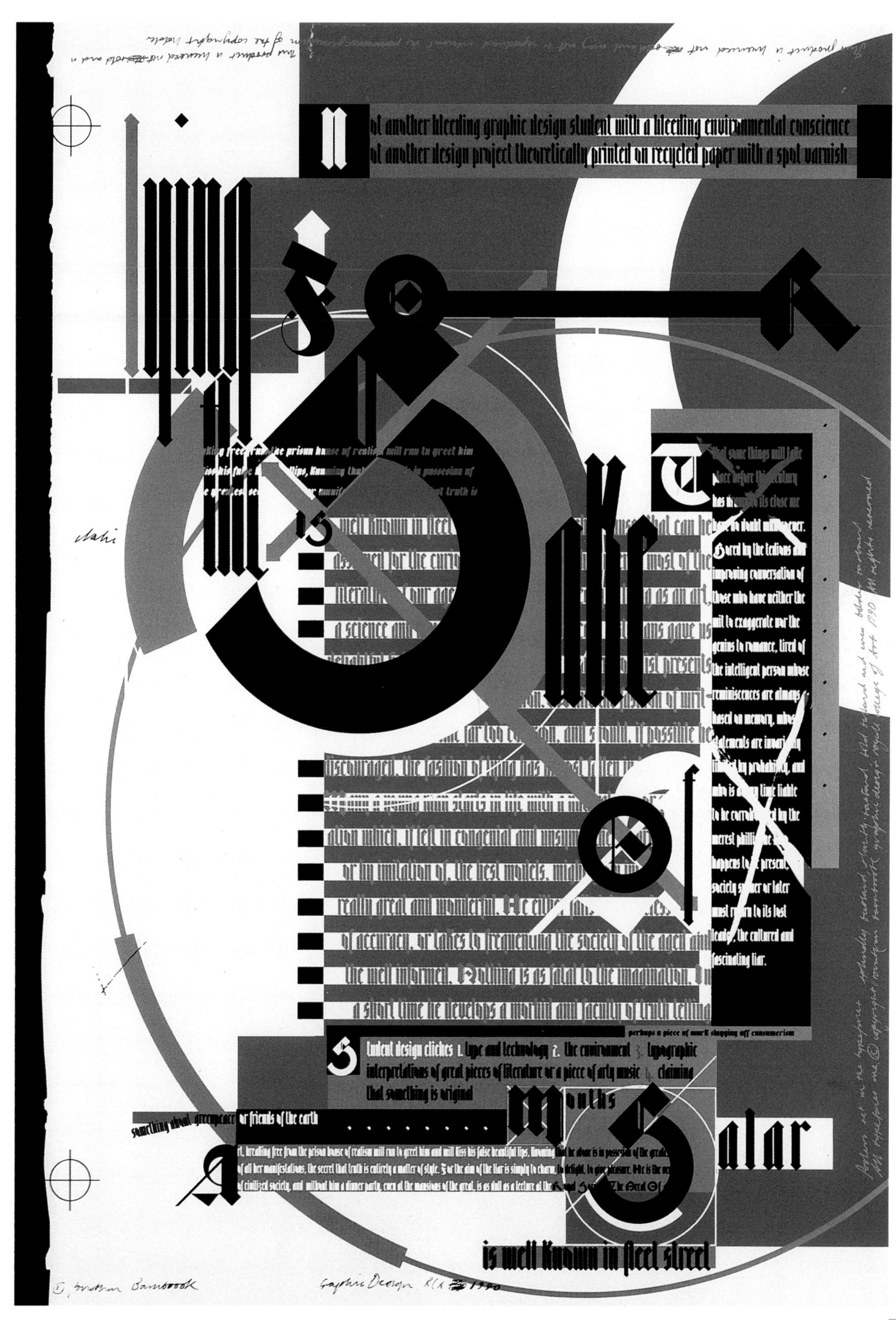
Not another bleeding graphic design student with a bleeding environmental conscience
Not another design project theoretically printed on recycled paper with a spot varnish
is well known in fleet street
Bored by the tedious and improving conversation of those who have neither the wit to exaggerate nor the genius to romance, tired of the intelligent person whose reminiscences are always based on memory,
statements are invariably
leader, the cultured and fascinating liar.
perhaps a piece of work slagging off consumerism
Student design cliches 1. type and technology 2. the environment 3. typographic interpretations of great pieces of literature or a piece of arty music 4. claiming that something is original
something about greenpeace or friends of the earth
Mouths
alar
is well known in fleet street
© Jonathan Barnbrook
Graphic Design RCA 1990

This is Prototype. Each letter is upper and lower case serif and sans serif. The letterforms are created by collaging parts from about ten other typefaces including Gill, Perpetua, Futura and Bembo. It was important to keep all the components the same to emphasise that it was 'brought together' on a computer rather than hand drawn

Prototype. UK, 1990. Design **Jonathan Barnbrook**

opposite: *Fudoni Bold Remix.* The Netherlands, 1991. Design **Max Kisman**

ABCDEFGH
abcdefgh
IJKLMNOPQ
ijklmnopq
RSTUVWXYZ
rstuvwxyz
1234567890

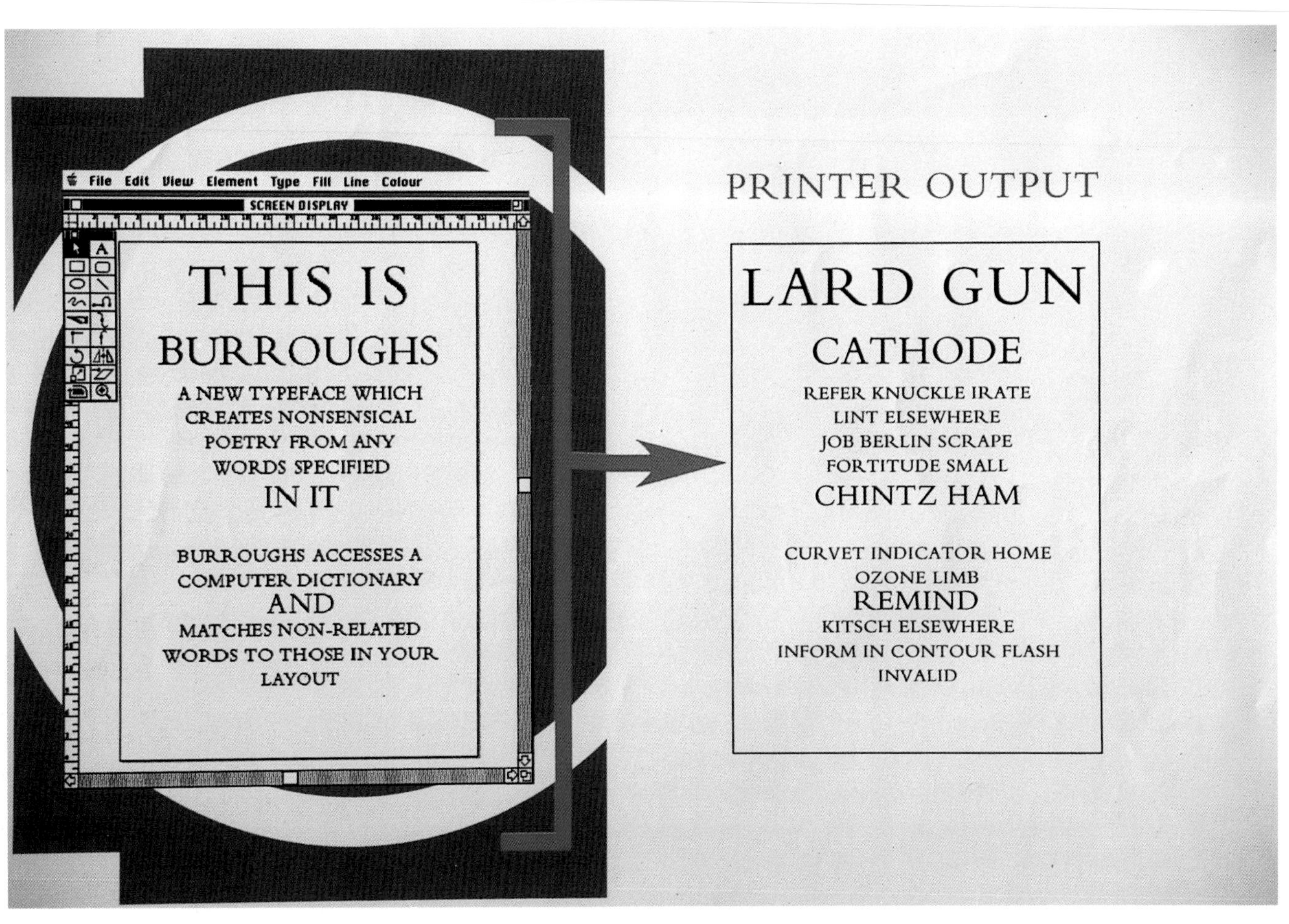

above: *Burroughs.* UK, 1991. Design Jonathan Barnbrook

Beowolf 23. Random font. FontShop, The Netherlands, 1990. Design Erik van Blokland Just van Rossum

ABCDEFGH
abcdefgh
IJKLMNOPQ
i j k l m n o p q
RSTUVWXYZ
rstuvwxyz
1234567890

opposite: *Boem Paukeslag Remix.* Poster
Application of Extended Maxm!x
Typ/Typografisch Papier, The Netherlands, 1991. Design Max Kisman

BOEM

PAUKESLAG

daar ligt alles PLAT

O ______ o

weer razen violen celli bassen koperen triangel

trommels PAUKEN

razen rennen razen rennen razen RENNEN

drama in volle slag hoeren slangen werpen zich op eerlijke

mannen het gezin wankelt de fabriek wankelt

de eer wankelt ligt er

alle begrippen VALLEN

HALT!

Repressed Victorian Roman

(ABCDEFGHIJKLMNOPQRSTUVWXYZ)

[abcdefghijklmnopqrstuvwxyz]

(ABCDEFGHIJKLMNOPQRSTUVWXYZ) [1234567890]

[abcdefghijklmnopqrstuvwxyz]

[1234567890]

BiC SHAVER

8/11 Although his theories regarding architecture and society have been widely read and accepted as the seeds of the modern movement, John Ruskin's bizarre fear of sexual activity haunted him for many years. These horrors, although shrouded in secrecy throughout his lifetime, and by his principal biographers, are confirmed in a series of letters and diary entries found, long after his death, under a floor board in his study.

10/13 After marrying Effie Gray, who was born in the room in which Ruskin's grandfather had committed suicide, he declared her "unfit for consumation", adding that he would reconsider when

12/15 she reached the age of twenty-five (he was twenty-eight and she was nineteen). Six years later, on her twenty-fifth birthday, Ruskin had still not reckoned with his

14/17 legedary disdain for pubic hair, and told her that she was still unfit, citing religious reasons for his abstention. Quite shortly after, the marriage was anulled, and Effie was remarried to the Pre-

16/19 Raphaelite painter, John Millais.

above: *Repressed Victorian Roman.* USA, 1989

opposite top: *Canicopulus Script.* USA, 1989

opposite: *Barry Sans Serif.* USA, 1989 Design **Barry Deck**

Canicopulus Script

(ABCDEFGHIJKLMNOPQRSTUVWXYZ
[abcdefghijklmnopqrstuvwxyz]
[1234567890]

(ABCDEFGHIJKLMNOPQRSTUVWXYZ)
[abcdefghijklmnopqrstuvwxyz]
[1234567890]

Eric Gill

There had been a string of infidelities put up with by his infinitely suffering wife Ethel Mary. Now we know the names. Here the biographer's task was simple enough: a trip to Los Angeles to read Gill's diaries in which he noted such encounters along with much mundane description [illegible] and the facts of his personal life necessary for invoicing clients and making tax returns. But these affairs were not, except in a few cases, matters of the heart. The picture we are given is of a mildly pathological character, a copper patriarch trying to keep jealous tabs on his extended family. There were incestuous

12 / 15 episodes (sisters and daughters), experiments with prostitutes, even with a dog. Gill announced his difference immediately in his dress. His standard garment came to be a penis-freeing smock, the rationale for which

he advanced in several essays and pamphlets. And his attitude to women was quite consciously medieval. He wanted them simple and undecorated, covered up in public and confined to domestic and agricultural activities. Despite himself, he did fall for the provocation offered by several modern or "new" women of his acquaintance. As MacCarthy points out, the missionary trait

14 / 17 ran in the Gill family: a grandfather and a brother served in the South Seas. For Eric, "missionary" could be understood in every sense of the word.
-Robin Kinross, Blueprint

16 / 19

BARRY SANS SERIF

(ABCDEFGHIJKLMNOPQRSTUVWXYZ)
[abcdeFghijklmnopqrstuvwxyz]
{1234567890}

(ABCDEFGHIJKLMNOPQRSTUVWXYZ)
[abcdeFghijklmnopqrstuvwxyz]
{1234567890}

BARRY DECK

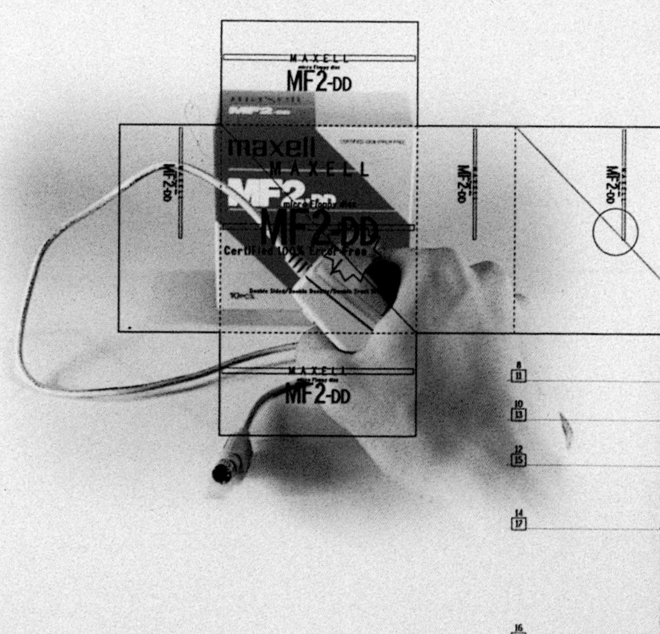

The latest Force to rear its ugly head on the ever-unfolding continuum of the postscript Font design Frontier, Former disciple of the infamous vectorist school and recent sleaze-baron of autotrace typography, is Barry Deck. He cuts his punches in a Frenzy of mouse clicks and key commands, producing a vulgar Flow

8 / 11 of vector-based bezier curve coordinates which are infinitely reproducible. Fueled by almost two grueling years of damn nearly continuous sexual Frustration as a graduate student at California *Institute of the Arts, he designs Fonts which combine influences*

10 / 13 From the past with lewd reFerences to the boundlessness of his own lust (as Focused on Fetishized typographical Form), and the vital energy and singleminded *internal and external drive necessary to blow these*

12 / 15 little characters right out of the laserwriter and into the Future. Held in his hand For days at a time, the indispensable mouse becomes an extension of the phallus, and the outcome re*produces itself in endlessly reconfiguring or-*

14 / 17 gies of language and dyslexic "FluFFemes" on the printed page. The typefaces produced under these conditions, with this methodology, exhibit the sort of spontaneity and passion that exists within sexuality itself. A combination oF all Barry relishes in typography, Barry Sans *SeriF is one such Face.*

16 / 19

ABCDEFGHIJKLMN
OPQRSTUVWXYZ
abcdefghijklmnop
qrstuvwxyz
[1234567890]
№ @!%$&?

ABCDEFGHIJKLMN
OPQRSTUVWXYZ
abcdefghijklmnop
qrstuvwxyz
[1234567890]
№ at !%$ ampers-AND &?

Template Gothic. USA, 1990. Design Barry Deck

Surfer. Magazine pages. Application of Template Gothic and Industry Sans Serif
Surfer Publications, USA, 1991. Art director David Carson

last bLaSt

A thing to remember about Pipeline: At a certain size it will cap over gently on the outside and lure you into the pit with this neighborly little drop. The ugly transformation begins a second or two after you get to your feet, when the wave starts to look like a Nicaraguan hotel in an 8.0 earthquake. Marvin Foster surfs Pipe enough to know that friendly faces don't always tell the truth. Sequence: Don King/Lightwaves.

opposite:
Industry Sans Serif Bold. USA, 1991

Circa 91. Poster/flyer. Application of Industry
The Museum of Contemporary Art, USA, 1991
Design Barry Deck

KAREN FINLEY

ANDY SOMA

LAWRENCE STEGER

BRENDAN DEVALLANCE

NANCY FOREST BROWN

IRIS MOORE

Live musical entertainment by

BIG HAT

AND

MAESTRO SUBGUM
AND THE WHOLE

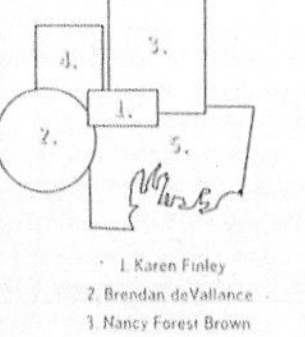

1. Karen Finley
2. Brendan deVallance
3. Nancy Forest Brown
4. Big Hat
5. Maestro Subgum and the Whole

Hear recorded excerpts from "Works in Progress"
by Los Angeles radio performance artist
JOE FRANK

OPEN BAR UNTIL 11PM

Hours:

Gallery: Tuesday-Saturday 11:00-5:00, Sunday 12:00-5:00 Office: Monday-Friday 10:00-6:00

Y · O · U · R
N · A · M · E
H · E · R · E

FilmForum continues its programming in the LACE Performance Space. For further information call [213] 276-7452.

LACE is supported in part by Art Matters Inc., Border Grill, CITY, the California Arts Council, Community Redevelopment Agency of the City of Los Angeles, Cultural Affairs Department of the City of Los Angeles, the James Irvine Foundation, S.K. Kojima and Co., L.A. Eyeworks, Meet the Composer, MIKA Company, the National Endowment for the Arts, Norton Family Foundation, Proton Corporation, Rockefeller Foundation, Yamaha International, and the FRIENDS and SUPPORTERS of LACE.

LACE NEEDS VOLUNTEERS! Learn the technical aspects of lighting for performance, the ins and outs of media installation, and gain first-hand experience putting together a visual arts exhibition! Face the challenges of development and get involved in fundraising for LACE! LACE is a laboratory where volunteers are given the opportunity to participate in all aspects of gallery and performance production and development techniques. Please call 213 624-5650 to volunteer your time and receive hands-on experience in the process, and a free one-year membership to LACE.

lay
n c
ing
nce
nfo

Non-Profit
U. S. Postage
Paid
Permit #35671
Los Angeles, CA

L A C E
Los Angeles Contemporary Exhibitions
1804 Industrial Street
Los Angeles, CA 90021
213.624.5650
September 89

STAFF

Anne Bray, Video Coordinator
Erica Bornstein, Performance Coordinator
Danae Falliers, Acting Development Coordinator
Laurie Garris, Acting Director
Jinger Heffner, Exhibitions Coordinator
Deborah King, Administrative Assistant
Jane Leslie, Bookkeeper
Dan Bernier, Bookstore Manager
June Scott, Development Assistant
Joy Silverman, Executive Director

INTERNS/VOLUNTEERS

Brian Baltin, Naomi Putterman/Performance Interns
Caroline Czirr/Video Intern
Alyssa Resnick/Exhibitions Intern
Sarah Vogwill/Bookstore Intern

MEMBERSHIP

___ MEMBER $30
Receives the LACE bi-monthly calendar with advance notice and invitations to all openings. 10% discount at the LACE Bookstore. Members-only discount to LACE performances, and with select Los Angeles merchants.

___ FAN $100
Receives all of the above PLUS one LACE publication.

___ FRIEND of LACE $250
Receives all of the above PLUS your name in lights on our illuminated, digital display, PLUS invitations to attend at least two exceptional events which highlight noteworthy people and ideas.

___ SUPPORTER $1000
Receives all the benefits of the FRIENDS, PLUS an invitation to attend a special Supporters-only Artists' event. PLUS your name on a permanent earthquake support plate on the LACE building. Your $1000 contribution literally "supports" LACE!

___ ARTIST/STUDENT/SENIOR MEMBER $20
Same benefits as Member.

Make checks payable to Los Angeles Contemporary Exhibitions or LACE

NAME: __________
ADDRESS: __________
CITY/STATE/ZIP: __________
PHONE: __________

SEND TO:
Los Angeles Contemporary Exhibitions
1804 Industrial Street
Los Angeles, CA 90021

Flyer. Application of Keedy
Los Angeles Contemporary Exhibitions, USA, 1989

opposite top: *Keedy Sans Bold.* USA, 1989

opposite: *Hard Times Regular.* USA, 1990

Design Jeffery Keedy

A B C D E F G H
a b c d e f g h
I J K L M N O P Q
i j k l m n o p q
R S T U V W X Y Z
r s t u v w x y z
1 2 3 4 5 6 7 8 9 0

A B C D E F G H
a b c d e f g h
I J K L M N O P Q
i j k l m n o p q
R S T U V W X Y Z
r s t u v w x y z
1 2 3 4 5 6 7 8 9 0

F State. UK, 1991

opposite: Application of F State. *State* poster. FontShop, UK, 1991. Design Neville Brody

POSTER DESIGN **NEVILLE BRODY** TYPEFACE **F STATE** POSTER ®1991 FONTSHOP INTERNATIONAL ©1991 NEVILLE BRODY

FUSE A LINE THROUGH THE CHAOS OF COMMUNICATION

index

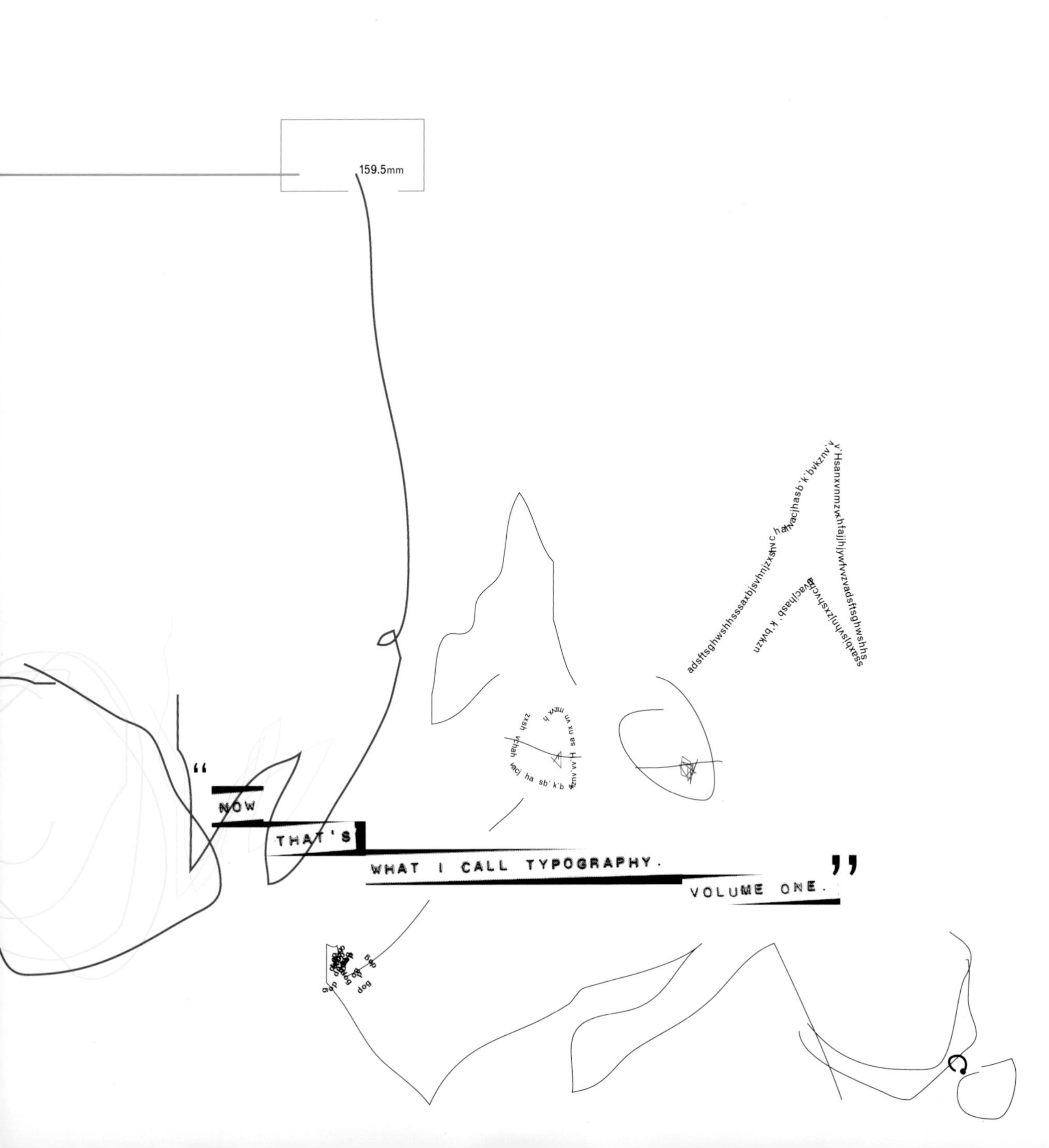
159.5mm
“NOW
THAT'S
WHAT I CALL TYPOGRAPHY.
VOLUME ONE.”
dog